Getting Started with Talend Open Studio for Data Integration

Develop system integrations with speed and quality using Talend Open Studio for Data Integration

Jonathan Bowen

[PACKT] open source*
PUBLISHING   community experience distilled

BIRMINGHAM - MUMBAI

Getting Started with Talend Open Studio
for Data Integration

First published: November 2012

Production Reference: 1251012

Published by Packt Publishing Ltd.
Livery Place
35 Livery Street
Birmingham B3 2PB, UK.

ISBN 978-1-84951-472-9

www.packtpub.com

Cover Image by Dean Taylor (dean.taylor@bt.com)

Credits

Author
Jonathan Bowen

Reviewers
Mark Chapman
Carbone Olivier
Philip Yurchuk

Acquisition Editor
Mary Nadar

Lead Technical Editor
Azharuddin Sheikh

Technical Editors
Veronica Fernandes
Ankita Meshram

Copy Editors
Insiya Morbiwala
Aditya Nair
Alfida Paiva
Laxmi Subramanian

Project Coordinator
Yashodhan Dere

Proofreader
Maria Gould

Indexer
Rekha Nair

Production Coordinator
Melwyn D'sa

Cover Work
Melwyn D'sa

Foreword

Talend's open source approach shatters the traditional proprietary model by supplying open, innovative, and powerful software solutions with the flexibility to meet the needs of all the organizations. By publishing the code of its core modules under the GNU Public License or the Apache License, Talend offers the developer community the ability to improve products and make enhancements that can benefit everyone.

Contributions from the community are critical to the success of Talend's products. They take many different forms: code contributions, extensions such as connectors and components, documentation and tutorials, community support and help, and more.

Documentation is probably one of the most important aspects of the usability experience. Without good learning and reference materials, the best software is impossible to fully master. Contributions from the community to this usability experience are hence very important and they participate to the broad adoption effort.

It should be no surprise then that Talend is supportive of initiatives such as this book. By providing an angle enriched by his real-life experience, the author guides the user of Talend Open Studio through a learning experience that is complementary to the user documentation provided by Talend.

Enjoy!

Yves de Montcheuil

VP of Marketing,
Talend

Foreword

As with any software, there are many different ways to learn how to properly use Talend Open Studio for Data Integration. There are many helpful resources now available online, thanks to the Talend company and the community. Undoubtedly, it may be difficult to choose which training path to take: Which tutorial shall I begin with? Which topics in the forum will be of use? Have I understood the explanatory video?

The method described by Jonathan Bowen in this book is straightforward. It is based on hands-on examples. There's no need for previous knowledge and anyone can try to perform the exercises.

Throughout the chapters, you will discover the main features of Talend Open Studio and learn the best practices. Take your time when setting up the technical environment and when solving all of the exercises. Learning will be easier that way.

Interested readers should consider studying for Talend Certification. Keep upgrading your skills with online resources as described in the last chapter.

Olivier Carbone

Knowledge Manager,
Talend

About the Author

Jonathan Bowen is an E-commerce and Retail Systems Consultant and has worked in and around the retail industry for the past 20 years. His early career was in retail operations, then in the late 1990s he switched to the back office and has been integrating and implementing retail systems ever since.

Since 2006, he has worked for one of the UK's largest e-commerce platform vendors as Head of Projects and, later, Head of Product Strategy. In that time he has worked on over 30 major e-commerce implementations.

Outside of work, Jonathan, like many parents, has a busy schedule of sporting events, music lessons, and parties to take his kids to, and any downtime is often spent catching up with the latest tech news or trying to record electronic music in his home studio.

You can get in touch with Jonathan at his website: www.learnintegration.com.

Acknowledgement

I am grateful to the editorial team at Packt – Theresa, Mary, Yashodhan, Azhar in particular – for helping with the production of this book. Their advice and guidance has been critical in getting it published. I would also like to thank the technical reviewers – Mark Chapman, Olivier Carbone, and Philip Yurchuk for their feedback. My friend and colleague, Dean Taylor, provided the book's cover photograph. Nice one Dean!

I have had two significant lucky breaks in my technical career: firstly, when I joined STS Systems, a retail systems vendor (thanks Peter!) and secondly, when I joined Fresca, a UK e-commerce platform provider (thanks Sarah, Gavin, and Justin!). Both experiences had a huge impact on me and greatly influenced my career path and technology skills. This book is, in large part, the result of those influences. I've also been fortunate to work with many fantastic people over the years that have contributed to my technical education in one way or another. A big thanks to you all!

I'd like to thank my parents and family for their support and encouragement, not just while writing this book, but since day one!

Finally, this book is dedicated to the three most important people in my life – Tanya, William, and Rose.

About the Reviewers

Mark Chapman is the Pre-Sales Manager for Talend in the UK, the leading Open Source Integration software vendor. He joined Talend in October 2009 as a Technical Consultant and is now the primary hands-on Pre-sales Manager for Integration (ETL and ESB), Data Quality (DQ), Master Data Management (MDM), and Business Process Management (BPM) for the Enterprise sector.

Mark has over 25 years of business experience in the Information Technology industry, the past 18 years as a consultant for Enterprise Master Data Management software vendors including Search Software America (now Informatica), Datactics, Datanomics (now Oracle), and Talend. Mark works with organizations from all sectors and sizes to understand how EDM technologies encompassing ETL, AI, DQ, MDM, and BPM can be deployed to meet the needs of the business.

http://uk.linkedin.com/in/markvchapman

Olivier Carbone began his career in the world of training and in 2006, he joined the open source software vendor, Talend. He worked on the team that produced the beta version of Talend Open Studio and subsequently was responsible for producing Talend training tools. He also worked in Talend's marketing team.

In 2008, he was appointed as Customer Care Manager at Talend. His role was to ensure that the services from Talend were on par with the customers' expectations. Continuing to satisfy his customers, he took the role of the Head of the Professional Services (training + expertise + support) and has enjoyed managing teams of French consultants.

In September 2011, he came back to R&D to work on a government project linked to e-learning and to build the internal social networks.

Olivier also belongs to the social network (`http://www.apprendre2point0.org`) dedicated to the impact of technology on our way to learn/work. Since 2007, he has invested a lot of time to write the first pages of this story and define the rules of practice.

He aims to share with us his experiences on his blog at `http://ocarbone.free.fr/blog/`.

Philip Yurchuk is an independent Enterprise E-commerce and Web Application Consultant. He started his career at NASA's Jet Propulsion Laboratory developing satellite mission planning software. At Boeing, he developed and managed systems software and web applications. He then began consulting, starting with an engagement managing the development of a high volume consumer web application for Toyota. Since then, he has worked as a project manager and developer on several e-commerce sites for major retail brands. He has a bachelors degree in Computer Science from Rensselaer Polytechnic Institute. Outside of work, he is a typical geek who enjoys movies, music, books, board games, and blogging at `http://philip.yurchuk.com`.

www.PacktPub.com

Support files, eBooks, discount offers, and more

You might want to visit www.PacktPub.com for support files and downloads related to your book.

Did you know that Packt offers eBook versions of every book published, with PDF and ePub files available? You can upgrade to the eBook version at www.PacktPub.com and as a print book customer, you are entitled to a discount on the eBook copy. Get in touch with us at service@packtpub.com for more details.

At www.PacktPub.com, you can also read a collection of free technical articles, sign up for a range of free newsletters and receive exclusive discounts and offers on Packt books and eBooks.

http://PacktLib.PacktPub.com

Do you need instant solutions to your IT questions? PacktLib is Packt's online digital book library. Here, you can access, read and search across Packt's entire library of books.

Why Subscribe?

- Fully searchable across every book published by Packt
- Copy and paste, print and bookmark content
- On demand and accessible via web browser

Free Access for Packt account holders

If you have an account with Packt at www.PacktPub.com, you can use this to access PacktLib today and view nine entirely free books. Simply use your login credentials for immediate access.

Table of Contents

Preface

We've all been there. Your boss drops you an e-mail saying:

> *Good news, we've just bought system X, which is going to make our lives a lot easier. First though, we need to hook it up to system Y for daily product and inventory feeds and system Z to post the financials back for invoicing. Should be easy, right? It's going to be live in two months. Any problems, please let me know. Oh....if you can get some extracts for the data warehouse at the same time, that would be great too.*

What to do? Well, you could ask your senior developer to code some integration jobs from scratch, but they might be hard to maintain, particularly if he/she left the company. In addition, you know he/she is working flat out on another important project. Alternatively, you could ask your boss if you can invest in a proprietary integration suite, with a legion of highly paid consultants. That will certainly do the job, but the budget, and timeline might not stretch to this.

Or you can take the new junior developer who joined your company a couple of weeks ago, dust off your business analyst and testing skills, and get the job done on time, on budget with Talend Open Studio for Data Integration.

Getting Started with Talend Open Studio for Data Integration is an introductory guide to solving this problem and many others like it.

What this book covers

Chapter 1, Knowing Talend Open Studio, introduces the reader to Talend Open Studio for Data Integration and what it can be used for. It also covers the installation of Talend Open Studio for Data Integration.

Chapter 2, Working with Talend Open Studio, introduces some common concepts the reader will come across when using Talend Open Studio for Data Integration, including creating a workspace to contain integration jobs, a tour of the Talend Open Studio for Data Integration interface, and use of metadata and schemas. We'll also build a simple "hello world" job.

Chapter 3, Transforming Files, gets into the detail of Talend Open Studio for Data Integration integrations and looks at using Talend Open Studio for Data Integration to transform files from one format to another.

Chapter 4, Working with Databases, looks at databases—how to get data out and how to get data in.

Chapter 5, Filtering, Sorting, and Other Processing Techniques, introduces common data operations: filtering, sorting, and aggregating.

Chapter 6, Managing Files, shows how to manage files during integration jobs. We'll look at renaming, moving, copying, and deleting files; how to timestamp a file; connecting to remote servers to FTP files; and zipping and unzipping files.

Chapter 7, Job Orchestration, will look at more complex integrations and how "one-shot" tasks can be combined to form multi-step jobs. We'll create subjobs and link them together using "if/then" logic. Integrations often produce temporary files, so we'll look at ways to clean up afterwards.

Chapter 8, Managing Jobs, covers the process of packaging, deploying, and scheduling jobs in a live environment.

Chapter 9, Global Variables and Contexts, looks at contexts and we explore how the same job can be used in different environments. We introduce dynamic variables, allowing our integration jobs to run flexibly, based on the current runtime information, rather than introducing complex, hardcoded routines.

Chapter 10, Worked Examples, brings together all of the knowledge from previous chapters in a series of worked examples. A real-life integration project is explored and developed to illustrate the use of Talend Open Studio for Data Integration "in the wild".

Appendix A, Installing Sample Jobs and Data, details how to obtain and use the sample data files required to follow the job development examples in the book. All of the jobs created throughout the book are also provided for reference.

Appendix B, Resources, highlights some resources and further reading to expand your knowledge of Talend Open Studio for Data Integration.

What you need for this book

The hardware and software requirements for this book are:

- A computer running Windows, Linux, or Mac OS with Java installed
- Talend Open Studio for Data Integration
- A text file/XML editor
- A MySQL database instance

Who this book is for

This book is for developers, business analysts, project managers, business intelligence specialists, system architects, and consultants who need to undertake integration projects. The book assumes a certain level of technical aptitude and readers should be comfortable with some of the following concepts and technologies:

- Relational database management systems with some SQL (structured query language) experience
- XML
- Java
- File Transfer Protocol (FTP)
- Programming flow and logic

Conventions

In this book, you will find a number of styles of text that distinguish between different kinds of information. Here are some examples of these styles, and an explanation of their meaning.

Code words in text are shown as follows: "Create a file delimited metadata for the currencies.csv file."

A block of code is set as follows:

```
String datestamp=TalendDate.getDate("YYYYMMDD");

globalMap.put("dateStamp",datestamp);
```

Any command-line input or output is written as follows:

```
sh [file name].sh
```

New terms and **important words** are shown in bold. Words that you see on the screen, in menus or dialog boxes for example, appear in the text like this: "Go to the **Debug Run** tab and click on **Traces Debug**".

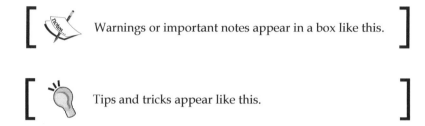

> Warnings or important notes appear in a box like this.

> Tips and tricks appear like this.

Reader feedback

Feedback from our readers is always welcome. Let us know what you think about this book—what you liked or may have disliked. Reader feedback is important for us to develop titles that you really get the most out of.

To send us general feedback, simply send an e-mail to feedback@packtpub.com, and mention the book title through the subject of your message.

If there is a topic that you have expertise in and you are interested in either writing or contributing to a book, see our author guide on www.packtpub.com/authors.

Customer support

Now that you are the proud owner of a Packt book, we have a number of things to help you to get the most from your purchase.

Downloading the example code

You can download the example code files for all Packt books you have purchased from your account at http://www.packtpub.com. If you purchased this book elsewhere, you can visit http://www.packtpub.com/support and register to have the files e-mailed directly to you.

Errata

Although we have taken every care to ensure the accuracy of our content, mistakes do happen. If you find a mistake in one of our books—maybe a mistake in the text or the code—we would be grateful if you would report this to us. By doing so, you can save other readers from frustration and help us improve subsequent versions of this book. If you find any errata, please report them by visiting http://www.packtpub.com/support, selecting your book, clicking on the **errata submission form** link, and entering the details of your errata. Once your errata are verified, your submission will be accepted and the errata will be uploaded to our website, or added to any list of existing errata, under the Errata section of that title.

Piracy

Piracy of copyright material on the Internet is an ongoing problem across all media. At Packt, we take the protection of our copyright and licenses very seriously. If you come across any illegal copies of our works, in any form, on the Internet, please provide us with the location address or website name immediately so that we can pursue a remedy.

Please contact us at copyright@packtpub.com with a link to the suspected pirated material.

We appreciate your help in protecting our authors, and our ability to bring you valuable content.

Questions

You can contact us at questions@packtpub.com if you are having a problem with any aspect of the book, and we will do our best to address it.

Knowing Talend Open Studio

1

Ever since the *second* computer system came along, integrating systems has been a key part of the work of IT teams.

Today's IT landscape is increasingly complex, with **enterprise resource planning (ERP)**, **customer relationship management (CRM)**, finance, warehousing, human resources, and e-business systems, both within and outside the enterprise, all needing to exchange data. The real-time nature of business today and the fast pace of business change add to the need to have a set of tools and skills that make the business of integrating systems quick and easy. New systems come along all the time, but it is also a requirement to respond quickly to new business opportunities that drive system integrations. Company takeovers and mergers, new markets and customers, new suppliers, and joint ventures are commonplace events that all require data to be exchanged on a one-off or regular basis to make them work.

As you might expect, for such a critical systems-development activity, there is no end of options to choose from to fulfill the need. From complex multi-million dollar integration suites from the major systems vendors to humble, yet powerful, scripting languages such as Perl, there is something for every budget and taste. So what is Talend Open Studio for Data Integration and why should you consider it for your next integration project?

What Talend Open Studio is

Talend Open Studio for Data Integration is an open source graphical development environment for creating and deploying custom integrations between systems. It comes with over 600 pre-built connectors that make it quick and easy to connect databases, transform files, load data, move, copy and rename files, and connect individual components in order to define complex integration processes.

Talend Open Studio for Data Integration is a code generator, and so does a lot of the "heavy lifting" for you. As such, it is a suitable tool for experienced developers and non-developers alike. Talend Open Studio for Data Integration is easy to use and reduces the time taken to develop integrations from weeks and months to days or even hours.

Integration jobs are created from components that are configured rather than coded and jobs can be run from within the development environment or executed as standalone scripts.

Use cases

Some common use cases for Talend Open Studio for Data Integration include:

- **Data migration from one database to another**: This is a common scenario when new systems are implemented or existing systems are upgraded. Data has to be populated into the new or upgraded system and database schemas may be subtly or completely different, requiring some modification of the data prior to loading. Data migrations tend to be "one-off" activities, not integrations that are deployed on an ongoing basis. The Studio facilitates data migrations through its many database connectors and actions.

- **Regular file exchanges between systems**: The humble flat file is still a cornerstone of many systems integrations. Their low-tech approach makes them particularly suitable for batch processes when real-time data flows are unnecessary. File exchanges will often require some form of file transformation, either data content, data format, or both. The Studio has the ability to manage many different file formats and, with its file management capabilities such as FTP and archiving (zipping), is able to facilitate a full end-to-end file exchange process.

- **Data synchronization**: Enterprises often have multiple data repositories of the same data. For example, data about customers might reside in the CRM system, the finance system, and the distribution system. They will probably have similar but different data models across these systems and every time a change is made in one, the same change needs to be made in the others — typically a time-consuming and manual process. The Studio can be used to keep the data in sync across systems with jobs that automate and transform the data transfer.

- **ETL (Extract, Transform, and Load)**: A key component process of a data warehouse or business intelligence system, ETL processes extract data from operational systems, transform the data, applying a series of rules or functions, and load the data into a database or data warehouse system.

History of Talend Open Studio

Talend was founded in 2005 and is an open source software vendor providing solutions for data integration, data quality, master data management, enterprise service bus, and business process management.

Talend's first product, Talend Open Studio for Data Integration, was launched in 2006, under the name Talend Open Studio, and has since been downloaded over 20 million times. Talend has continued to develop its product portfolio and has added complementary tools that provide a single platform for application, data, and process integration. The Talend Open Studio brand has since been adopted across the range of Talend's products.

Benefits of Talend Open Studio

An obvious question to ask is "Why should I use Talend Open Studio above other similar products? What can it do for me?" Talend Open Studio for Data Integration offers a number of benefits:

- The Studio is open source, free to download and use, with access to the source code, allowing users to extend the product to their particular needs if required.
- The Studio is a great productivity-booster. It's easy to learn and quick to develop with. Even novice developers will be building complex integrations in no time.
- The Studio's pre-built components handle many common and not-so-common tasks. Developers can focus on the end-to-end process, rather than the low-level technical details.
- Talend has an active and open user community. Practical, problem-solving advice is easy to access.

Installing Talend Open Studio

Before we can begin, we need to install the Studio. Talend provides installation guides and other material on its wiki at the following URL:

```
http://www.talendforge.org/wiki/doku.php?id=doc:installation_guide
```

We will also cover the basic installation instructions here.

Prerequisites

The Studio is a cross-platform application, running on Windows, Linux, and Mac OS. A list of hardware and software prerequisites can be found at `http://www.talend.com/docs/community/prerequisites.html`.

As a minimum, you will need a supported operating system, Java, and of course, the Studio itself.

Installation guide

The installation process for the Studio is essentially the same across all supported operating systems. We will show how to complete the installation on Windows, but you can follow the same steps on other platforms.

Follow the instructions given to install the Studio on Windows:

1. Check to see if Java is installed on your computer by opening a command window and running the following command:

   ```
   java -version
   ```

2. If Java is present, you will see a message showing which version is installed, as shown in the following screenshot:

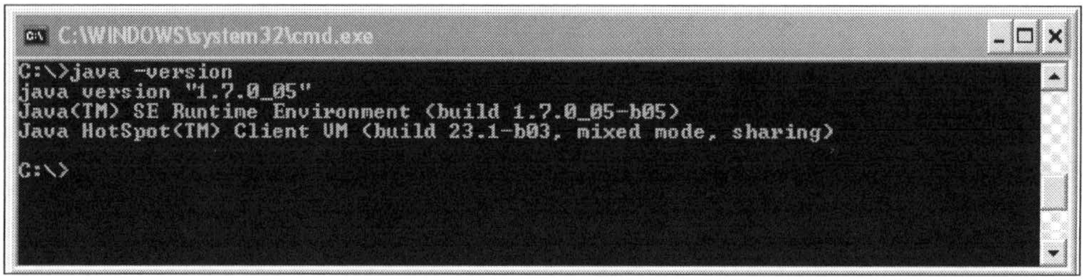

   In the preceding screenshot, you can see that Version 1.7.0_05 of Java is installed. If Java is not present, you will get an error message, as shown in the following screenshot:

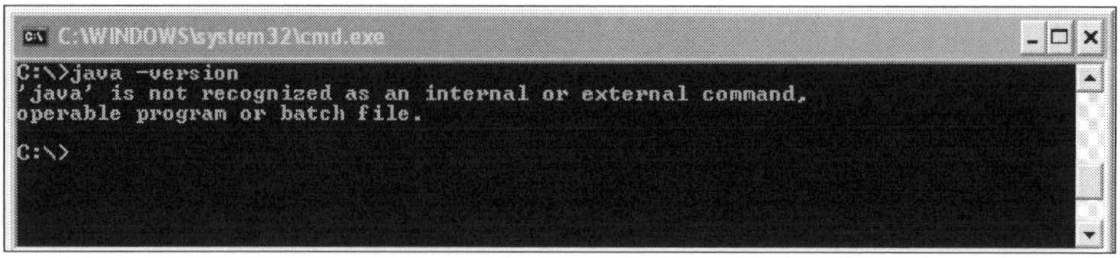

3. If you need to install Java, visit the following URL to download a Java installer:

   `http://www.oracle.com/technetwork/java/javase/downloads/index.html`

   There are various versions of the Java Standard Edition JDK for different operating systems. Choose the appropriate version for your computer and download the installer to your computer.

4. Once the installer is downloaded, click on the executable file to run it. Follow the instructions on the installer as it progresses.

5. Now that Java is installed, we can download and install the Studio. Start by going to the Talend download page at the following URL:

   `http://www.talend.com/download.php`

6. Choose the **Data Integration** tab and click on the **Download** button for **Talend Open Studio for Data Integration,** as shown in the following screenshot:

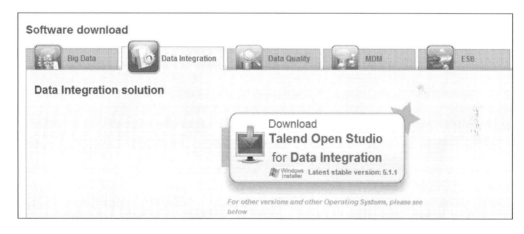

7. Once it has downloaded, double-click on the executable to extract the Studio files as shown in the following screenshot:

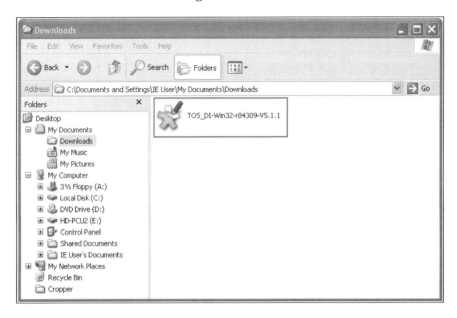

8. Follow the installation instructions on-screen. You will be prompted to choose an installation directory. Enter an appropriate location such as C:\Talend, as shown in the following screenshot:

Once the installation is complete, you can start the Studio and start to develop jobs. See *Chapter 2, Working with Talend Open Studio,* for details on how to start the Studio.

Other useful software

In order to follow the sample jobs throughout the book, you may wish to install some additional software.

Text editor

A decent text editor will be very useful to view CSV and XML files. There are hundreds of text editors — both free and paid-for — and here are some recommendations if you don't already have a favorite:

- If you are using a Linux operating system, you will probably have at least one good text editor installed as part of your distribution. gedit (http://projects.gnome.org/gedit/) is the official text editor of the GNOME project and will do the job admirably.

- Windows users can download Notepad++ (http://notepad-plus-plus.org/), which really is a double-plus compared to the default Notepad application that Windows provides.

- Mac users can pick up TextWrangler from http://www.barebones.com/products/TextWrangler/.

MySQL

Chapter 4, Working with Databases, focuses on using the Studio to extract from and insert data into a relational database system. The Studio supports many different database systems, but for the examples in this book, we have chosen to use MySQL.

MySQL is the most popular open source relational database and is used by many large-scale applications and websites. It is free to use and there are a number of tools you can use to administer databases. To follow the examples as they are, use MySQL. However, if you have another preferred database you wish to use, it should not be too difficult to modify the job examples to incorporate other database components instead of the illustrated MySQL components.

MySQL Community Server can be downloaded from the following URL:

http://dev.mysql.com/downloads/mysql/

Installation instructions for various operating systems can be found at the following URL:

http://dev.mysql.com/doc/refman/5.1/en/installing.html

Once you have installed the MySQL server, download and install the client tools, which you can use to administer the database, view data, and so on. The MySQL Workbench can be downloaded from `http://www.mysql.com/downloads/workbench/`.

MySQL Workbench documentation, including installation instructions, can be found at `http://dev.mysql.com/doc/workbench/en/`.

Readers who wish to use other database systems can find a full list of supported databases at `http://www.talendforge.org/components/`.

The list includes Oracle, DB2, MS SQL, Postgres, SQLite, and Sybase, among others. TOS also supports the JBDC API to connect to, and a relational database that supports this protocol.

Sample jobs and data

Each chapter of the book contains a number of example jobs that we will construct in a systematic manner. Readers are encouraged to follow the steps in order to get the most out of the book and consolidate their learning as they go. However, you can download and import the full set of example jobs if you wish.

Additionally, some jobs rely on database data and file-based data sources to work correctly. Again, these data sources can be downloaded and installed prior to working through the examples.

Appendix A, Installing Sample Jobs and Data, gives full instructions on downloading and installing the example jobs and data files.

 Note that some sample data files may have their encoding changed as they are downloaded, unzipped, and copied from one location to another. As a result you may occasionally get some encoding errors notified in the Studio. If this happens, open the offending file and ensure it is saved with the UTF-8 encoding.

Summary

Welcome to Talend Open Studio for Data Integration! In this chapter, we learned what the Studio is and what it can be used for. We walked through installing the Studio on your computer (along with some additional useful software).

Our next step is to log on to the Studio, become familiar with the Studio working environment, and create a simple job to illustrate the development workflow. All of this will be covered in *Chapter 2, Working with Talend Open Studio*.

2
Working with Talend Open Studio

Now that we have the Studio installed, we can start to build integration jobs. However, before we dive straight in with some complex developments, let's get familiar with the working environment, get ourselves organized, and start with something simple.

In this chapter, we will:

- Learn how to log on to the Studio
- Get a tour of the Studio's environment and find out the different elements that make up the Studio tool
- Learn how to create a new project and a new job
- Learn about metadata—what it is and how it is used in the Studio

Studio definitions

Let's start with a few definitions to make everything clear:

- A *workspace* is a directory on your computer that contains one or more projects
- A *project* is a logical grouping of one or more jobs
- A *job* is a group or one or more components that, when executed, implement a data flow or integration process

We will create each of these as we work through the chapter.

Starting the Studio

The Studio is a cross-platform development tool and supports Windows, Linux, and Mac OS in both 32-bit and 64-bit versions. To start the Studio, go to the directory where the Studio was installed, and double-click on the executable appropriate for your operating system.

1. When you start the Studio for the first time, you will be presented with a license notification. Click on **Accept** to proceed. We will then see the first-time start up screen and we are presented with a few options at this point. We can:
   - Import a demo project
   - Create a new project
   - Change some basic settings

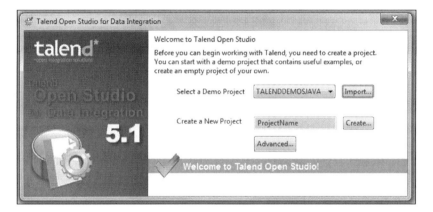

2. We will start by amending some settings. Click on **Advanced**. You will see the following screen:

3. The first thing we will do is change the workspace location. You can leave it with the default value if you want, but the path is a little convoluted, so it is worth changing it. Click on the **Change** button and select an appropriate path, such as `C:\Talend\Workspace`.

4. You will then see a prompt to restart the Studio. Click on the **Restart** button now.

5. Our next step will be to import the demo project provided with the Studio. We won't refer to this in the following chapters of the book, but it is an excellent reference project, giving lots of examples of how to complete specific tasks. Readers are encouraged to take time to review the demo project as they read this book. Make sure that the default demo project, **TALENDDEMOSJAVA**, is selected in the demo project drop-down and click on **Import**.

We will be prompted to enter a name and, optionally, a description for the new project as shown in the following screenshot:

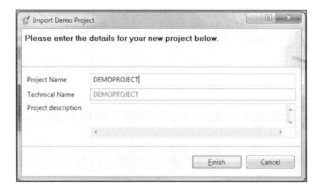

6. Enter a suitable name, such as DEMOPROJECT, and click on **Finish** (as shown in the preceding screenshot). The Studio will take a moment to import the job and when complete, we will be presented with the "standard" logon screen as follows:

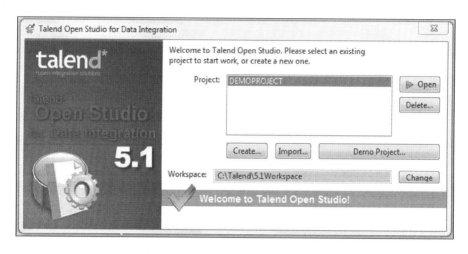

7. Make sure the demo project is highlighted and click on the **Open** button. We will see a form screen that gives you the ability to create an account for TalendForge, the Talend online community, as shown in the following screenshot:

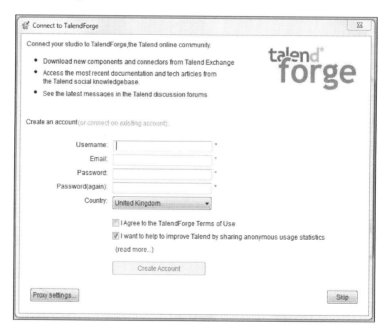

8. We will look at TalendForge later in this book; click on **Skip** for now. The Studio will start to load.

9. Once the Studio is open, it runs a **Generation Engine Initialization** process, which can take a few minutes to complete. We can choose to have this run in the background if you wish by clicking on the **Run in Background** button as shown in the following screenshot:

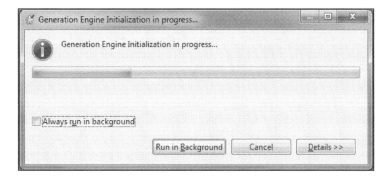

10. Finally, we will be presented with the Studio's welcome screen (as shown in the following screenshot), which lists the latest jobs that have been edited, links to documentation, and the latest Talend news:

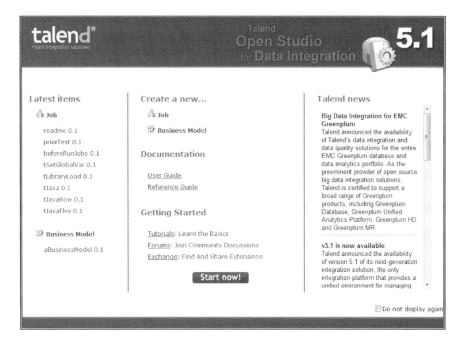

11. Click on the **Start now!** button.

Tour of the Studio

Let's look at the Studio environment. To help illustrate the different windows and views of the Studio tool, we will open a job from the demo project.

In the left-hand column of the Studio tool, we will see the **Repository** window. The **Repository** contains all of the artifacts associated with a project—**Job Designs**, **Business Models**, **Metadata**, and so on—as shown in the following screenshot:

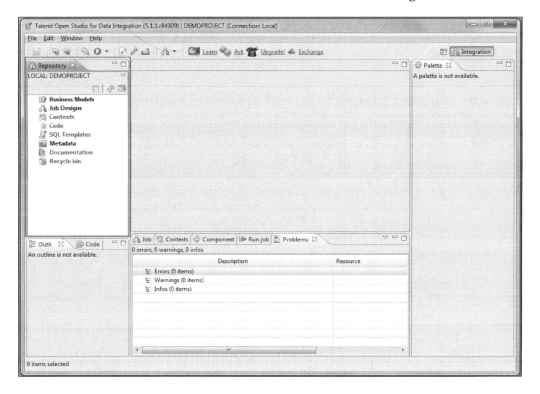

Expand the **Job Designs** section of the **Repository** and double-click on the job named **priorTest 0.1**. This will open the priorTest job as shown in the following screenshot:

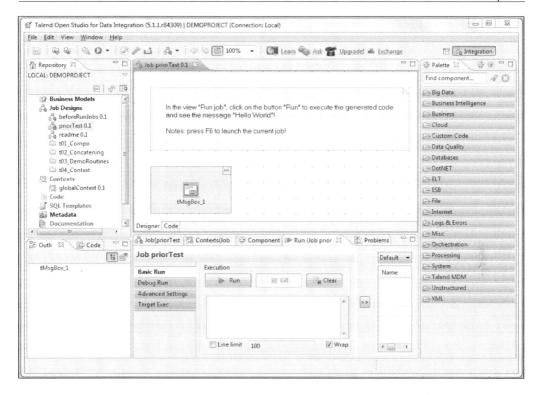

The Repository

As noted earlier, the **Repository** window, shown in the top-left of the Studio, contains all of the artifacts associated with a project. This will typically include:

- One or more job definitions
- Metadata items such as database connection details, FTP connection details, and file schema definitions
- Reusable code snippets
- Business Models that describe the non-technical workflows of a data integration job
- Contexts — global or job-specific variables

The design workspace

The design workspace is in the middle of the Studio and is the key development window, as shown in the following screenshot:

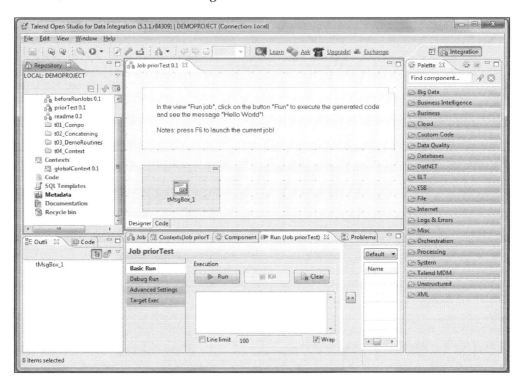

The design workspace is where developers place and configure components in order to build the required data integration job.

The Palette

The Palette is located on the right-hand side of the Studio, as highlighted in the following screenshot:

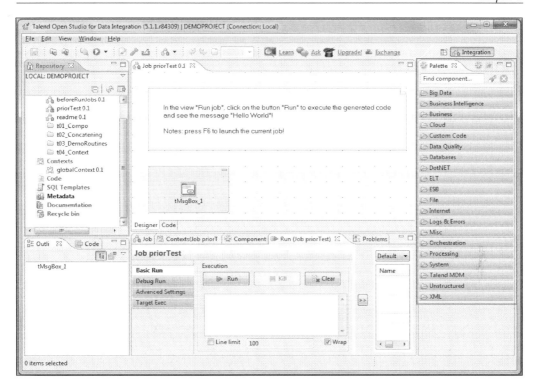

The Palette contains the component that can be used in the data integration jobs. The Studio comes with over 600 built-in components and third-party components can be downloaded and added to the Studio. Adventurous developers can even create their own components for use with the Studio.

The components in the Palette are grouped to help you find what you are looking for and some components will appear in more than one grouping where this makes sense. You can also search for components in the Palette. For example, type xml in the search box and press *Enter*. The list of components will be filtered by your search term, although still shown in their grouping folders. Expand some of the group folders to see the items contained inside.

Configuration tabs

The configuration tabs are below the design workspace and they display properties of the job or specific components that are selected in the design workspace. The configuration tabs are highlighted in the following screenshot:

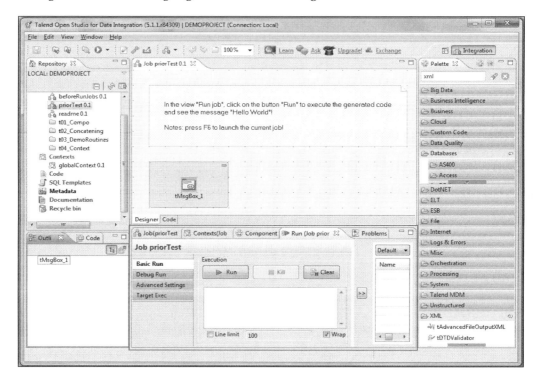

We will use this area a lot to configure how each component will work—for example, what SQL query to run in a database component or what fields to extract from a file in an XML component. We can also run jobs from here, viewing the output and debugging as we go.

Outline and Code panels

The Outline and Code panels are situated in the bottom left-hand corner of the Studio, as highlighted in the following screenshot:

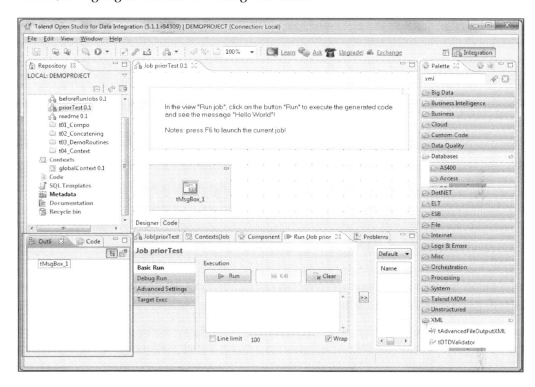

The **Outline** tab lists the components that have been added to the design workspace and gives quick access to the standard variables for each component. The Code panel displays the code associated with each component.

Creating a new project

Let's now create a new project, which we will use as a container for all of the example jobs illustrated in later chapters of the book.

Start the Studio (or if it is already open, go to **File | Switch Project**) and wait for the logon screen to appear. We will see our demo project in the list of projects but we won't open this project; instead, we'll create a new one. Click on the **Create** button as shown in the following screenshot:

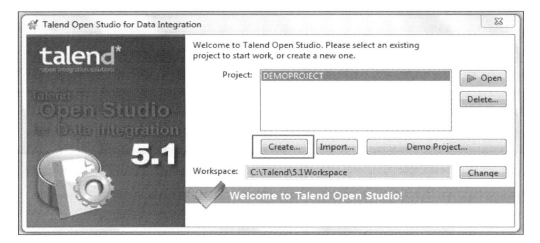

You will be prompted to enter a project name. Enter BEGINNERSGUIDE, optionally adding a project description if you wish, and click on the **Finish** button. You'll now see the new project in the project list. Highlight the BEGINNERSGUIDE project and click on the **Open** button.

Once the Studio is open, we will see the standard Studio layout as described previously. Let's create a simple job to illustrate the development process and give you some hands-on experience with the Studio.

Creating an example job

The Studio helpfully describes the development process for you on the default design workspace window.

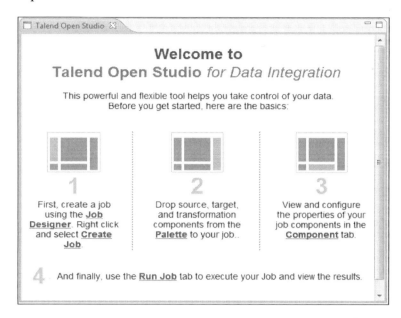

The basic process is as follows:

1. Create a job in the Repository.
2. Drop components from the Palette onto the design workspace of your job.
3. Configure the properties of the components.
4. Run the job and view the results.

Simple, right?

In the time-honored tradition of programming books, our first job will be a simple "hello world" job. Follow the given steps:

1. In the Repository, right-click on **Job Designs** and select **Create Job**.

2. We will be presented with the **New Job** window as shown in the following screenshot:

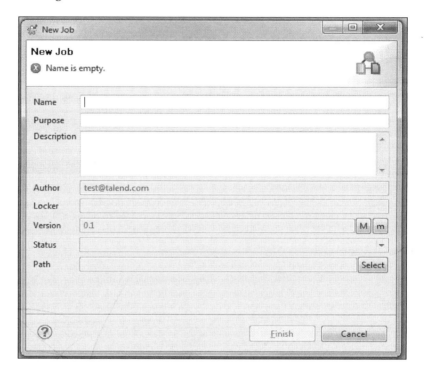

3. Enter HelloWorld into the **Name** field and click on **Finish**. Our new job will open, showing the design workspace window.

4. In the Palette, search for message. In the **Misc** folder, we have a component named tMsgBox. Drag this onto the design workspace.

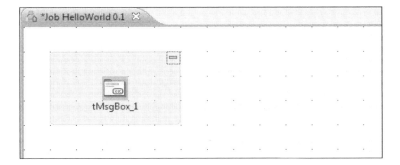

5. Click on the message box component and click on the **Component** tab of the configuration area below the design workspace. We will see the configuration options for the highlighted component.

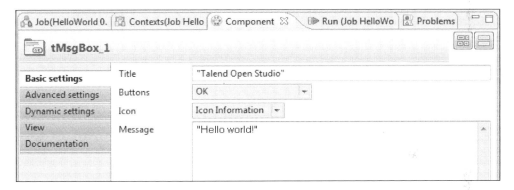

6. The Component tab shows the **Basic** and **Advanced Settings**, which is where the configuration properties for the component are set. The **Component** tab also shows:

   ○ **Dynamic settings**: This allows developers to change parameters to dynamic variables

   ○ **View**: This allows you to change the display format of the highlighted component

   ○ **Documentation**: Here developers can add any notes or documentation related to the component

In our job, we are configuring a message box component and you can see that the available settings relate to the component in question, allowing us to configure the message box title, buttons, icon, and message. For now, we can keep the default settings that come with the component.

7. To run the job, go to the **Run** tab.

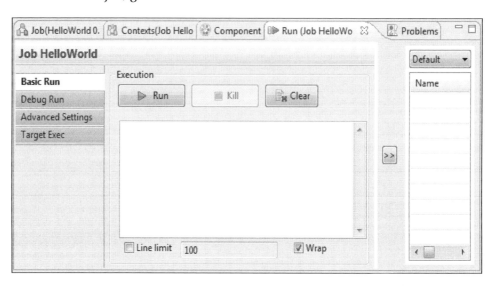

8. Click on the **Run** button—the job will compile and then execute, displaying a message box as configured.

 You can also press the *F6* key on your keyboard to launch a job.

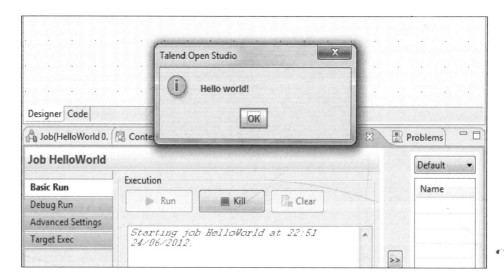

9. Click on **OK** and the job will complete. Try modifying some of the configuration parameters for the message box component and run the job again, noting the impact they have on the job output.

As you can see, this job is very simple and, like all "Hello World" jobs, doesn't do much. However, the job illustrates the principles of constructing jobs in the four simple steps outlined in the default design workspace screen. As we work through the book, the jobs will become more complicated (and will achieve more!), but the core principles remain.

Metadata

For the final part of this chapter, let's look at how the Studio uses "metadata". Metadata is defined as "data about data". It describes the data, but isn't the data itself. In the Studio context, metadata refers to reusable configurations that describe the data, its attributes, or its containers. For example, we could define metadata in the Studio that describes an XML schema, a web service definition, or an FTP connection. Once defined, these configurations can be used across multiple Studio jobs.

The benefit of metadata components is that they save developers time as they are defined once and used many times. They also provide a single place to update configurations for many jobs. For example, if the password to an FTP account changes and this FTP connection is used in 10 different jobs, the details would have to be updated 10 times. However, if you store this configuration in a single metadata component, it only needs to be updated once.

Let's work through an example of metadata configuration by creating a reusable database connection. Work through the steps outlined as follows:

1. In the **Repository** window, expand the **Metadata** section and right-click on **Db Connections**. Click on **Create Connection**.

2. In the pop-up window, enter a name for the connection—let's call ours
   DEMO_DB. You can also enter additional information in the **Purpose** and
   Description boxes. There are other configuration options for **Version**, **Status**,
   and **Path**, but these are not mandatory, so we will leave them for now.

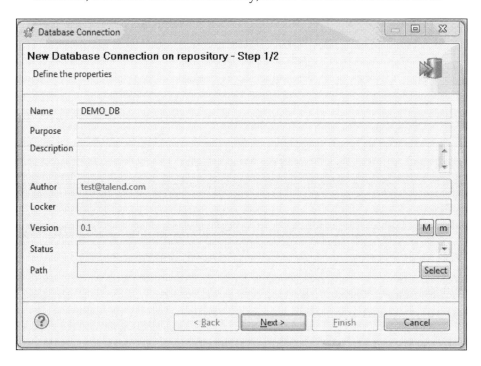

3. Click on the **Next** button.

4. We now need to configure the database connection.

> You may need to get the database connection details from your database
> administrator if you are working with an existing database. Note that,
> while broadly similar, the connection parameters that are required do
> vary depending upon which database system you use, so seek some
> expert advice on the specifics of your database if you are not sure.

5. The Studio has built-in connection drivers for most of the common database
   systems (and some not so common). It can also use generic ODBC or JDBC
   drivers for those database systems that support these protocols. We are using
   MySQL, so in the **DB Type** drop-down, find and select **MySQL**. Selecting
   this will configure some default parameters such as the **Db Version** and
   the connection string. Note that the **Db Version** can be changed
   where appropriate.

6. Enter the value for the **Login** and **Password** fields.

7. Enter the value for the **Server field**. This will be the hostname or IP address of your database server.

8. Enter the **Port** details.

9. Enter the **Database** name to which you want to connect.

10. Once all of the values have been entered, click on the **Check** button to test the connection. If all has been set up correctly, you will get a **Connection Successful** pop up. If not, go back and check the values that you have configured.

11. Click on **Finish** to save the connection. You will see the connection in the metadata area of the Repository.

12. Now right-click on the **DEMO_DB** metadata entry in the **Repository** and select **Retrieve Schema**. We can use the **Retrieve Schema** function to automatically configure the database tables, views, and synonyms within the metadata. The **Schema** pop-up window will appear.

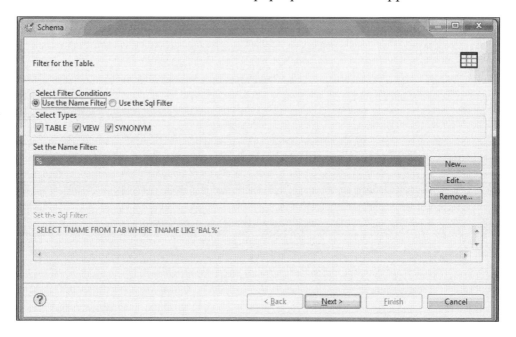

13. We might not wish to configure all of the tables, views, and synonyms for a given database, so we can use the **Name** or **SQL** filters to select certain database objects only. We can also use the **TABLE**, **VIEW**, and **SYNONYM** checkboxes to configure objects of certain types only. For our database, we can stay with the default settings. Click on **Next**.

14. On the next screen, expand the demo_db entry in the **Name** column to reveal the tables within our database. Select the checkbox next to demo_db to select all of the tables.

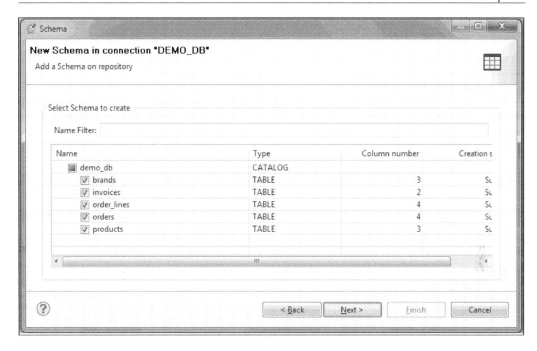

15. Click on **Next** to show the final schema configuration window.

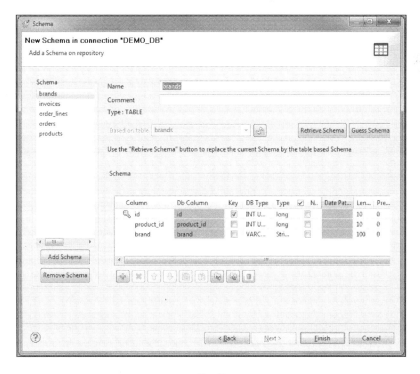

16. In this screen we can see the schema for each table as identified by the Studio. We can accept the defaults or make any changes we wish, by clicking on the table name in the **Schema** pane on the left-hand side and modifying the columns and data types in the main pane. Click on **Finish** to accept the configuration.

In later chapters, we will see how to make use of the configured connection in a Studio job.

Although each type of metadata is set up in a different way, the principle of creating a reusable data structure is consistent throughout. Readers are encouraged to make as much use of metadata as possible, particularly when working in a collaborative environment with two or more developers. The timesaving benefits and consistency benefits will be clear.

Summary

In this chapter, we looked at the Studio working environment and introduced some of the standard tasks you will undertake as a developer, such as creating projects, jobs, and metadata. We created a "Hello World" job that illustrated a simple development process and executed the job to see how the Studio presents its results.

In the next chapter, we will get truly hands on with the Studio and create some jobs that transform data files.

3
Transforming Files

Let's start our "deep dive" into the world of Talend Open Studio for data integration by looking at some common file integration techniques. Of all the methods of integrating systems, using files and file exchanges is probably one of the oldest and most common. With the rise of other, more modern, integration methods over the last few years, web services for example, integrating files might be seen as a bit unfashionable. But don't be fooled; exchanging files between systems can be an excellent way to integrate. To support this, lots and lots of applications have file-based integration APIs.

In this chapter, we will learn how to:

- Transform files from one format to another
- Use the Studio's expression editor to modify data
- Build advanced and multi-schema XML files
- Use lookups to enrich data
- Get familiar with the Studio development environment by following the detailed step-by-step examples

Transforming XML to CSV

Let's start with a simple file format transformation. Many modern applications use **Extensible Markup Language (XML)** formats to get data in and out. Other, often simpler, systems use a **Comma Separated Format (CSV)**. Common, desktop-based systems, such as Excel and Access, have wizards for taking data in the CSV format. We'll work through the process of taking a simple XML file and extracting its data into a comma-separated format.

Before we dive in and actually start to configure a the Studio job, let's look at the data that we want to transform. Our input file is an XML product catalogue named `catalogue.xml`, which is present in the datafiles of this chapter. Open this in the XML viewer of your choice. You can see that the data is pretty self-explanatory. The file contains data about **Stock Keeping Units (SKUs)**. There are a number of repeating SKU elements, each containing an skuid, skuname, size, colour, and price.

```
catalogue.xml
 1    <?xml version="1.0" encoding="UTF-8"?>
 2    <catalogue>
 3        <sku>
 4            <skuid>1233212406</skuid>
 5            <skuname>Summer Dress</skuname>
 6            <size>6</size>
 7            <colour>Green</colour>
 8            <price>39.99</price>
 9        </sku>
10        <sku>
11            <skuid>1233212408</skuid>
12            <skuname>Summer Dress</skuname>
13            <size>8</size>
14            <colour>Green</colour>
15            <price>39.99</price>
16        </sku>
17        <sku>
18            <skuid>1233212410</skuid>
19            <skuname>Summer Dress</skuname>
20            <size>10</size>
21            <colour>Green</colour>
22            <price>39.99</price>
23        </sku>
```

We want to extract this data into a spreadsheet-style format with similar columns to the XML elements, that is skuid, skuname, size, colour, and price.

So let's create the job step-by-step:

1. Create a new job in the Studio and name it XML2CSV. (I've also created a new folder named Chapter3 to contain the jobs for this chapter and I'll follow this convention for other chapters throughout the book.)

2. Next, we'll define the metadata for the `catalogue` file we want to read. In the **Repository** window, expand the **Metadata** section, right-click on **File XML**, and select **Create file xml**. The **New Xml File** wizard will open:

3. Enter `catalogue` into the **Name** field and click on **Next**.

4. As we are creating metadata for a data source or input to the process, select **Input XML** on the step 2 screen and click on **Next**.

5. In step 3, we need to provide an XSD file or a sample XML file so that the Studio can determine the XML schema. In our case, we will provide a sample XML file. Click on **Browse** and navigate to the `catalogue.xml` file. Select it and click on **Open**. The Studio will determine the file encoding automatically and will provide a view of the schema structure. Click on **Next** to move to step 4:

6. Step 4 of the process is where we determine how the Studio should read the XML files. Specifically, the Studio needs to know which elements to loop on and which elements should be extracted. Let's deal with the loop first.

7. Our catalogue file is a series of SKUs. So, in order to extract data for each SKU, we need to set this as our loop element. We want the Studio to loop over all of the SKUs when the job runs. In order to configure this, we need to map the SKU to the **Xpath loop expression** box. Click on the SKU element in the **Source Schema** pane and drag it to the **Xpath loop expression** box:

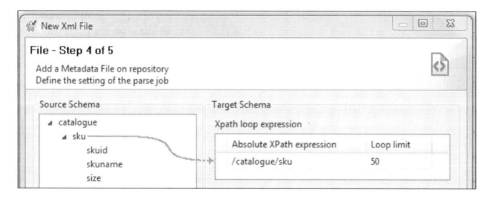

8. The **Loop limit** field determines how many times the job will loop over the selected element. By default, this is configured to **50**, but let's change this to **0**, which is the number used to configure no limit.

9. Now, we can configure the fields we want to extract from the `catalogue` file. Drag the **skuid**, **skuname**, **size**, **colour**, and **price** fields to the **Fields to extract** pane:

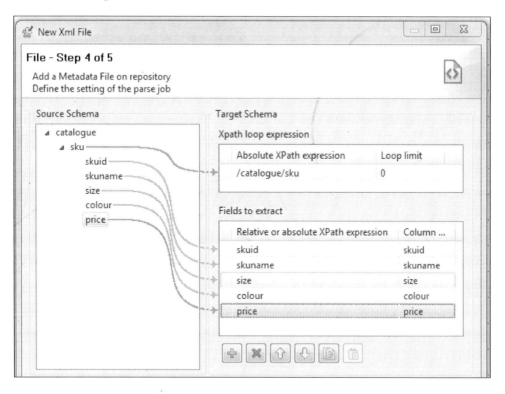

XPath is a query language for finding information in an XML document. It uses path expressions to navigate to the required elements. XPath is a big subject in its own right, and it is outside the scope of this book to go into detail on the subject. However, W3C Schools provides an excellent tutorial on the subject at `http://www.w3schools.com/xpath/`, and readers may wish to take some time to read through this.

10. Click on the **Refresh Preview** button in the bottom left-hand corner of the window, and the Studio will read the file and preview the extract of the data in a tabular format. Click on **Next** to move to step 5.

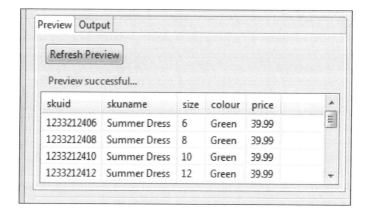

11. Step 5 of the metadata setup allows us to confirm or alter the schema as determined by the wizard and add this to the **Repository** window. The Studio has determined data types, field length, and precision values. In this case, we can make a couple of changes. Our **skuid** field is a unique key, so we can note as such in the schema by checking the **Key** checkbox for the **skuid** row. As **skuid** is a key, we would need it to be present for every record, so it cannot be nullable. Uncheck the **Nullable** checkbox for the **skuid** row. Finally, for this step, change the **Name** field to `catalogue`. Click on **Finish**:

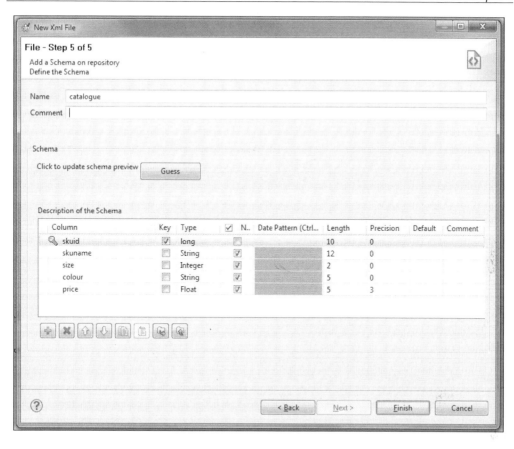

Often, XML files will come with an **XML Schema Definition (XSD)** file so that data types can be determined directly. If you don't have an XSD file, then some assumptions can be made from the data we have. Although, it is important to bear in mind that sample data sets may not give the full picture, so some caution is advised here. For example, the metadata wizard has determined that size is an integer based upon the data presented in the file, but we might subsequently come across the sizes of *S*, *M*, and *L*, making the data type incorrect. If you are using an XML file as the basis for the schema, ensure that it covers all of the data types you would expect or, alternatively, edit the schema definition as shown previously in step 5.

12. With our metadata configured, we can now build the job. From the **Repository** window, expand the **Metadata** section, click on the newly created catalogue metadata and drag it onto the Job Designer. You'll be presented with a list of components compatible with the metadata we have defined. In this case, we can observe two components, namely **tFileInputXML** and **tExtractXMLField**. Our job needs the **tFileInputXML** component, so select this and click on **OK**. The component will now be visible on the Job Designer.

13. In the **Component** palette, search for `delimited` and find the **tFileOutputDelimited** component (it is in folder **File | Output**). Drag this onto the Job Designer next to the **tFileXMLInput** component.

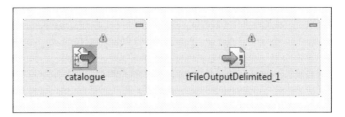

14. We then need to connect the two components. There are a number of different connection types available in the Studio. For this job, we will use the **Main** connector. This connection type is probably the most used in the Studio and represents a straightforward passing of data between two components. To connect it in this way, right-click on the **tFileInputXML** component and select **Row | Main**. This will create a line from the component to your cursor. Place your cursor over the **tFileOutputDelimited** component and click on it. This will create a connection line between the two components. (It will also merge the gray background box, signifying that the two components are now part of a larger integration process.)

 Note that the process of connecting the two components will synchronize the schemas from the catalogue XML component to the delimited output component.

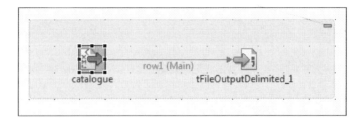

15. Let's now configure the **tFileOutputDelimited** component. Click on the component, and select the **Component** tab in the panel below the Job Designer. Some default configurations are presented, and we'll change a few of these.

16. Change the filename to the full path of the output file you require. This might be something similar to `C:/Talend/Workspace/GETTINGSTARTED/DataOut/Chapter3/catalogue-out.csv`.

We're now ready to test our job!

In the bottom panel below the Job Designer, click on the **Run** tab and then click on the **Run** button. This will save the configurations you have made, compile the job, and then run it.

The **Run** tab will show some statistics as the job executes and, if a runtime error occurs, will show error details to allow you to diagnose any issues. The Job Designer will also indicate how many rows of data have been extracted for the input file we are working with.

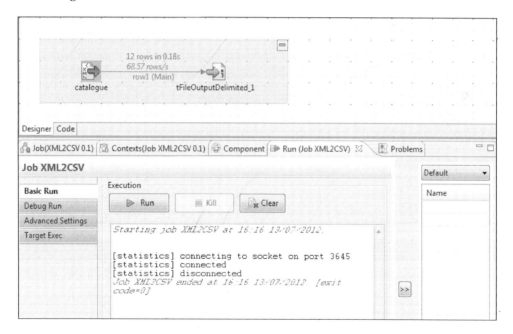

Browse to your output folder, and you will see the output file similar to the one shown in the following screenshot:

```
catalogue-out.csv
1    1233212406;Summer Dress;6;Green;39.99
2    1233212408;Summer Dress;8;Green;39.99
3    1233212410;Summer Dress;10;Green;39.99
4    1233212412;Summer Dress;12;Green;39.99
5    1233212414;Summer Dress;14;Green;39.99
6    1233212416;Summer Dress;16;Green;39.99
7    3455437806;Cotton Skirt;6;Pink;29.99
8    3455437808;Cotton Skirt;8;Pink;29.99
9    3455437810;Cotton Skirt;10;Pink;29.99
10   3455437812;Cotton Skirt;12;Pink;29.99
11   3455437814;Cotton Skirt;14;Pink;29.99
12   3455437816;Cotton Skirt;16;Pink;29.99
13
```

Success! Let's move on to another file transformation example, from CSV to XML.

Transforming CSV to XML

Working the other way around, we will now transform a simple CSV file into an XML format. Again, this is a common integration scenario, where, for example, data needs to move from a spreadsheet to a format suitable for loading into another application via its native API.

Start by creating a new job in the `Chapter3` folder and call it `CSV2XML`. We're going to use the CSV output from our previous task as an input file this time, so take a copy of `catalogue-out.csv` from your `DataOut` folder and drop it into the `DataIn` folder. To avoid confusion, let's rename this to `csv2xml-catalogue.csv`.

As in the previous example, we'll start by declaring the metadata for the input file before completing the main configuration of the job. Perform the following steps:

1. In the **Metadata** section of the **Repository** window, right-click on **File delimited** and select **Create file delimited**. The metadata wizard window will appear. Enter `csv_catalogue` into the **Name** field and click on **Next**:

2. In step 2, we need to add our sample input file so that the schema can be determined. Click on the **Browse** button and navigate to the sample file in our `DataIn` folder. The wizard will show a preview of the file in the **File Viewer** pane:

3. Click on **Next** to view the parse settings for the file. Here we can define field and row separators, and header and footer rows, for example. The wizard will have made a guess at the settings based on the file presented, and we'll keep the selections it has made. Click on **Next** to move to step 4.

4. In the final step, we can set the schema definition. Again, the wizard will have made a best guess based on the file presented, but there are a few things that we need to change. The columns do not have meaningful names, so modify them to **skuid**, **skuname**, **size**, **colour**, and **price**. We'll also make **skuid** a key field and not nullable. Finally, change the **Name** field to be `csv_catalogue`. When finished, your settings should be as follows:

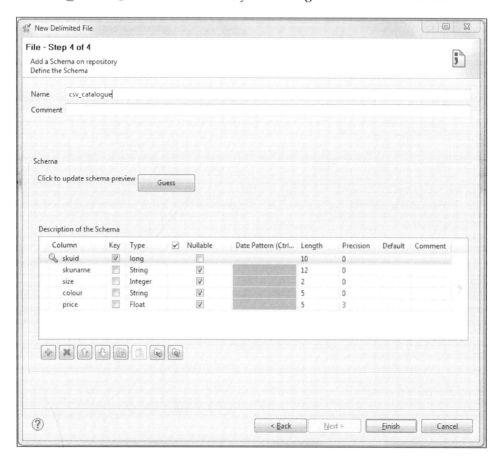

5. Click on **Finish** to complete the metadata configuration.

6. Now click on the file delimited metadata we have created and drag it onto the Job Designer. As before, we are presented with a list of components that can be used with the metadata we have defined. We want a simple delimited file input, so select the **tFileInputDelimited** component and click on **OK**.

7. Let's now configure the output side of this job. Search for xml in the palette, and locate the **tFileOutputXML** component. Drag this onto the Job Designer next to the delimited file input:

8. We can now join the two components together as before. Right-click on the delimited file input and select **Row | Main**. Drop the line attached to your cursor onto the XML output component by clicking on it.

    We need to add a few more configurations to the XML output component.

9. Under **Basic settings**, enter the output filename and path we require (or browse to it by clicking on the ellipsis button).

10. The next configuration item, **Row tag**, is the name of the XML element that will wrap around each row of data. If you are working to a predefined XML schema, then you can determine this from the XSD. In this case, let's set this to sku, as each row of our data is an SKU and its associated data.

11. Moving onto the **Advanced settings** tab, we'll need to add a root tag to the XML output. Again, this might be determined from the XML schema, but in our case, let's use the value **catalogue**. Click on the + button of the **Root tags** pane to add a new row and then change the **newline** value to catalogue.

12. Let's also change the file encoding to **UTF-8**.

Again, we have accepted the default values for a number of the configuration settings and we'll revisit some of these in different scenarios throughout the book.

Let's run the job. Go to the **Run** tab in the bottom panel, and click on the **Run** button to save, compile, and run the job.

 You can also run jobs by pressing the *F6* button on your keyboard. It's a useful shortcut when you are running jobs a number of times during the development/debug phase.

Go to your `DataOut` folder, and you should see the XML output file as shown in the next screenshot:

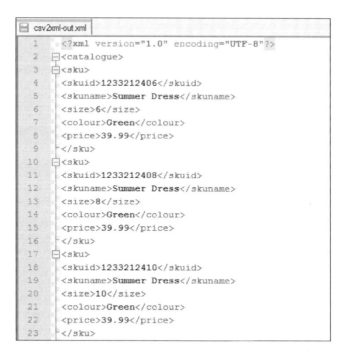

```
csv2xml-out.xml
 1    <?xml version="1.0" encoding="UTF-8"?>
 2    <catalogue>
 3    <sku>
 4      <skuid>1233212406</skuid>
 5      <skuname>Summer Dress</skuname>
 6      <size>6</size>
 7      <colour>Green</colour>
 8      <price>39.99</price>
 9    </sku>
10    <sku>
11      <skuid>1233212408</skuid>
12      <skuname>Summer Dress</skuname>
13      <size>8</size>
14      <colour>Green</colour>
15      <price>39.99</price>
16    </sku>
17    <sku>
18      <skuid>1233212410</skuid>
19      <skuname>Summer Dress</skuname>
20      <size>10</size>
21      <colour>Green</colour>
22      <price>39.99</price>
23    </sku>
```

So, our first two jobs have taken us on a quick round-trip from XML to CSV and back again. They have also illustrated that the Studio can perform integration transformations (admittedly, quite simple transformations thus far) by configuring, rather than coding. Let's make things a little more complex by introducing the Studio's tMap component, which among other things, allows us to perform functions against fields, using its expression editor.

Maps and expressions

In most integration scenarios, we are unlikely to find that all data fields can be passed from one system to another without any modification. Because different systems model the same objects in different ways, there's often the need, to not only change the file format, but also to change the data model and content in some way.

For our next job design, we'll do another CSV to XML transformation; but this time, the data models of the input and the output (and hence the schemas) will be different. We'll use the Studio's mapping component and Expression editor to help us deal with these differences.

To start off, let's look at our two data models to examine the differences. Our CSV file is a customer datafile and has the following fields:

- Customer ID
- First Name
- Last Name
- Address1
- Address2
- Town City
- County
- Postcode
- Telephone

We know that all of these fields have a string data type and that all fields are mandatory, except for Address2.

The XML file we want to produce has a similar, yet different set of fields, as follows:

- id (left-padded with zeros to make its length 8)
- name (for example, John Smith)
- address_1 (for example, house number, street name, and district)
- address_2 (any other address fields)
- telephone_number (must be numbers only, without spaces or other characters)

Our first decision, then, is completely outside of the Studio. How are we going to map the CSV fields to the XML fields? The following table shows the mappings we will make for this integration job; although, of course, other mappings could be equally valid:

XML Field	CSV Mapping
id	Customer ID field (left-padded with zeros to make its length 8)
name	First Name and Last Name
address_1	Address1 and Address2
address_2	Town City, County, and Postcode
telephone_number	Telephone with non-numeric characters removed

Rather than trying to get everything right on the first go, let's approach this in an iterative way, implementing the transformations we need, step by step, and checking the results as we go:

1. Let's create a new job and call it `Expressions` in the `Chapter3` folder of the Studio. There is a sample datafile for our CSV schema (`expressions.csv`). Copy that into your `DataIn` folder.

2. As in our previous examples, we'll start by creating the metadata for the input file. Right-click on **File delimited** in the **Metadata** section of the **Repository** window and select **Create file delimited**. As our input file contains customer data, let's name this metadata definition `customer`. Follow the same steps that we took in the previous example job to define the metadata, using the `expressions.csv` file.

3. As we have seen, the Studio does a good job of guessing the settings, but in step 3 of the configuration, we can make some changes. Our sample file contained column names in the first row, so in the **Preview** tab of step 3, we can configure the metadata to reflect this. Check the checkbox named **Set heading row as column names** and then click on the **Refresh Preview** button. Our column headers are now populated by the first row of data:

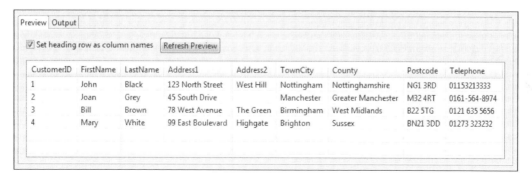

4. In step 4 of the wizard, you can see that the column names have been carried forward as the schema column names. As previously, let's make the **id** field, **CustomerID**, a key and not nullable. Click on **Finish** to complete the metadata configuration.

5. Now click on our newly created delimited metadata and drag it onto the Job Designer. Choose **tFileInputDelimited** from the component list.

6. Search for tMap in the **Palette** window and drop this onto the Job Designer. The **tMap** component is used to map data inflows to data outflows, and we'll use this to define the mapping we have noted previously:

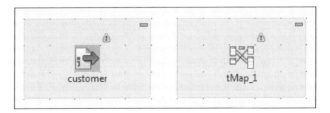

7. Right-click on the delimited customer input, and select **Row | Main** and join it to the **tMap** component.

8. Double-click on the **tMap** component and the **Map Editor** will appear. The **Map Editor** is a powerful tool that allows you to map, transform, and route the dataflows within your job.

 The **Map Editor** has a number of panels for configuring mappings and transformations. The input panel on the top left-hand side shows all of the incoming dataflows. The variable panel in the middle allows you to configure mappings to variables. The output panel on the top right-hand side is used to define the outgoing dataflows and the mappings to them. At the bottom of the **Map Editor** is the **Schema editor,** which shows a schema view of all the inputs and outputs. Behind the **Schema editor** is the **Expression editor,** which allows you to edit any of the expressions used.

9. Our first step in the **Map Editor** is to configure the data output that we need. In the output pane on the right-hand side, click on the + button to create a new output. You'll be presented with a pop-up window to name the output:

10. Let's accept the default **New output** name by clicking on **OK**. A new output is created in the output pane and a new, empty schema is created in the schema pane.

11. Click on the **+** button of the **out1** schema five times, to add new rows to the schema. Change the names of the new rows added to match our output schema, as defined in the previous table. The **id** field needs to be of data type integer, to match the input data coming from the delimited file. Let's also make the **id** field of the new output a key and not nullable:

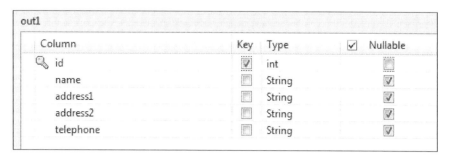

out1

Column	Key	Type	☑	Nullable
🔍 id	☑	int		☐
name	☐	String		☑
address1	☐	String		☑
address2	☐	String		☑
telephone	☐	String		☑

12. Before we configure the mappings in the **Map Editor**, let's configure the XML output. In the **Palette** window, search for xml and drag a **tFileOutputXML** component onto the Job Designer.

13. Right-click on the **tMap** component, select **Row | out1**, and drop the connector onto the XML output component:

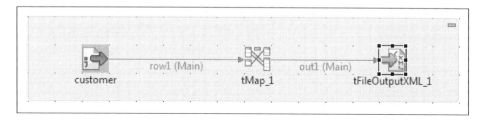

14. Click on the XML component and then the **Component** tab to reveal its configuration settings. We will make some changes to the default settings. Starting with **Basic settings**, set the **File Name** field to something appropriate in your DataOut folder.

15. Change the **Row tag** field to customer (as each row will be a customer).

16. Moving to the **Advanced settings** tab, add a **Root tag** field and name it customers.

17. Change the **Encoding field** to **UTF-8**. So far, so good. We now need to define the mappings in the **Map Editor**. Double-click on the **tMap** component to open this.

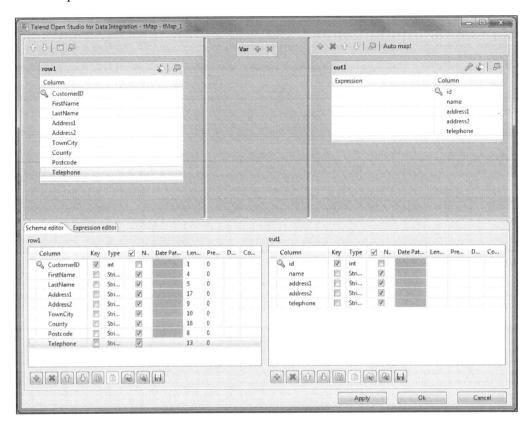

The mapping functionality is supported by a simple, drag-and-drop interface. Let's try this out by clicking on the **CustomerID** field under **row1**, and dragging it to the **Expression** column on the **id** row of the **out1** schema:

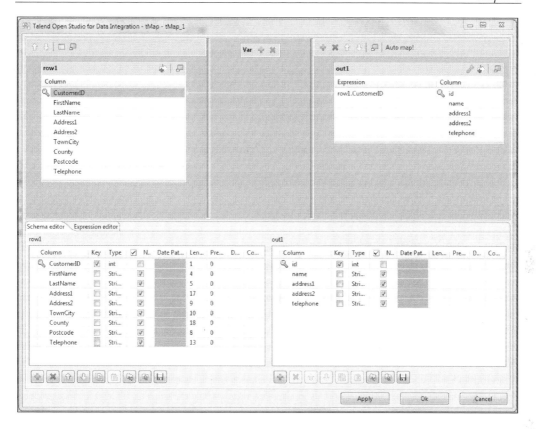

The component draws a line between the two fields, as shown in the previous screenshot, and also fills in the **Expression** column of the **out1** schema with **row1. CustomerID**. You could also type this directly into the **Expression** column rather than using the drag-and-drop option, if you prefer.

Before we go any further, let's click on **OK** on the mapping window and run the job to check that everything is connected. The job will save, compile, and run, and you should see the following output in your `DataOut` folder:

```
expressions-out.xml
1      <?xml version="1.0" encoding="UTF-8"?>
2      <customers>
3      <customer>
4        <id>1</id>
5        <name></name>
6        <address_1></address_1>
7        <address_2></address_2>
8        <telephone_number></telephone_number>
9      </customer>
10     <customer>
11       <id>2</id>
12       <name></name>
13       <address_1></address_1>
14       <address_2></address_2>
15       <telephone_number></telephone_number>
16     </customer>
17     <customer>
18       <id>3</id>
19       <name></name>
20       <address_1></address_1>
21       <address_2></address_2>
22       <telephone_number></telephone_number>
23     </customer>
24     <customer>
25       <id>4</id>
26       <name></name>
27       <address_1></address_1>
28       <address_2></address_2>
29       <telephone_number></telephone_number>
30     </customer>
31     </customers>
32
```

Great! It works! There are lots of empty elements, but we can soon fix that.

Open the **tMap** component again. Let's work on the **FirstName** and **LastName** fields. In this instance, we cannot perform a straight drag-and-drop function, so to start the mapping process for these fields, click on the **Expression** column of the **out1** schema on the **name** row. You will see an ellipsis button appear at the end of the line. Click on this to reveal the **Expression Builder**.

The **Expression Builder** is a really useful tool that allows you to build data transformations in Java code from a library of functions and expressions. You can also type Java code into the **Expression Builder,** if there is a Java function you want to use that is not in the function library. You'll find that you use the **Expression Builder** a lot, particularly with complex integration transformations, so take some time to practice with it. If your Java coding is a little rusty, simply Google what you want to do. There is a wealth of Java tutorials and code snippets on the Internet.

We're going to build an expression that joins the first and last names so that we can pass the output to the **name** field in the output schema. To do this, double-click on **row1.FirstName**. This will then appear in the **Expression** window:

Place your cursor at the end of the expression, and then double-click on **row1.LastName**. It will appear at your cursor position, which is after **row1.FirstName**. The expression must be valid Java syntax, so we need to do a bit more work before we can test the job again. Between **row1.FirstName** and **row1.LastName** type a +, which is the Java string concatenation operator. The **Expression** window should now show the following:

```
row1.FirstName+row1.LastName
```

Click on **OK** in the **Expression Builder**, and then click on **OK** again on the mapping window. Let's see what happened, by running our job again.

Well it's definitely progress, but not quite what we had expected.

```
expressions-out.xml
1    <?xml version="1.0" encoding="UTF-8"?>
2    <customers>
3    <customer>
4    <id>1</id>
5    <name>JohnBlack</name>
6    <address1></address1>
7    <address2></address2>
8    <telephone></telephone>
9    </customer>
```

The first and last names have been joined together, but it is a continuous string, rather than the normal convention of [first name] [space] [last name]. Let's quickly resolve that by opening the **Expression Builder** again and editing the expression to the following:

```
row1.FirstName+" "+row1.LastName
```

Run the job again to check the output:

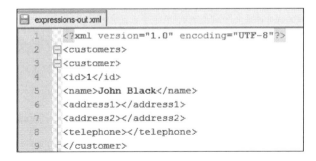

```
expressions-out.xml
1    <?xml version="1.0" encoding="UTF-8"?>
2    <customers>
3    <customer>
4    <id>1</id>
5    <name>John Black</name>
6    <address1></address1>
7    <address2></address2>
8    <telephone></telephone>
9    </customer>
```

Let's complete the mapping for the other fields by creating expressions for them, as follows:

- For address_1:
  ```
  row1.Address1+", "+row1.Address2
  ```

- For address_2:
  ```
  row1.TownCity+", "+row1.County+", "+row1.Postcode
  ```

You can see here that we've added a comma and a space between each address field.

Let's also drag-and-drop **row1.Telephone** onto the **Expression** column of **out1. telephone_number**.

Let's run the job again. We're getting closer to our required output, but there are a few more changes that we need to make as per the requirements.

```
expressions-out.xml
1    <?xml version="1.0" encoding="UTF-8"?>
2    <customers>
3    <customer>
4    <id>1</id>
5    <name>John Black</name>
6    <address_1>123 North Street, West Hill</address_1>
7    <address_2>Nottingham, Nottinghamshire, NG1 3RD</address_2>
8    <telephone_number>01153213333</telephone_number>
9    </customer>
```

1. The `<id>` is displaying an integer, but we want this to be left-padded with zeros, up to a maximum of 8 characters. To implement this, click on the expression ellipsis button of the **id** field in the **Expression** column of the **out1** schema, and change the expression from **row1.CustomerID** to the following:

    ```
    String.format("%08d",row1.CustomerID)
    ```

2. This is the Java expression for left-padding with zeros.

3. On **address_1** of the second customer record, the output is `<address_1>45 South Drive, </address_1>`. The **Address2** field in the input file is not mandatory. We get the slightly odd result of the output for the **address_1** field because its format is `[Address_1] [comma] [space]`. As we know that there will always be an **Address_1** field, but not necessarily an **Address_2** field, we can make the `[comma] [space]` output conditional, based upon the presence of an **Address_2** value. In the expression for **address1** in **out1**, enter the following:

    ```
    ("").equals(row1.Address2)?row1.Address1:row1.Address1+", "+row1.
    Address2
    ```

> The previous code is the Expression Builder format for an `if-then-else` statement; the developers named it as the ternary condition. It takes the following form:
>
> ```
> [test]?[value if true]:[value if false]
> ```
>
> So in the previous code, the expression will evaluate if the **row1. Address2** field is empty. If it is empty, then the output will be as follows:
>
> ```
> row1.Address1
> ```
>
> If it is not empty, then the output will be as follows:
>
> ```
> row1.Address1[comma][space]row1.Address2
> ```

4. We need to standardize the telephone number output and remove any spaces, hyphens, or other non-numeric characters. Let's change the expression for the **map_output telephone_number** to the following:

```
row1.Telephone.replaceAll( "[^\\d]", "" )
```

5. This is the Java expression to remove all non-numeric characters.

Let's run the job one more time to check the output. You should see something similar to the following screenshot, in the DataOut folder:

```
expressions-out.xml
 1    <?xml version="1.0" encoding="UTF-8"?>
 2    <customers>
 3    <customer>
 4      <id>00000001</id>
 5      <name>John Black</name>
 6      <address_1>123 North Street, West Hill</address_1>
 7      <address_2>Nottingham, Nottinghamshire, NG1 3RD</address_2>
 8      <telephone_number>01153213333</telephone_number>
 9    </customer>
10    <customer>
11      <id>00000002</id>
12      <name>Joan Grey</name>
13      <address_1>45 South Drive</address_1>
14      <address_2>Manchester, Greater Manchester, M32 4RT</address_2>
15      <telephone_number>01615648974</telephone_number>
16    </customer>
17    <customer>
18      <id>00000003</id>
19      <name>Bill Brown</name>
20      <address_1>78 West Avenue, The Green</address_1>
21      <address_2>Birmingham, West Midlands, B22 5TG</address_2>
22      <telephone_number>01216355656</telephone_number>
23    </customer>
24    <customer>
25      <id>00000004</id>
26      <name>Mary White</name>
27      <address_1>99 East Boulevard, Highgate</address_1>
28      <address_2>Brighton, Sussex, BN21 3DD</address_2>
29      <telephone_number>01273323232</telephone_number>
30    </customer>
31    </customers>
```

As you can see from this example, the Expression Builder is a powerful tool, allowing us to format data and add logic to our integration jobs.

We've looked at some simple file transformations and used expressions to modify data. Let's move on to look at another the Studio component called **tAdvancedFileOutputXML**, which deals with complex XML structures.

Advanced XML output for complex XML structures

The XML output format we used in the last example was pretty straightforward. Every piece of data is contained within its own XML element; however, it is very common for XML files to be more complex, with subelements being repeated within a parent element, and data items being held in XML attributes rather than in elements.

In this example, we will produce an XML file that contains data about customer orders that have been dispatched. This file will contain the following information:

- The order ID
- The order-line ID
- The product SKU for each line
- The quantity of each dispatched SKU
- The dispatch date (in the format `yyyy-MM-dd hh:mm`)
- The courier tracking ID (so that customers can track their order)

The XML format we need to adhere to is as follows:

```
<?xml version="1.0" encoding="UTF-8"?>
<DISPATCH_DOCKET>
  <ORDER ID="1000">
    <ORDER_LINE ID="1" SKU="123456789" QUANTITY="1" DISPATCHED_
DATE="2011-01-01 12:00" TRACKING_ID="ABC12345"/>
  </ORDER>
</DISPATCH_DOCKET>
```

Note that the XML elements, `<ORDER>` and `<ORDER_LINE>`, do not contain data between their opening and closing tags, as in the previous example; but instead, data is stored in the attributes of each of these elements. The Studio component we will use in this example is **tAdvancedFileOutputXML**. It allows us to build up complex XML structures and explicitly assign data to elements or attributes, as appropriate.

To make things a little more interesting, we are using our input CSV file with slightly different data. It contains `order_id`, `line_id`, `sku`, `quantity`, `shipping_status`, and `courier_docket_code`, so we'll have to do some manipulations to map this to the output file. An example file is shown in the following screenshot:

Note that the input file contains data from orders in various different states, for example, shipped, sourced, and picked. Our output file is concerned only with dispatched (or shipped) orders, so we'll need to filter the data to get what we want.

Let's start building the new job as follows:

1. Create a new job and name it `AdvancedXMLOutput`.

2. We'll start, as before, by creating the metadata for the order status delimited file. Follow the same steps that we outlined previously, using the `order_status.csv` sample file as an input to the metadata definition. On step 4 of the definition, we can define our key fields. In this example, we have a composite key; **order_id** on its own is not a unique key, but is the combination of **order_id** and **line_id**. It does provide a unique reference for each row, so make both the columns key fields, as shown in the following screenshot :

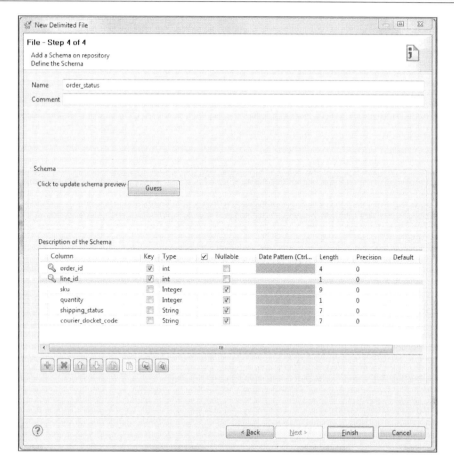

3. When you have completed the metadata setup, drag-and-drop an instance of the order status metadata onto the Job Designer. Select a **tFileDelimitedInput** component from the pop-up window.

4. From the **Palette** window, search for and add a **tMap** and **tAdvancedFileOutputXML** component to the Job Designer.

5. Right-click on the input delimited file, select **Row | Main**, and connect this to the **tMap** component. Double-click on the **tMap** to open the Map Editor.

6. Click on the + button at the top of the output pane to add a new data output. We now need to define the output schema and mappings we require.

   As most of the output elements are the same as the input elements, we can drag-and-drop these from the input pane on the left-hand side, to the output pane on the right-hand side. Multiselect **order_id**, **line_id**, **sku**, **quantity**, and **courier_docket_code** from the input panel, and drag them over to the newly created output pane:

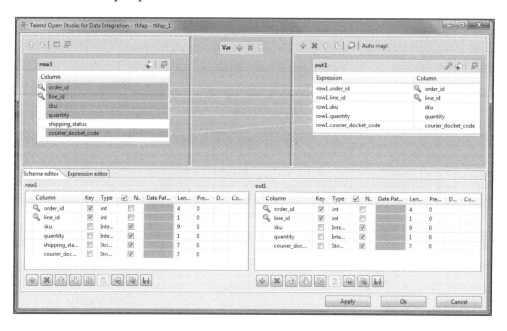

7. We also need the dispatch date in the output schema, so click on the + button in the **out1** pane of the **Schema editor** tab, to add a new column to the schema and change its name to **dispatch_date**. Change its data type to **Date** and amend the **Date Pattern** field to **yyyy-MM-dd hh:mm**. For consistency with the element order of the output file, let's also use the up arrow button to move the date above the **courier_docket_code** column.

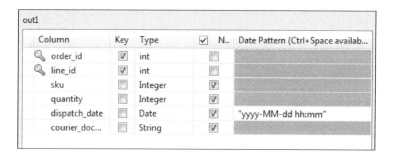

8.   The output file requires a dispatch date, but this data is not contained in the input file. In the real world, we might have a number of choices at this point. For example, we could change the input file to include a dispatch date so that it can be mapped to the output file. In our case, we will generate a relevant date using the Studio date functionality. Click on the ellipsis in the **Expression** column of the dispatch date, which will bring up the Expression Builder. In the **Categories** section in the bottom left-hand corner, scroll through and click on **TalendDate**. This will show a number of date functions in the middle **Functions** window. Find the function **getCurrentDate** and double-click on it. The function syntax will appear in the expression code window. Click on **OK** in the Expression Builder window to save the changes.

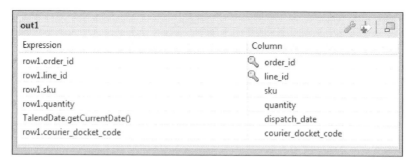

9.   As noted previously, our input file contains the data for orders that are yet to be dispatched, so we want to remove this data from the output. The **tMap** component contains an expression filter that allows us to do just that. In the top right-hand corner of the **out1** schema is a white arrow icon with a green **+** sign (highlighted in red in the following screenshot):

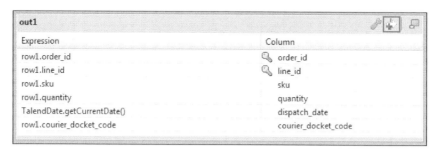

10. Click on this to reveal the expression filter editor. We want to filter our data to where the shipping status on the input file is shipped, rather than when it is picked, sourced, or anything else. To implement this, drag the **shipping_status** field from the input schema across to the expression filter box. It will show as **row1.shipping_status**. Edit this so that it shows as the following:

```
("shipped").equals(row1.shipping_status)
```

11. This will only allow rows with **shipping_status** of **"shipped"** through to the **out1** schema. Click on **OK** in the **tMap** component to save the changes.

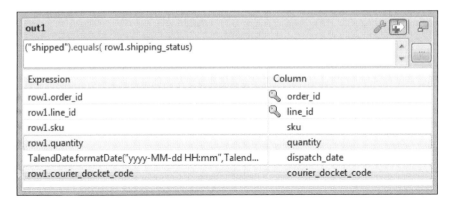

12. We now need to configure the XML output. Click on the **tAdvancedFileOutputXML** component. In the **Basic settings** tab, click on the **Configure Xml Tree** button. In the window that pops up, you can see our schema in the left-hand pane and an empty **XML Tree** window on the right-hand side. Our job here is to construct the **XML Tree** column and then assign data elements from the left-hand window to this tree.

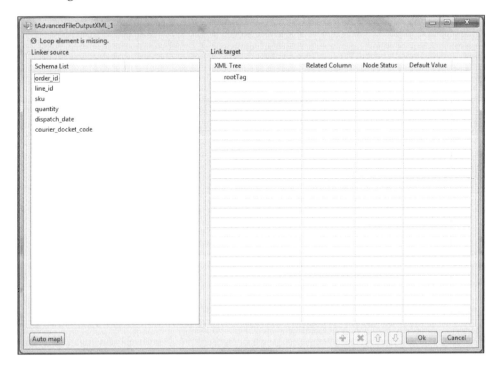

13. We'll start with the **rootTag** field. From our example output file, we can see that the root tag is `<DISPATCH_DOCUMENT>`. Click on the **rootTag** in the **XML Tree** column and change its value to **DISPATCH_DOCUMENT**. The `<ORDER>` element is a subelement of `<DISPATCH_DOCUMENT>`, and `<ORDER_LINE>` is a subelement of `<ORDER>`. Right-click on **DISPATCH_DOCUMENT** in the **XML Tree** column and select **Add Sub-element**. Enter ORDER in the pop-up window and click on **OK**:

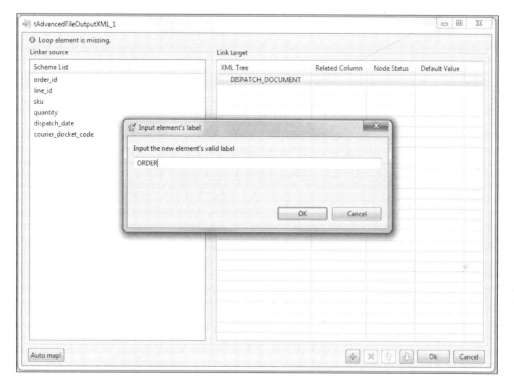

14. Follow the same process for creating the subelement **ORDER_LINE**. We can now create the attributes.

15. Right-click on **ORDER** and select **Add Attribute**. In the pop-up window, enter the attribute value ID and click on **OK**. You'll see the attribute appear below the **ORDER** field in the **XML Tree** column (attributes are prefixed with the @ symbol).

16. On the **ORDER_LINE** element, we need to add **ID, SKU, QUANTITY, DISPATCHED_DATE**, and **TRACKING_ID** as attributes, so go ahead and do this by following the procedure outlined previously. Your **XML Tree** will look similar to what is shown in the following screenshot, when you have finished:

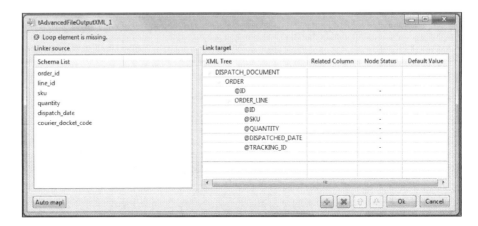

17. Now let's connect our data inputs with the new **XML Tree**. As we saw with the **tMap** component, linking can be achieved by dragging-and-dropping. Click on the **order_id** item in the left-hand pane and drag it onto the **@ID** element of the **XML Tree** tab. You will be presented with a pop-up window that offers a number of linking options:

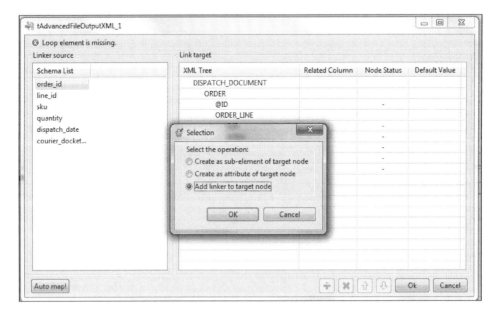

18. The first two options allow you to assign data items to and create the XML tree in one go. Alternatively, you can use the last option, which links the data items to an already existing XML tree. Try both methods, as you develop your integration jobs, and see which works best for you. As we have already created our XML tree, we'll use the last option, which is **Add linker to target node**. Click on **OK**, and the Studio will draw a connection line between the data item and **XML Tree**:

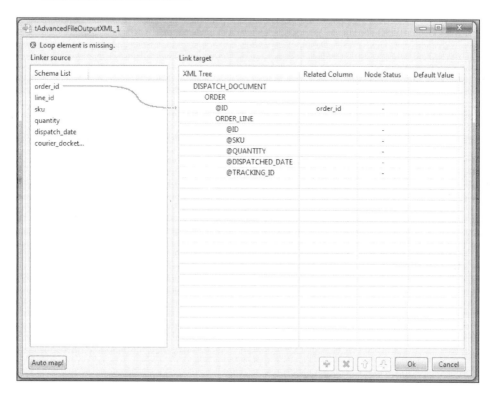

19. In the same way, connect **line_id** to **@ID**, **sku** to **@SKU**, **quantity** to **@QUANTITY**, **dispatch_date** to **@DISPATCHED_DATE**, and **courier_docket_code** to **@TRACKING_ID**.

20. You will notice that the XML tree builder is showing a warning in the top left-hand corner of the window, **Loop element is missing**. We need to specify the element that we want the the process to loop over. This will typically be the element that defines a row. In our case, our rows are based on order lines, so we will use the **ORDER_LINE** element of the **XML Tree** tab as our loop element. Right-click on **ORDER_LINE** in the XML tree and select **Set As Loop Element**.

21. We can also optionally set a **group by** element. This is the element that the loop element is grouped by. For some XML outputs this may not make sense, but in our output, we are outputting the order lines and we want to group them by order. Right-click on **ORDER** in the XML tree and select **Set As Group Element**. Click on **OK** to accept the changes.

22. Amend the **File Name** parameter under the **Basic settings** tab, and change the **Encoding** value to **UTF-8** on the **Advanced settings** tab.

23. Run the job and check the output. You should see something similar to the following screenshot:

```
advancedxmloutput.xml

 1    <?xml version="1.0" encoding="UTF-8"?>
 2
 3    <DISPATCH_DOCKET>
 4      <ORDER ID="1233">
 5        <ORDER_LINE ID="1" SKU="896538289" QUANTITY="2" DISPATCHED_DATE="2012-07-15 09:02" TRACKING_ID="A434223"/>
 6        <ORDER_LINE ID="2" SKU="566738940" QUANTITY="1" DISPATCHED_DATE="2012-07-15 09:02" TRACKING_ID="A434223"/>
 7        <ORDER_LINE ID="3" SKU="583948930" QUANTITY="1" DISPATCHED_DATE="2012-07-15 09:02" TRACKING_ID="A434223"/>
 8        <ORDER_LINE ID="4" SKU="478309030" QUANTITY="1" DISPATCHED_DATE="2012-07-15 09:02" TRACKING_ID="A434223"/>
 9      </ORDER>
10      <ORDER ID="1236">
11        <ORDER_LINE ID="1" SKU="100232434" QUANTITY="2" DISPATCHED_DATE="2012-07-15 09:02" TRACKING_ID="A434567"/>
12        <ORDER_LINE ID="2" SKU="323454565" QUANTITY="1" DISPATCHED_DATE="2012-07-15 09:02" TRACKING_ID="A434567"/>
13        <ORDER_LINE ID="3" SKU="456565678" QUANTITY="1" DISPATCHED_DATE="2012-07-15 09:02" TRACKING_ID="A434567"/>
14        <ORDER_LINE ID="4" SKU="765345345" QUANTITY="1" DISPATCHED_DATE="2012-07-15 09:02" TRACKING_ID="A434567"/>
15      </ORDER>
16    </DISPATCH_DOCKET>
17
```

You can see that the Studio's advanced XML output gives us complete flexibility to build files to a given specification.

Working with multi-schema XML files

The XML files we have worked with so far were straightforward and only dealt with a single collection of elements. However, many systems produce or consume XML files that contain multiple collections of elements; these are called multi-schema XML files. Here's an example:

```
<?xml version="1.0" encoding="UTF-8"?>

<catalogue>
  <skus>
    <sku>
      <skuid>432345</skuid>
      <skuname>Check Shirt</skuname>
      <size>S</size>
      <colour>Green</colour>
      <price>29.99</price>
    </sku>
  </skus>
  <inventory>
```

```
    <sku>
      <skuid>432345</skuid>
      <stock_on_hand>12</stock_on_hand>
    </sku>
  </inventory>
</catalogue>
```

This shows a product catalogue file with two schemas, one for the product details and one for the inventory. There's nothing in the XML structure to connect the two schemas. In essence, these are two separate XML structures joined together for convenience. In order to process this file in the Studio, we could simply create two XML file input components, and have one input read the SKUs schema and the other read the inventory schema. However, the Studio makes things a little easier for us, by offering a multi-schema XML file input component. We'll create a job that reads the XML files and writes the output to the **Run job** console using the **tLogRow** component.

> The tLogRow component is great for quickly testing the output of a job before writing it into a more complex structure, such as an XML file, or before loading it into a database.

We'll use the input file, `ms-catalogue.xml`, from the `Chapter 3` example files as our input data. Copy this to your `DataIn` folder. Follow these steps to create the job:

1. Create a new job and name it `MultiSchema`. The Studio does not offer a metadata component for a multi-schema XML file, so in this case, we will configure directly in the component.

2. In the **Palette** window, search for `MSXML` (multi-schema XML), and from **File | Input** , drag-and-drop a **tFileInputMSXML** component onto the Job Designer.

3. Now search for `logrow` in the **Palette** window and drop two **tLogRow** components onto the Job Designer.

4. Click on the **tFileInputMSXML** component and configure its properties.

5. Set the **File Name** to the datafile in your `DataIn` folder.

6. Next we'll set the **Root XPath Query** field, which in our case will be `/catalogue`.

7. Click on the checkbox to **enable XPath in the column**. This will allow us to define an XPath loop for each schema.

8. In the **Outputs** section, click the + button to add a schema.

9. In the schema column of the newly created row, click on the ellipsis button. You'll get a pop-up box where you can define the name of the schema; let's call this **SKUs**.

10. A follow-on pop-up window will allow you to define the schema components for the **skus** schema. Click the + button five times and add the following elements:

    ◦ skuid

    ◦ skuname

    ◦ size

    ◦ colour

    ◦ price

11. Leave the data types as **String**, except for price, which we will change to **Float**, with **Precision** as **2**. Click on **OK** to save the schema.

12. In the **Schema Xpath Loop** column, enter the XPath loop for the **skus** schema. Note that this is relative to the **Root XPath Query** field that we configured in step 6 previously, so we'll set this to **skus/sku**.

13. We now need to set the XPath queries for the individual fields. Click on the ellipsis in the **XPath Queries** column and enter the following values in the **Schema XPathQueries** column of the pop-up window:

    ◦ sku

    ◦ skuname

    ◦ size

    ◦ colour

    ◦ price

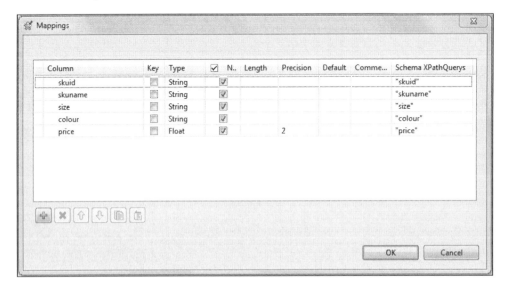

14. Follow steps 8 to 12 to configure the component for the inventory schema.

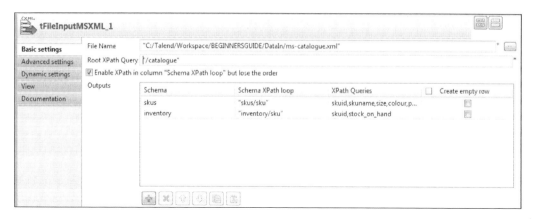

15. Let's now connect our multi-schema XML component to the log rows. Right-click on the **tFileInputMSXML** component, select **Row | skus**, and drop the connector onto **tLogRow1**. Right-click on the **MSXML** component again, select **Row | Inventory**, and drop the connector onto **tLogRow2**:

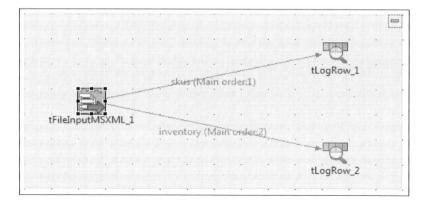

16. We're now ready to run our job. Go to the **Run** tab in the bottom panel and click on **Run**. You will see the data scroll past in the **Run job** console. You will see the inventory data returned, followed by the product data:

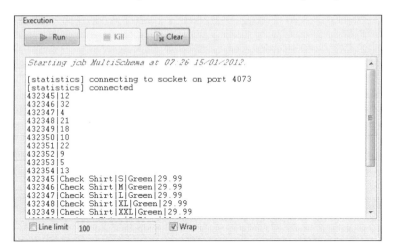

Nice work! Obviously, we could send the output to different files rather than the **Run Job** console if required.

Enriching data with lookups

So far, we have looked at integration scenarios where we have transformed files from one format to another, but in all cases the data we needed in the output file was contained, in some form, in the input file. However, it is commonplace in real-life scenarios that we need to transform data to the requirements of one system, but the originating system does not actually contain the data we need. It's time to improvise!

In this section, we'll create a job that passes data from one component to another, but on the way, uses a lookup data to replace some data. Imagine that we need to transform some customer data. Our original file is simple, containing the following fields:

- Company name
- Address
- City
- State
- Zip code

The following is a sample file:

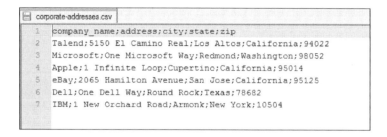

Let's name this file as `corporate-addresses.csv` and drop it into your `DataIn` folder.

The output file required by the receiving system is exactly the same as this, with one exception. Its **state** field is only two characters long (as it is expecting the standard USPS two-character state code).

Our original system does not hold the two-character state code, so we'll have to get this data from somewhere else and merge it into the original file. In this case, a quick search on the Internet will direct us to a number of sources of state name and state code data. For this job, we're going to keep the lookup data in a pretty low-tech container. Fire up your trusted text editor and write the state data into the file, in the following format:

```
[State Name],[State Code]
```

Make sure that each state name/state code pair is on a new line. The following a snippet of what you should have when you have completed this:

We'll name this file as `states.csv` and drop it into the `DataIn` folder too.

Of course, the state lookup data could be held in lots of different containers, such as an XML file, relational database, even a third-party web service; but for now we'll work with a plain old text file.

Let's start by creating a new job named `StateLookup`. Then, follow these steps:

1. Create file delimited metadata for the two input files, `corporate-addresses.csv` and `states.csv`, following the same steps as used previously.

> When creating the corporate addresses metadata, the wizard defines zip as a data type of integer, based on the data presented in the file. This is okay if the file contains US-only addresses, but might not be okay if the file contains a mix of US and other addresses. If this were to be the case, you would modify the data type here to string, to cope with other zip code formats.

2. Drag each metadata component onto the Job Designer, selecting **tFileInputDelimited** in each case.

3. Now search for `join` in the **Palette** window, grab a **tJoin** component, and drop it onto the designer. This is the component that will join our two data streams.

4. Right-click on the corporate addresses file component, select **Row | Main**, and drop the connector onto the **tJoin** component.

5. Right-click on the `states` file component, select **Row | Main**, and again drop this onto the **tJoin** component. You'll notice that, even though we selected **Row | Main** in both cases, the resulting connector is slightly different. The first connector we made in step 4 is noted as **Main**, while the second is called **Lookup**. The order in which we connect the components to the **tJoin** is important. Join the primary data stream first, and one or more lookup components subsequently.

> If you join connections in the wrong order or wish to change which is the Main dataflow and which is the Lookup dataflow, you can do this by right-clicking on one of the connectors and selecting **Set this connection as Lookup** or **Set this connection as Main**.

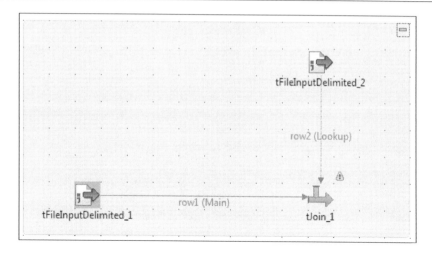

6. Search for `delimited` in the **Palette** window and drag a
   tFileOutputDelimited component onto the Job Designer. Edit its **File Name**
   so that the output is created in your `DataOut` folder. Let's call the output file
   `address-lookup-out.csv`.

7. Now click on the **tJoin** component. In its **Basic settings**, click on the **Edit
   Schema** button.

8. We need to copy some of the input fields into the **tJoin** component. You can
   see in the left-hand side window that both of the input schemas are shown in
   separate tabs. Holding down the *Ctrl* key, click on **company_name**, **address**,
   city, and **zip** from our main delimited input file. Click on the top-arrow
   button in the middle bar of the window to copy these over to the **tJoin_1**
   schema. (Clicking on the two-arrow button will copy all the fields from the
   left-hand side window to the right-hand side window.)

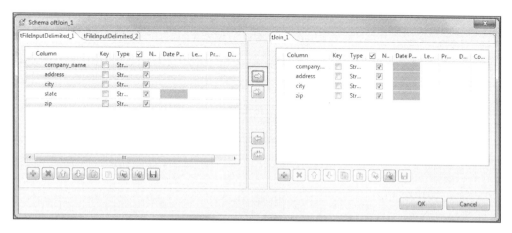

9. Now click on the second tab in the left-hand side window showing the schema for the second delimited file input. Select the **state_code** column and copy this over to the right-hand side window, using the top-arrow button.

10. In the right-hand side window, click on the **state_code** column and move it up one place on the list of fields by clicking on the up arrow button:

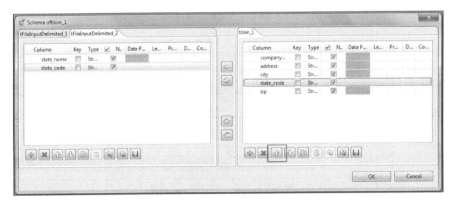

11. Click on **OK** to save the changes, and when prompted to propagate the schema changes, click on **Yes**. This will copy the **tJoin** schema over to the delimited output component.

12. In the **Basic settings** tab of the **tJoin** component, click on the checkbox **Include lookup columns in output**.

13. In the **Column mapping** box, add a row and select **state_code** from the **Output column** drop-down menu. In the **Lookup column** section, select **row2.state_code**.

14. In the **Key definition** table, add a row and select **state** as the **Input key attribute** field, and **row2.state_name** as the **Lookup key attribute** field;

What have we just done here? In the **Key definition** table, we've noted that the **state** field in the main input file maps to the **state_name** field in the lookup file. We've also configured in the **Column mapping** table, that in the **Output column** section, the **state_code** field should be populated with values from the lookup file **state_code** field.

15. Right-click on the **tJoin** component, select **Row | Main**, and drop this onto the delimited output component.

16. It's time now to run the job. You should get the following output in your DataOut folder:

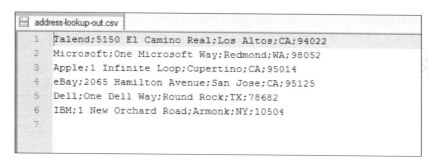

Notice that the **state** field has now changed from the full state name to the two-character state code.

For the final exercise in this chapter, let's build some jobs that use the most familiar of datafiles—Excel.

Extracting data from Excel files

Spreadsheets are a ubiquitous business tool in the modern world, and there is a vast amount of critical data that resides in these common desktop files. As the tools are so commonplace and easy to use, spreadsheets are often the tool of choice for storing and manipulating all kinds of data. In this section, we'll look at a couple of ways to pull data from a spreadsheet. One of the most-used features of spreadsheets is the sheets functionality, which is the ability to add another page within the spreadsheet file. Sheets within a file may be closely related (for example, each sheet represents sales data for a given month) or may be less closely related (for example, a customers spreadsheet may contain customer data, such as the first name, last name, and e-mail in sheet 1, and address data in sheet 2). Instead of taking spreadsheet data and converting it into the CSV format before transforming it, the Studio has Excel components that allow us to address multiple spreadsheets within a single file.

Extracting data from multiple sheets

In the first example, let's look at extracting data from multiple sheets within a spreadsheet, but where each sheet has the same columns or schema. Our example datafile has three sheets representing categories of garment. Each sheet has a **product_code** field and a **product_name** field. Our task is to extract data from each sheet and export it into a single CSV file. Perform the following steps:

1. Create a new job named `Spreadsheet1`.

2. As is our common practice, let's create a metadata component for our input Excel file. Right-click on **File Excel** in the **Metadata** section of the **Repository** window and select **Create file Excel**.

3. In step 1 of the wizard, change the **Name** field to `products` and click on **Next**.

4. In step 2, browse to the `products.xls` file in the `DataIn` folder. The wizard will show the available sheets in the Excel file and a preview of the data for each sheet.

5. Check **All Sheets** in the **Set sheets parameters** pane to configure all the sheets to be read by the job. In the lower right-hand pane, we need to select a sheet that will serve as a schema guide for the wizard. Let's leave this as **dresses**, as selected by the wizard. Click on **Next**.

6. In step 3, let's set the heading row as the column name, as we have done previously. Note that the heading rows from the second and third sheets are showing the preview as data, as shown in the next screenshot. Don't worry about this for now; we'll return to it when we configure the job.

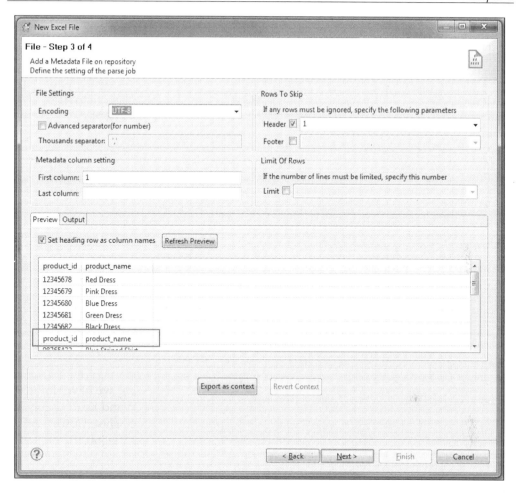

7. Click on **Next**. Change the schema name to `products` in step 4 and click on **Finish**.

8. Now drag the products' Excel metadata onto the Job Designer. Click on the **Component** tab below the Job Designer and check the checkbox named **Affect each sheet (header & footer)**. This forces the header configuration to apply to each sheet and resolves the issue we noted earlier, that the header data was appearing in the data output.

9. Search for `delimited` in the **Palette** window and drag a **tFileOutputDelimited** component onto the Job Designer.

10. Right-click on the Excel component, select **Row | Main**, and connect it to the delimited output component:

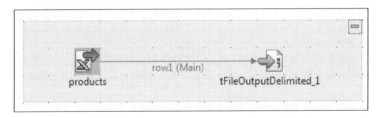

11. Turning to the delimited output component, set the output **File Name** to product-excel-out.csv in your DataOut folder.

12. Click on the **Include Header** checkbox, which will add the header row to the output file.

13. Run the job and check the output; it should look like the output shown in the following screenshot:

Joining data from multiple sheets

In the second example, let's imagine our spreadsheet has two sheets—one that contains basic customer information, for example, title, name, e-mail; and another that contains customer address data. The two sheets are linked by a unique customer ID. We want to extract the data from both these sheets, join it together based on the unique customer id, and present it as a single output file. We'll use two different Excel input components to access the different sheets (and the schemas that they contain) and a **tMap** component to join the two dataflows. Perform the following steps:

1. Create a new job named `Spreadsheet2`.

2. Let's now create two metadata components from different worksheets in the same Excel spreadsheet (`customers.xml` in the `DataIn` folder). Follow the same steps that we have used previously, but on step 2 of the wizard, ensure that the correct worksheet is checked, rather than **All sheets**. In the following screenshot, you can see just the addresses sheet being configured:

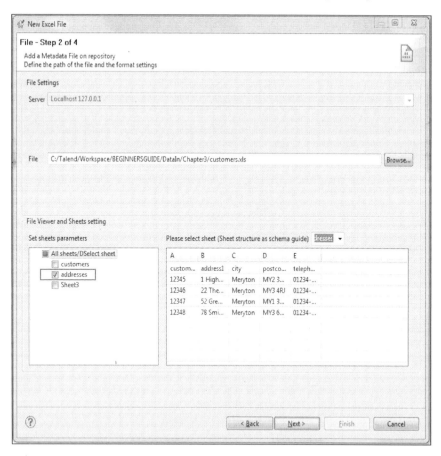

3. Once the metadata is configured, drop an instance of each from the **Metadata** section in the **Repository** window, to the Job Designer. From the **Palette** window, search for tMap, and drop this onto the Job Designer too:

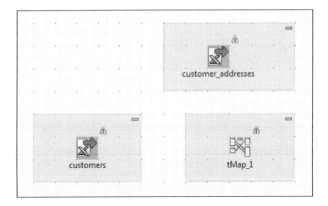

4. Now let's join everything together. Right-click on the customers input file, select **Row | Main**, and drop the connector onto the **tMap** component. Do the same with the customer_addresses input file. Note that we see the customers connector as **Main** and the customer_addresses connector as **Lookup** again. Remember that the first connection becomes the main flow and the second or subsequent connections become lookup flows:

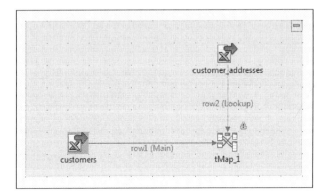

5. Double-click on the **tMap** component to open the Map Editor. The first thing we need to do is join the two input rows. We have previously noted that **customer_id** is the common field and the key that joins the two sets of data. To join **row1** and **row2**, simply click on **customer_id** in **row1** and drag it to the expression box of **customer_id** in **row2**:

6. The component draws a line between the two **customer_id** fields to show the connection.

7. In the output pane of the Map Editor, click on the **+** button to create a new output. Change the name of the output to **customer_addresses**, to make it more meaningful:

8. Now we can drag-and-drop fields from the input pane to the output pane, building up the mapping and the schema as we go. Multiselect all of the fields from **row1** and drop them onto the **customer_addresses** output pane. Select **address1**, **city**, **postcode**, and **telephone_number** from **row2**, and drop these onto the **customer_addresses** output pane too. Your final mapping configuration should be similar to what is shown in the following screenshot:

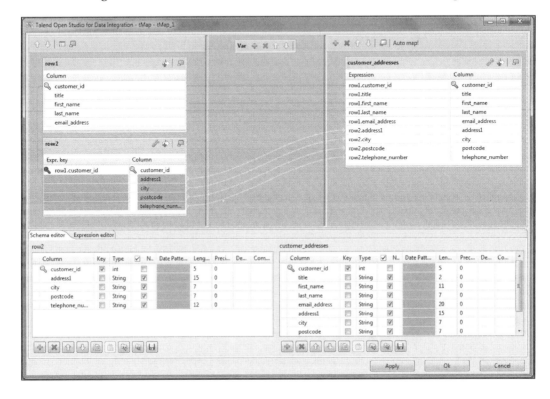

9. Now search for a delimited output file in the **Palette** window and add this to the Job Designer. Right-click on the **tMap** component, select **Row | customer_addresses**, and drop the connector onto the delimited output component.

10. Change the **File Name** field of the delimited output component to something appropriate in the **DataOut** folder. The final job configuration should be as shown in the following screenshot:

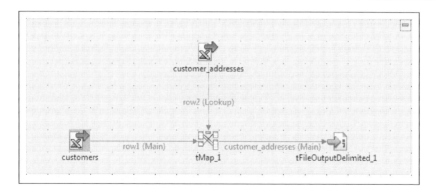

 It is best practice to layout lookup components, as shown in the previous screenshot. Specifically, the **Main** component is placed on the left-hand side, with one or more **Lookup** components above the main dataflow feeding into it as dataflows from left to right. The positioning does not, of course, change the output of the job in any way, but this is a Talend convention and makes jobs easier to read, particularly in a collaborative development environment, where many developers may work on a job over time.

11. Let's run the job. You should see the data from both the sheets joined into the single delimited file.

Referring back to the original spreadsheet, you can see that there are five distinct customers in the customer sheet, but only four customers in the address sheet. This has been represented correctly in the output file. Take a look at the last line; it has the customers' title, name, and e-mail, but a series of empty fields for the address data:

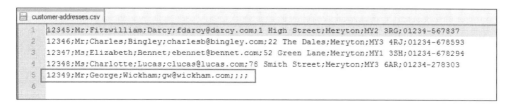

This is because joins created in the **tMap** component are, by default, **left outer joins**.

 Left outer joins is a common concept in database SQL queries, and where there are two database tables, X and Y, which are joined by a query, a left outer join will result in all the records from the left-hand table X being returned, even if there is no matching record in the right-hand table Y.

The result of a left outer join can be clearly seen in the data output from our job.

However, you may not always want the result set to behave in this manner, and you can set the join type, which is a so-called inner join, so that only those records that are represented in both data sets appear in the output.

To configure this in our job, go back to the **tMap** component and click on the spanner icon of **row2**. You'll see some other configuration options revealed:

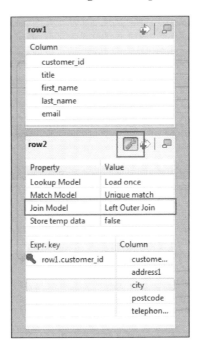

Click on the words **Left Outer Join** and an ellipsis button is revealed. Click on this button, and the pop-up window will show two options for the **Join Model** field, **Left Outer Join** and **Inner Join**. Click on **Inner Join** and then click on **OK**. Click on **OK** to close the **tMap** window and run your job again. This time, you will see that only four rows are returned, only those customer records that have an address.

If you wish to capture the records rejected by the inner join (those that do not have an address), you can define another output in the **tMap** component to achieve this. Double-click on the **tMap** component and perform the following steps:

1. Click on the **+** button of the output pane to add a new output. Change its name to **customer_addresses_rejects** and click on **OK**.

2. Multiselect all of the fields from the **row1** input pane and drag these onto the new output. We don't need any fields from **row2** as we know that any records sent to this new output will not have address data.

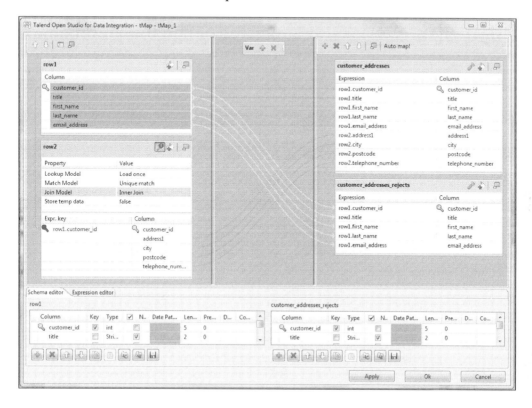

3. Click on the spanner icon for the **customer_addresses_rejects** output pane. This will reveal its settings. Click on the value box of the **Catch lookup inner join rejects** row to reveal the ellipsis button. Click on the button and select **True** from the options. Click on **OK** to accept this change, and then click on **OK** to close the Map Editor and save its settings.

4. Add another delimited file from the **Palette** window to the Job Designer. Right-click on the **tMap** component, select **Row | customer_addresses_ rejects**, and drop the connector onto the new delimited file component.

5. Change the **File Name** parameter of the delimited component and run the job. You will see the four records going to the original delimited output as before, but now the single rejected record will pass to the new delimited component:

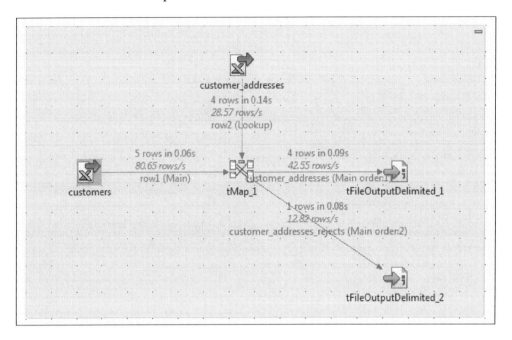

Summary

This was the first time we got our hands dirty with the Studio, the Studio, and we looked at some common integration scenarios based on common file formats. We looked at transforming files from one format to another—CSV to XML, for example. We also explored the **tMap** component and its built-in Expression editor. We built jobs using the multi-schema XML component, and saw how we can map data to the most complex XML structures using the advance XML output component. We also saw how to join data from different sources using both the **tJ join** component and the join functionality within **tMap**.

Let's move on to look at how the Studio can work with another common systems component—the relational database.

4
Working with Databases

Databases, specifically relational databases, are at the heart of most modern applications and business systems and it is likely that anyone involved in integrating systems will need to interact with databases in some way.

In this chapter, we'll look at using the Studio to work with databases. We will learn about the following topics:

- Extracting data from a database table
- Joining data across database tables
- Writing data to a database table
- Synchronizing data between databases
- Modifying data in a database
- Dynamic database lookup in an integration job

The jobs we create in the chapter use a simple database which is in the `Chapter 4 ResourceFiles` folder for this chapter. Let's take a moment to look at the database and familiarize ourselves with the data it contains.

There are four tables in the database: products, brands, orders, and order lines. The entity relationship diagram in the next screenshot shows the connections between the tables:

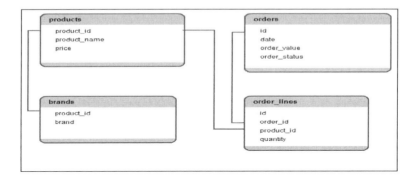

As we go through this chapter, we'll use one or more of the tables in each job that we produce. You may want to view the content of the tables in your database browser before proceeding.

Database metadata

As we saw in *Chapter 3, Transforming Files*, we will use metadata components to define connection details for our database. Work through the following steps to create the metadata configuration for our database:

1. In the **Repository** window, expand the **Metadata** section and right-click on **Db Connections**. Click on **Create Connection**. The **Database Connection** wizard will appear as shown in the following screenshot:

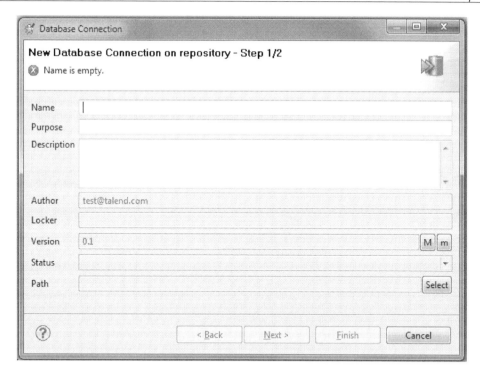

2. Enter a name for the connection. Let's call ours DEMO_DB. You can also enter additional information in the **Purpose** and **Description** boxes. There are other configuration options for **Version, Status,** and **Path,** but these are not mandatory, so we'll leave them for now.

The **Version** option allows you to modify the version of the database connection metadata as you may modify this over time and wish to keep older versions. The **Status** option allows you to set an arbitrary status for the connection. The default values are **development**, **testing**, and **production**, but these can be modified to suit your purpose. Finally, the **Path** option allows you to define a directory hierarchy and position for this database connection. For example, you might have a metadata directory structure that defines your database connections on server A and server B.

3. Click on **Next.**

4. We now need to configure the database connection.

 You may need to get database connection details from your database administrator if you are working with an existing database. Note that, while broadly similar, the connection parameters that are required do vary depending upon which database system you use, so seek some expert advice on the specifics of your database if you are not sure.

5. The Studio has built-in database connection drivers for most of the common database systems (and some not so common). It can also use generic ODBC or JDBC drivers for those database systems that support these protocols. We are using MySQL, so in the **DB Type** drop-down menu, find and select **MySQL**. Selecting this will configure some default parameters, such as the **Db Version** field and the **String of Connection** fields. Note that **Db Version** can be changed wherever appropriate.

6. Enter the value for the **Login** and **Password** fields.

7. Enter the value for the **Server** field. This will be the hostname or IP address of your database server.

8. Enter the **Port** details.

9. Enter the **Database** name to which you want to connect.

10. Once all of the values have been entered, click on the **Check** button to test the connection. If all has been set up correctly, you will get the **Check Connection** pop-up window saying that the connection has been successful. If not, go back and check the values that you have configured.

11. Finally, click on **Finish** to save the connection.

Having set up the database connection metadata, we need to add to this by retrieving the schema of the database. This will allow us to easily query tables from the database in our jobs without having to explicitly define them each time. Perform the following steps:

1. In the **Repository window, expand the Metadata section**, right-click on the **DEMO_DB** connection, and select **Retrieve schema**.

2. The window that appears allows us to define which database objects are added to the schema.

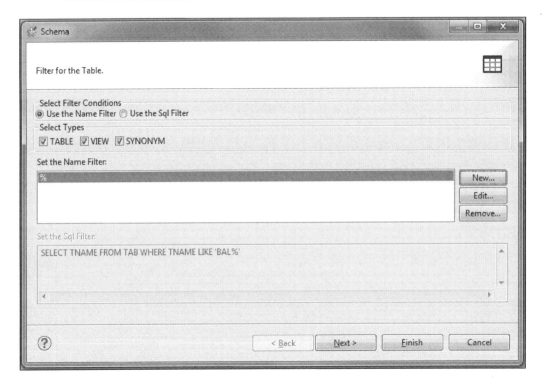

3. By default, the schema wizard will retrieve all objects types, tables, views, and synonyms, and all objects by name (the name filter is set to %, which is the SQL wildcard notation). We could modify these settings so that, for example only tables with a specific name or name pattern are returned, but let's accept the default settings for now. Click on **Next**.

4. The next screenshot shows the objects returned by the previous name pattern query. We can now explicitly set which objects we want to set in our schema. In our case, we want all of the database tables to be in our schema, so expand the **demo_db** line to reveal the tables and check the box next to **demo_db** to select all tables.

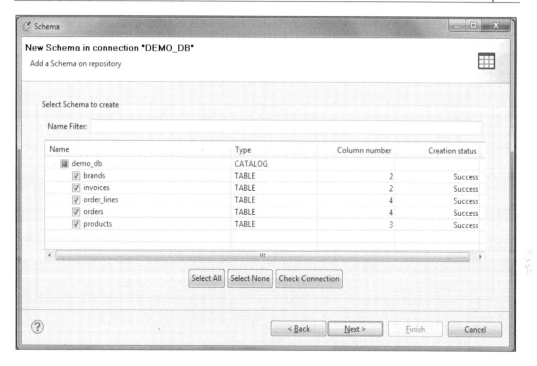

5. Click on **Next**. The Studio will work out the schema for each table based on the table definition within the database, but on the next screenshot, we can modify the schemas as necessary. Again, we'll go with the defaults for now, so select **Finish** to complete the schema's setup.

6. Expand the **DEMO_DB** metadata connection to show the items within the **Table schemas** folder.

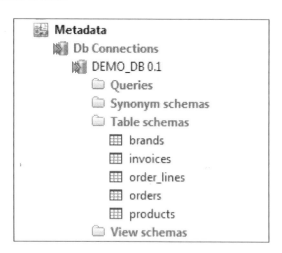

Now that our database connection is set up, we'll start to do something useful with it. Let's kick off with a simple extract from our database.

Extracting data from a database

One of the most common integration tasks is to take data from an application database and write it to a file where it might be processed by another system or converted to a report. In this first example, we'll take data from a single database table and export it to a delimited file.

If you're following the examples using the source code provided for this chapter, have a quick look at the tables provided. You'll see that there are two tables, **products** and **brands**. The tables are joined by a product ID that is present in both tables. For the first example, we will simply extract the data from the **products** table.

Perform the following steps:

1. Under **Job Designs** in the **Repository** window, create a new folder named Chapter4 and, within this, create a new job named DBExtract.

2. Expand the **DEMO_DB** metadata we created previously to show the **Table schemas**. Click on the **products** table and drag this onto the Job Designer. You will be presented with a window which shows lots of possible component types that can be used with this table definition.

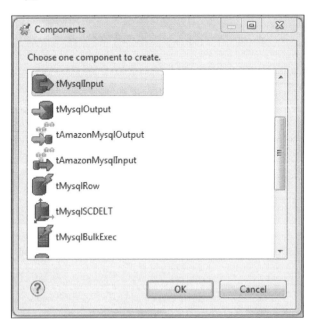

3. Select **tMySQLInput** and click on **OK**. The component will appear in the Job Designer.

For the job we're building, we'll need a **tMySQLInput** component. This somewhat-confusingly named component, for the beginner at least, extracts data from a database and passes the result onto another component. In a similar, but opposite vein, the **tMySQLOutput** component writes data into a database! The Studio names these and other components from the perspective of the job, not the data source or the data target. So, a **tMySQLInput** component is an input source to the job.

4. Now highlight the component in the Job Designer and click on the **Component** tab in the panel below the Job Designer. You can see all of the connection details pre-configured into the component. You can also see the SQL query that is needed to extract data from this table.

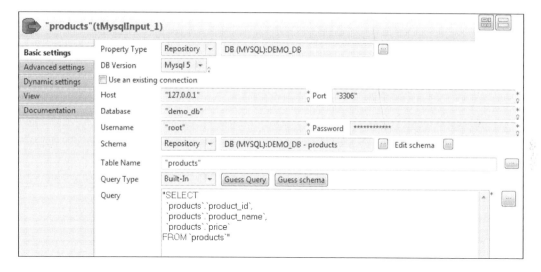

The SQL queries we will use throughout this book will be relatively straightforward and readers with modest SQL experience should be able to follow along. Those readers who need a primer or refresher on SQL will find a lot of material on the Internet to help them. Simply search for SQL Tutorial in your favorite search engine.

5. Let's now connect our database component to a file component. In the **Palette** window, search for `delimited` and drag a **tFileOutputDelimited** component onto the Job Designer.

6. Right-click on the **tMySQLInput** component, select **Row | Main,** and connect it to the delimited output component.

7. Now go to the **Component** tab of the delimited output. Set its **File Name** to something suitable in your `DataOut` folder. Run the job and, once complete, open the new delimited file and check the output.

```
  products-out.csv
 1    383741444;Fuji 16MP Digital Camera - Black;120.0
 2    383741454;Fuji 16MP Digital Camera - Silver;120.0
 3    383741464;Fuji 16MP Digital Camera - Pink;120.0
 4    383741474;Fuji 16MP Digital Camera - Red;120.0
 5    383741484;Olympus 14MP Digital Camera Black;120.0
 6    383741494;Olympus 14MP Digital Camera Silver;120.0
 7    383750454;Fuji 14MP 30x Optical Zoom Camera;120.0
 8    383751734;Panasonic 14MP Digital Camera Blue;115.0
 9    383751744;Panasonic 14MP Digital Camera Red;115.0
10    383751754;Panasonic 14MP Digital Camera Pink;115.0
11    383751824;Panasonic 16MP Digital Camera Black;160.0
12    383751834;Panasonic 16MP Digital Camera Silver;160.0
13    383751844;Panasonic 16MP Digital Camera Red;160.0
14
```

Congratulations! Your first database extract is complete. Let's move on to extracting data from multiple tables.

Extracts from multiple tables

The previous extract example was based on data from a single table, but we frequently need to retrieve data from multiple tables in a denormalized form. Most modern applications that use a relational database will have a normalized structure, so, by definition, extracting data in a denormalized form will involve joining data from different tables.

In the Studio, we can join the data within the database extract component, using the database itself to do the work or outside of a component, within the job, where it is Java that does the data crunching. Let's take a look at examples of both.

Joining within the database component

Our first example is straightforward and presents an SQL query to the database component that joins two database tables. Carry out the following steps to recreate this job:

1. Create a new job in the repository and call it DBInternalJoin.

2. In the **Repository window,** expand the **Metadata** section, click on the **DEMO_DB** connection (highlighted in red in the following screenshot), and drag it onto the Job Designer.

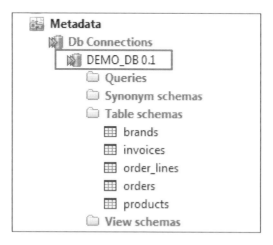

3. The available components window will appear. Choose **tMySQLInput** from the list.

4. Click on the **Component** tab below the Job Designer. You can see that the database connections are visible, but because we selected the parent component from the **Repository** window, rather than a specific table within the schema, there isn't a query or schema defined for this component yet. Let's create these now.

5. Click on the ellipsis button to the right of the **Query** box and the SQL Builder window will appear. We can use this to define the tables, fields, and specific query that will be used in our job.

6. The SQL Builder can be used in a number of ways, but in this example we'll use the query designer functionality to build our query. In the **Database Structure** pane, expand the **demo_db** item to reveal the tables. Right-click on the **products** table and select **Generating Select Statement**. This will add the table to the query designer pane in the top right-hand side of the window. You can also see the query in SQL just below the query designer.

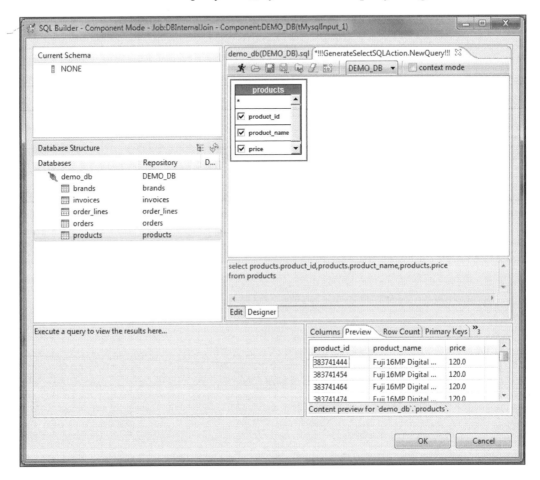

7. Now right-click in the query designer and select **Add Tables**. Select **brands** and then click on **OK** to add the **brands** table to the query designer.

8. The **product_id** field is a key field in the **products** table and a foreign key (http://en.wikipedia.org/wiki/Foreign_key) in the **brands** table, so we will link these two fields together. Right-click on the **product_id** field in the **products** table, select **Equal,** and drop the connector onto the **product_id** field in the **brands** table. Notice that this action changes the text SQL query below the query designer and adds a **where** clause.

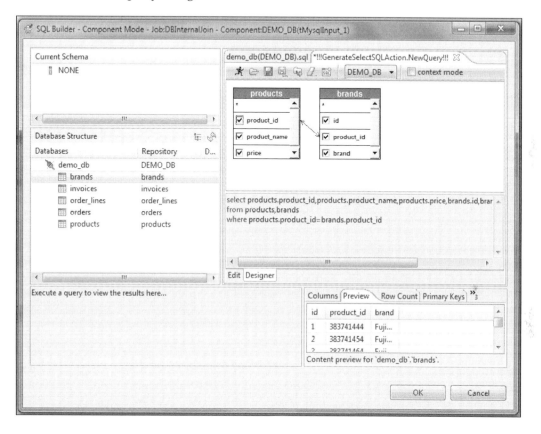

9. Let's now view the output of this query. Click on the running man icon above the query designer and you will see the output in the query results pane in the bottom left-hand side of the window, highlighted in the following screenshot:

10. We can see that the result set contains some redundant information. The **product_id** is shown twice and the **id** field in the **brands** table is simply an incrementing id and is not required for our particular data-set. To resolve this, untick the checkboxes next to **id** and **product_id** in the **brands** table, as shown in the following screenshot:

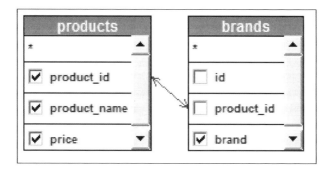

11. Execute the query again to view the resulting output. Now that we are happy with the result set, click on **OK** to save the query into the component.

12. We can use the query we have defined to set the schema of the component. Click on the **Guess schema** button and the Studio will work out what the schema should be, based on the query we have designed. The Studio will present the schema once it has completed its guesswork. Click on **OK** to save the schema or modify it as necessary.

13. With the database component now complete, let's add our output component to the job design. Search for `delimited` in the **Palette** window and add a **tFileOutputDelimited** component to the Job Designer.

14. Right-click on the **DEMO_DB** component, select **Row | Main,** and drop the connector onto the delimited output component. Set the **File Name** parameter of the delimited output component to something suitable in your `DataOut` folder.

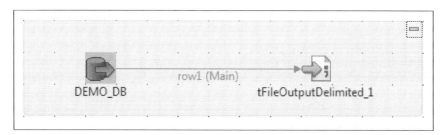

15. We can now run the job. The output should be as shown in the following screenshot:

```
join_within_db.csv
1   383741444;Fuji 16MP Digital Camera - Black;120.0;Fujifilm
2   383741454;Fuji 16MP Digital Camera - Silver;120.0;Fujifilm
3   383741464;Fuji 16MP Digital Camera - Pink;120.0;Fujifilm
4   383741474;Fuji 16MP Digital Camera - Red;120.0;Fujifilm
5   383741484;Olympus 14MP Digital Camera Black;120.0;Olympus
6   383741494;Olympus 14MP Digital Camera Silver;120.0;Olympus
7   383750454;Fuji 14MP 30x Optical Zoom Camera;120.0;Fujifilm
8   383751734;Panasonic 14MP Digital Camera Blue;115.0;Panasonic
9   383751744;Panasonic 14MP Digital Camera Red;115.0;Panasonic
10  383751754;Panasonic 14MP Digital Camera Pink;115.0;Panasonic
11  383751824;Panasonic 16MP Digital Camera Black;160.0;Panasonic
12  383751834;Panasonic 16MP Digital Camera Silver;160.0;Panasonic
13  383751844;Panasonic 16MP Digital Camera Red;160.0;Panasonic
```

In the next section, we'll look at a different way to approach this task by joining data *outside* of the database query, within the Studio itself.

Joining outside the database component

The second example demonstrates a scenario where the join is outside of the database component and uses a the Studio join component to do the heavy lifting.

Again, perform the following steps:

1. Create a new job and call it DBExternalJoin.

2. As in the previous example, we are joining data from the **products** table with data from the **brands** table. As our metadata for these tables is already set up, we can easily add these components to the job. In the **Metadata** section of the **Repository window**, expand the **DEMO_DB** connection and expand the **Table schemas** section to show the different tables available in our metadata.

3. Click on the **products** table and drag this onto the Job Designer. Select **tMySQLInput** from the **Components** pop-up window. Do the same with the **brands** table. Arrange the components as shown in the next screenshot. The **products** data will be our main dataflow and the **brands** data will be our lookup dataflow. As noted previously, it is best to have the lookup flows above the main dataflow, which operates from left to right.

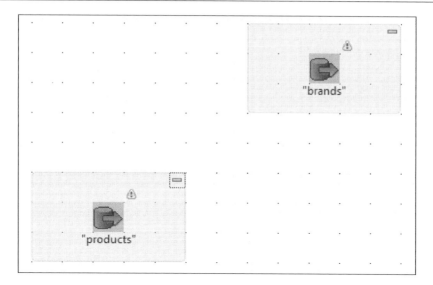

4. Search for map in the **Palette** window and drop a **tMap** component onto the Job Designer. Join the **products** component to the **tMap** component, using a **Row | Main** connector and then do the same for the **brands** component. Note that the products dataflow should be a **Main** flow, with the brands dataflow shown as a **Lookup** flow.

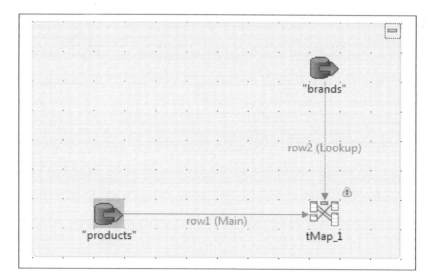

5. Double-click on the **tMap** component to open the Map Editor.

6. Let's connect the two input dataflows within the Map Editor by clicking on **product_id** from **row1** and dragging this to the expression key box of **product_id** in **row2**.

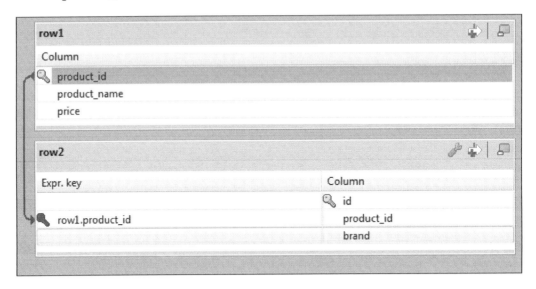

7. Now add a new output flow to the Map Editor by clicking on the green + button at the top of the right-hand pane. You'll be prompted to name the output flow. Let's call it `product_brand`.

8. We can now drag the fields we require from the input flows to the output flow. Drag all three fields from **row1** and the **brand** field from **row2** to the output flow.

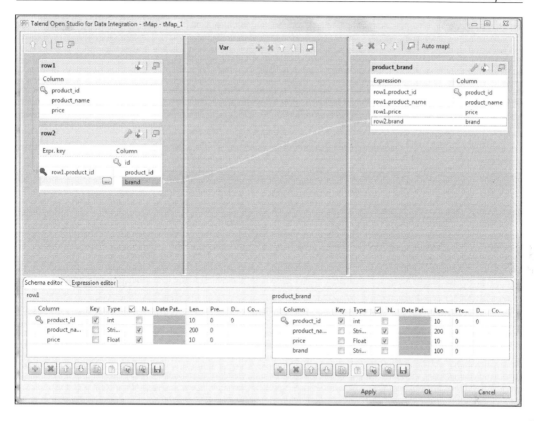

9. Click on **OK** to save the mapping.

10. Now search for `delimited` in the **Palette** window and add a **tFileOutputDelimited** component to the Job Designer. Right-click on the **tMap** component and select **Row | product_brand**, connecting this to the delimited output. Change the **File Name** of the delimited output component to something suitable in your **DataOut** folder.

11. With the configuration complete, we can run the job normally. However, for this execution let's use the Traces Debug mode, which runs the job and also shows the dataflows as they happen. On the **Run** tab, click on **Debug Run** and then click on the **Traces Debug** button to run the job. The job will run at a slower speed than a normal execution and will display each row of data as it comes from the main input source and as it passes to the main output target, as shown in the following screenshot:

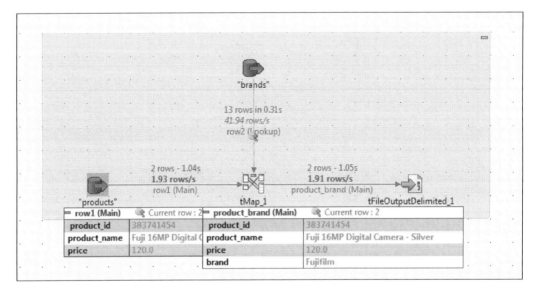

12. This is a really useful way of viewing the data as it runs, allowing developers to validate the output in real time. You will notice that the job can be paused at any point if you want to inspect the data in detail.

13. As a final check, view the output file produced by the job. You will find, as expected, that the output is identical to that produced by the previous job.

The obvious question that arises from these two examples is, when do I use an internal join instead of an external join. There's no hard and fast rule about this and sometimes it will come down to the skill of the developer creating the job. Arguably, it is easier for a less experienced SQL coder to use an external join, whereas an experienced database developer will naturally lean towards creating the SQL query in one go, and so will use a single **tMySQLInput** component. With regard to the performance of the Studio job, one might choose to use an external join when the SQL query required contains outer joins, sub-queries, or both. Sometimes it can be more efficient to have the Studio join data from two or more components, each with simple queries, than for this to be accomplished on a single MySQL component with a single complex SQL query. It may also come down to assessing the capabilities of your database server compared to your Talend job server. This might include the physical hardware characteristics and system resources available, but also the typical activity that each server might undertake. For example, if you are extracting data from a database which has heavy use from its own application, it may make more sense to join the data outside of the database, rather than within it. When in doubt, build the job using both methods and compare the performance results.

Let's follow this by looking at sending data in the opposite direction while inserting data from a file into a database.

Writing data to a database

Having extracted data from a database, the obvious next step is to put it back in. In the real world, we might come across this scenario when we need to exchange data between one application and another. A common way of facilitating this exchange is to extract some data out of an application database A, write it to a file, then take the same file, and import it into an application database B. As different applications (often from different vendors) are unlikely to be integrated at the application or at the database level, this intermediate step provides a bridge between one application and another.

A word of caution before we proceed. In real-life scenarios, we should be cautious about writing data directly to a database. There is something quite final and irreversible about this sort of process and that is one of the reasons why so many applications have data import **Application Programming Interfaces (APIs)**. APIs provide a measure of protection for the underlying system where new data can be programmatically checked and validated before importing. Before embarking on an integration that writes directly to a database, you should ensure that the correct analysis has been done and programs have been fully tested before unleashing to a production environment. It is all too easy to import new data into a database and damage the data integrity that exists. Additionally, data validations and integrity checks should be built into the integration jobs wherever possible. However, in some circumstances, directly writing into the database may be the only option, so it should not be ignored as an option, it is just to be used with care.

In this walk through, we're going to use the database from the previous example, along with some additional data in a file to load in. Before we get into the job itself, take a look at the datafile we're going to apply to the database. Open the file DB_IN_ UPDATE.csv in the Chapter 4 datafiles. If you compare this to the data extract from the previous example (or if you query the database) you will see that the datafile contains seven rows that are already in the database, albeit with different prices, and six new rows that are not in our database. This highlights a very real integration challenge, the need to deal with updates to data differently to brand new records. Sometimes, this can be accommodated by having two separate datafiles to import, one for updates and one for new records. The originating application may be able to distinguish updates from new records by created and updated timestamps or other mechanisms. But what if it can't? What if all you can get from your originating application is a set of data that you know has changed in some way, either updates or inserts? Sometimes, all we might get is a data set that contains some records that are identical, some that contain updates, and some records that are completely new, but with no way to distinguish between them. Fortunately, the Studio comes to our rescue as it can deal with these differences for us. Work through the following steps:

1. Create a new job in the **Repository window** and call it DBInsert.

2. As previously, we'll start by defining the metadata for our input file. Expand the **Metadata** section of the **Repository window** and right-click on **File delimited**, selecting **Create file delimited**.

3. On step 1 of the metadata definition, enter the name product_update and click on **Next**.

4. On step 2, click on **Browse** and navigate to the input file in your **DataIn** folder.

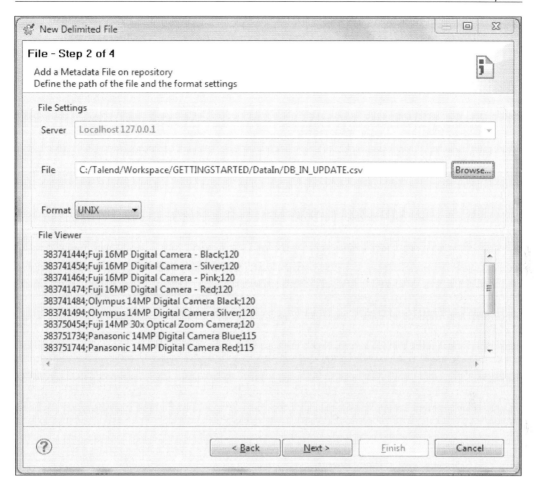

5. Click on **Next**. On step 3 we can accept the defaults noted by the Studio, so click on **Next** again.

6. On step 4, change the **Name** field to `product_update` and modify the column names to be `product_id`, `product_name`, and `price`. The Studio has detected the price as an integer, so modify this to be a float with precision of 2. Click on **Finish** to complete the setup.

7. Select our newly created **product_update** metadata and drag it onto the Job Designer. Choose **tFileInputDelimited** from the **Components** window.

8. The data we present in the file is going to update the **products** table in the database, so expand the **Table schemas** folder of the **DEMO_DB** metadata, select the **products** table, and drag this onto the Job Designer too. Our database is a data target in this job, rather than being a data source as in previous jobs, so we need to select **tMySQLOutput** in the **Components** window.

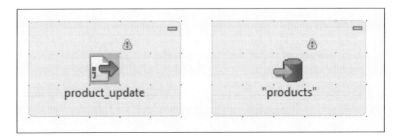

9. Now, let's join our components. Right-click on the delimited input component, select **Row | Main** and drop this onto the **products** database component.

10. We now need to set two configuration parameters for the database update component, **Action on table** and **Action on data**. We'll take a moment to look at all of the options as they have a big impact upon how the component works.

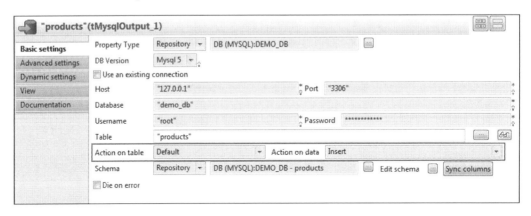

Action on table instructs the component on what to do with the database table we are targeting. The options are defined as follows:

Action on table	Result
Default	No operation is carried out on the targeted table.
Drop and create table	The targeted table is dropped (removed) and recreated. If the table does not already exist, then the drop command will fail and the job will terminate with an error.
Drop table if exists and create	Similar to the previous operation, but a check is done to see if the table exists before the drop command is issued. Use this in preference to the previous configuration if you are not sure whether or not a table exists.
Truncate table	Issues a truncate command prior to inserting the data. The truncate command quickly removes all data from the table and its action cannot be rolled back.
Clear table	Issues a delete command prior to inserting the data. A delete command will generally take longer to execute than a truncate command, but it can be rolled back if required.
Create table	Tries to create the table before inserting the data. The command will show an error if the table already exists, resulting in a job failure.
Create table if not exists	It is similar to the Create table operation, but the command checks if the table exists already and, if it does, does not issue the create table command.

Action on data instructs the component on what to do with the data it is trying to insert. The following table defines the options available:

Action on data	Result
Delete	Deletes the records passed by the input component if they exist in the target table. Records that do not exist are ignored.
Insert	Adds new records to the component. If duplicate entries are found, then the job will terminate.
Insert Ignore	Adds new records, but ignores duplicates based on the schema key.
Insert or Update	Adds new records or updates existing records. Note that this action tries to insert data first and if it cannot (because the records already exist), it will try to update the record.
Insert or update on duplicate key or unique index	Similar to the Insert or Update operation.

Action on data	Result
Replace	Adds new records. If an existing row has the same value as a new row based on a key or unique index, the old row will be deleted before the new row is inserted.
Update	Updates existing records, but ignores new records.
Update or Insert	Updates existing records and creates new records. Note that this action tries to update a record first and if it can't (because the record doesn't exist), then it will insert the record.

11. We'll set the **Action on table** to `Default` and **Action on data** to `Insert or update`. Note that table inserts or updates are based on the key field defined in the schema. In our job, it is the **product_id** field which is defined as the key, so it will use this to determine whether to insert data (if the new record's key value does not exist in the table) or update data (if the key record already exists in the table).

Okay, we're ready to run the job, so click on **Run** in the **Run** tab. When the job completes, take a look at the data in your database table. You should see the seven existing rows with new, updated prices. You should also see the six new records that were not present before.

Spend some time experimenting with the different table and data actions that TOS provides. For example, compare the results of an **Update** versus an **Insert Ignore** for the **Action on data** setting. In a similar manner, if **Action on data** is set to **Insert Ignore**, **Action on table** set to **Default** will quote different results to the same parameter set to **Drop table if exists and create**.

Database to database transfer

In a lot of the examples we have seen so far in the book, we have used files of different sorts to be the conduit for the data. Specifically, data is extracted to a file or imported from a file. However, it is perfectly possible for data to be passed directly from one system to another, which often means from one database to another. We will look at an example of this database-to-database transfer in this section. The job we will build will transfer data from our example database to a second database named DB2DB (there is a script to create the database and an associated table in the **ResourceFiles** folder of this chapter). The new database contains a table named **order_data** containing the following fields:

- order_date
- order_id
- line_id
- order_status
- product_id
- product_name
- brand
- unit_price
- quantity
- extended_price

All of these fields are contained within our original database, with the exception of **extended_price**, which we will have to construct. (Extended price is commonly defined as the unit price multiplied by the quantity.)

As you are probably starting to realize, there is often a number of different ways that a Talend job can be implemented. For this job we're going to use a database extract component, a **tMap** component, and a database import component.

1. Let's start by creating the metadata for our new database, DB2DB. Right-click on the **DB connections** element of the **Metadata section in the Repository window** and select **Create connection**. Enter DB2DB in the name field and click on **Next**.

2. Enter the database connection details on step 2 and click on **Finish**.

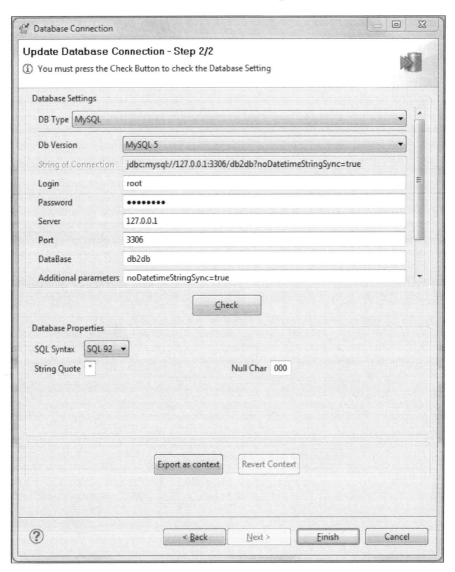

3. Right-click on the newly-created connection and select **Retrieve schema**. Follow the same steps on the schema wizard as we used previously.

4. Create a new job and name it DB2DB. We can approach the job in (at least!) two ways, joining data internally or externally as we saw earlier in the chapter. Both will work, but let's choose an external join for this job.

5. We're going to need a number of tables as source data in this job. From the **DEMO_DB** metadata, drop the **products**, **brands**, **orders**, and **order_lines** tables onto the Job Designer, selecting **tMySQLInput** in each case as the desired component.

6. Search for **tMap** in the **Palette** window and drop this onto the Job Designer too.

7. Right-click on each of the MySQL input components in turn, select **Row | Main,** and connect to the **tMap** component. The table we are inserting data into contains order data with the **order_id** and **line_id** field as a composite key. Therefore, it makes sense to have either the **orders** or **order_lines** component as the main dataflow into the **tMap** component, with the others as lookups.

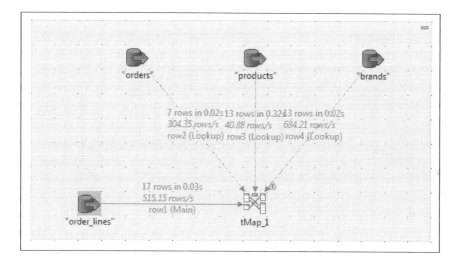

8. To make things a little easier to understand within the **tMap** component, it is worth taking a moment to rename the dataflows. You can do this by double-clicking on the **row1** name. This will make the label editable. Change **row1** to order_lines and do the same for **row2**, **row3**, and **row4**, changing the name to match the database table each dataflow is coming from.

9. Now double-click on the **tMap** component to open the Map Editor, where we can join the incoming dataflows.

10. Drag and drop fields from one dataflow to another to make the necessary joins. We need to join the **order_id** field from **order_lines** to the **id** field in **orders**, the **product_id** field in **order_lines** to the **product_id** field in **products**, and the **product_id** field in **products** to the **product_id** field in **brands**. Let's also make the join type on the **orders** and **products** dataflow an inner join, rather than the default left outer join. Once you have finished making the connections, your source dataflows should look like the following:

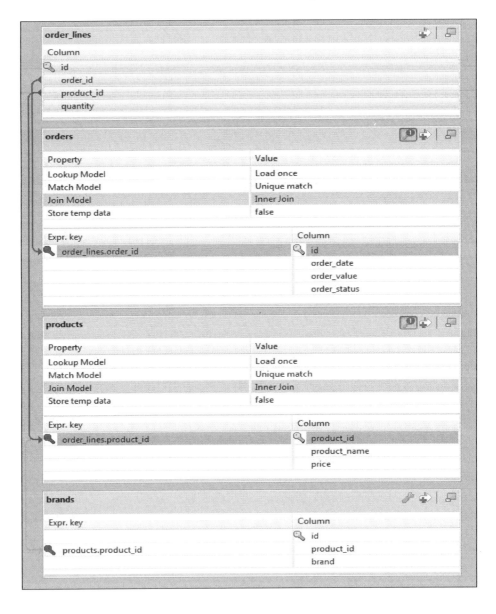

11. Let's now configure the target component of the job. In the **Repository window, expand the Metadata section,** expand the **DB2DB** connection in it that we created earlier, and select the **order_datatable** in the **Table schemas** folder. Drag this onto the Job Designer. In the **Component** pop-up window, select a **tMySQLOutput** component and click on **OK**.

12. Right-click on the **tMap** component, select **Row | New Output,** and drop the connector onto the **order_data** component. You will be prompted for a name for this dataflow, let's call it order_data.

13. Now double-click on the **tMap** component to open the Map Editor. You will see the input and output data sources, but no connections between them.

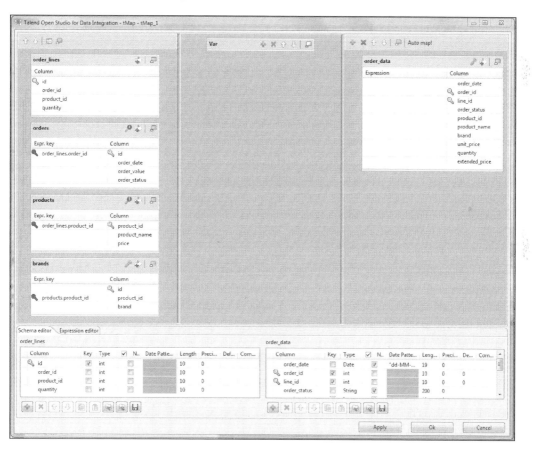

14. We can join data from the input sources to the target output in the normal manner, but let's use the Auto Map feature instead. The Studio joins fields from the inputs to those on the outputs based upon the field name. Click on the **Auto map!** button at the top of the right-hand pane and you will see that the Studio does a pretty good job of joining the fields:

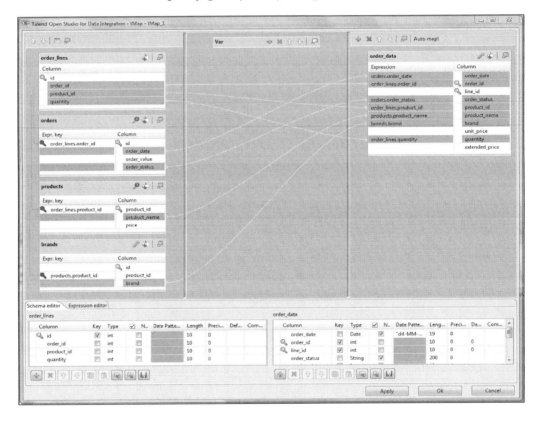

15. There are some fields that the Studio cannot match, so we'll join these by hand. Drag the **id** field in **order_lines** to the **line_id** field in **order_data**, the **price** field in **products** to **unit_price** in **order_data**; finally, open the Expression Builder of the **extended_price** field and enter the following expression or build it by clicking on the required fields and operators:

```
order_lines.quantity*products.price
```

16. Click on **OK** in the Map Editor to save the mappings.

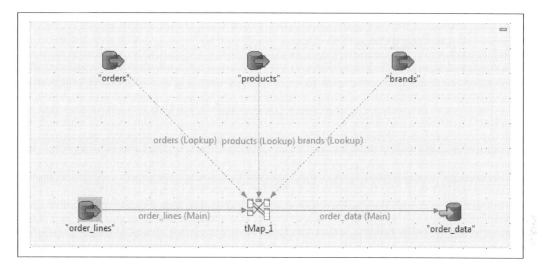

17. We are now ready to run the job. Click on **Run** in the **Run** tab. You should see 17 rows being pushed from the input database, through the **tMap** component to the output database. Open your database browser and you will see this similarly reflected in the **db2db.order_data** table.

Modifying data in a database

It is not unusual for data integrations to be simply about getting data from one system, modifying it, then passing it onto another system to consume the classic **Extract, Transform and Load** (ETL) scenario. However, sometimes we will also need to modify the data in the database that we are sourcing data from or, indeed, the database we are sending data to.

To illustrate this, imagine we have a database table containing customer orders. We need to extract the data out of this table and send it to another system so that the orders can be fulfilled. However, most of the time we will need to be selective about the data that we send over. We cannot select all rows from the table, because presumably some will have already been sent. We could filter our result set by date/time so that the job only runs once per hour and each time it sends data created in the last hour. This would probably work perfectly well for most scenarios, but even this kind of filter is not quite as good as knowing definitively whether an order record has been extracted or not. A better solution would be for each row to have a status and the status is updated as events happen.

So in the **orders** table example described earlier, an order might originally have a status of **ORDERED**, but once it is extracted then its status is changed to **EXTRACTED**. In this way, we can use the **order_status** field as the filter for our result set, that is, at any time we can extract all of the orders that have a status of **ORDERED**, knowing that they have not been extracted previously. Once we have extracted this data, we can change the **order_status** to **EXTRACTED**, so that they will not be extracted the next time (or ever again).

In order to facilitate this scenario, we need a job that will update data in the database table. Perform the following steps to create this job:

1. First, let's take a look at the data in our table. In the query browser enter the following:

```
SELECT * FROM orders
```

You will see the following data:

It shows a number of orders each with a unique ID, and order date/time, value, and order status. We want to update the **order_status** column so that its values are **EXTRACTED**.

2. Create a job and call it DBUpdate.

3. From our **Repository window,** expand the **Metadata** section, select the **orders** table from the **DEMO_DB** database connection, and drag-and-drop this onto the Job Designer. Choose **tMySQLRow** from the **Components** window that pops up.

4. Click on the component in the Job Designer and then click on the **Component** tab in the panel below it.

5. Under the **Basic settings tab**, you can see the connection details pre-configured, as shown in the following screenshot:

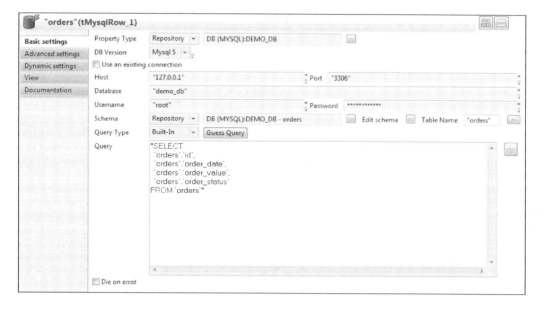

6. By default, the query is a **SELECT** query. For our purposes, we want this to be an **update** statement.

7. Delete the default query in the **Query** box and replace it with the following SQL statement:

```
"update orders set order_status= 'EXTRACTED';"
```

Notice the single quotes around the word EXTRACTED and the double quotes around the whole statement.

8. Our job is ready to run. Press *F6* on your keyboard to start the job. The job will complete quickly and, because we are not passing data from one component to another, there is no feedback to show how many rows have been updated. However, go back to your database browser and you should see that all of the order status values have been updated to **EXTRACTED**.

In reality, this job would probably be part of a larger job that would incorporate a number of steps. As was illustrated at the start of this example, it might be that data was extracted to a file before the **update** component was executed. It is also likely that the SQL update statement would be more complex. For example, it might set the order status to **EXTRACTED** where the current order status is **ORDERED** or where the order ID was in a specific set of values. We shall see examples of more complex, multi-step jobs later on in the book.

Our next exercise will look at an often-needed technique, that is, how to dynamically extract data from a database.

Dynamic database lookup

What do we mean by dynamic database lookup? Let's explain with an example scenario.

Let's suppose we have an integration process that passes some information to us and that each time the data set that is returned is different. For example, the information passed to us might be a list of product IDs that have been sold today; tomorrow it will be the product IDs that will be sold tomorrow, and so on. This information is very useful, but a little hard to work with as it is only a list of product IDs. We might want to know other information about the products, such as the product name or the product price.

As we have seen in a previous example, we could extract all of the product data from our database and, using a **tJoin** or **tMap** component, match this data with the incoming product order data, and create a file that has the product information appended to the order information. Although this approach would work perfectly well, it might not be the most efficient approach in some circumstances. If the incoming order data is relatively small in size compared to the database product data, then we are unnecessarily extracting all of the product data from the database in order to match it with the order data and, depending upon the size of the product database, this may take some time. A better approach would be to extract only the records we need based on the incoming data-set. Let's look at how we can do this:

1. We'll start by thinking about what we want the job to do. We want it to read the data input (products sold data) and turn this into a form such that we can pass it to a database read component where the query is as follows:

    ```
    select product_id, product_name, price from products where
    product_id in (...)
    ```

The . . . would be substituted each time by the current set of product IDs. Now that we have the general principles in mind, let's build the job.

2. Create a new job and name it `DynamicDBLookup`.

3. We will use a simple CSV file as the input data in this job. It is a list of product IDs and represents the order data described previously. Copy the reference file `products-sold.csv` to your `DataIn` folder.

products-sold.csv	
1	383741444
2	383751734
3	383741464
4	383741484
5	383751844
6	

4. Following the process we have used previously, define the metadata for this delimited file and, once complete, drop this onto the Job Designer, selecting **tFileInputDelimited** from the **Components** pop-up window.

5. In the **Palette** window search for `denormalize` and drop a **tDenormalize** component onto the Job Designer.

6. The **tDenormalize** component is typically used to group data by a specific field. For example, suppose we had the following data set:

```
England, London
USA, New York
USA, Seattle
Canada, Montreal
England, Nottingham
```

7. If we denormalize this data using the country as the grouping field, our data set will become as follows:

```
England, London, Nottingham
USA, New York, Seattle
Canada, Montreal
```

In our job, we just have a list of product IDs, but if we denormalize this data using the product ID as the grouping field, we can turn the list into a comma-separated string, perfect for passing through to our database-read component.

8. Right-click on the delimited input component, select **Row | Main**, and drop the connector onto the denormalize component.

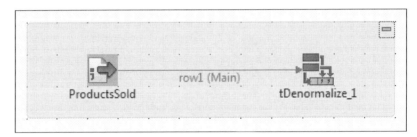

9. In the **Component** tab of the denormalize component, click on **Sync columns** to copy the schema from the delimited component to the denormalize component. The output from the denormalize component will be a comma-separated string as noted previously, so we also need to modify the datatype of the **product_id** field from integer to string.

10. We now need to configure the denormalize element. In the **To denormalize** box, click on **+** to add a new row to the table. By default, it will show the first field in the schema (in our case, **product_id**, the *only* field in the schema, so we can leave this as it is). The **Delimiter field** is shown as a semi-colon. This is the output delimiter and we want this to be a comma in our output, so modify this to "," accordingly. The final column in the table is **Merge same value**. If this is checked, then duplicate values in the input data will be merged, so that only one occurrence is output; if unchecked, then duplicate values will remain. In our case, it makes sense for duplicate values to be merged, so we can check the checkbox.

11. From the **Metadata section in the Repository window**, drop the products table metadata onto the Job Designer, selecting **tMySQLInput** from the resulting pop-up window.

12. Modify the default query to the following:

```
select product_id, product_name, price from products where
product_id in (...)
```

13. From the **Palette** window, search for `log` and drop a **tLogRow** component onto the designer.

14. Right-click on the database component, select **Row | Main,** and drop the connector onto the **tLogRow** component. The output of the database component will now display on the **tLogRow** component when the job runs.

 We now need to pass the results of the denormalize component to the input of the database component. However, we hit a problem here. The database component does not take a regular main input. You can validate this by right-clicking on the denormalize component, selecting **Row | Main**, and dropping the connector onto the database component. As you can see, TOS does not allow this action to happen. The database component will, however, accept an **iterate** connector and we can use the **tFlowToIterate** component that turns a flow input into an iteration as a vehicle for passing the dynamic data through, as a variable.

15. Search for `iterate` in the **Palette** window and drop a **tFlowToIterate** component onto the Job Designer, between the denormalize and database components.

16. Create a **Row | Main** connector between the denormalize and the flow to iterate components. Create a **Row | Iterate** connector between the Flow To Iterate component and the database components.

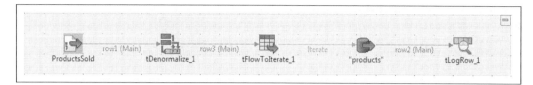

The **iterate** connection has the effect of invoking the database extract once for every row produced by the denormalize component. In our job, as we are turning a single column of data into a single row of data, we know that the database component will be run only once.

17. Finally, moving back to the database component, we're going to change the query so that it accesses the data being pushed from the denormalize component, via **row3 (Main)** to the **tFlowToIterate** component. Change the query to the following:

```
"select product_id, product_name, price from products where
product_id in ("+row3.product_id+")"
```

18. The query code in the previous item concatenates three strings, using the concatenate (+) function. The middle string is currently a variable, row3. product_id, and at run time, this will be substituted with the actual values produced by the denormalize component.

19. Let's run the job in Traces Debug mode to see it in action.

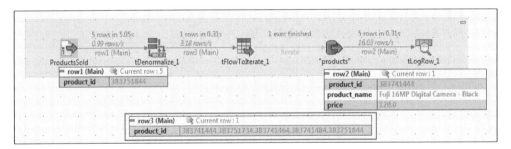

The **row3 (Main)** box, highlighted in red in the preceeding screenshot, shows the denormalized string of **product_id** that is formed and then gets passed to the products database component via the **iterate** connector. This string is then plugged into the query we defined in the database component, using the row3. product_id variable.

Each time a file of product IDs is presented, the extract query will run for exactly those IDs that are in the file.

Summary

Following our introduction to working with files in *Chapter 3, Transforming Files*, this chapter worked through some common integration scenarios with one of the mainstays of modern applications, the relational database. We set up a database connection as project metadata that could be reused on many jobs. We learnt how to extract simple data from a database (from a single table), and two different ways that we might extract and join data from multiple tables. We created jobs that wrote data to a database, first from a flat file to a database and secondly, from database to database. We learned how to modify data in a database table and, finally, we learned about the dynamic database lookup based on information from an input data source.

Our next chapter will reuse some of the techniques we discovered in *Chapters 3, Transforming Files* and in this chapter, to help us understand how to implement some common data operation functions, sorting, filtering, aggregating, and normalizing.

5
Filtering, Sorting, and Other Processing Techniques

As we pass data around from component to component, system to system, there is often the need to modify it in some way. This chapter introduces the Studio's processing components, which will become your "Swiss Army Knife" as you develop integration jobs. The processing group of components is used as intermediate data processing or transformation components, intercepting data flows between input and output components. For example, we might have a filtering component between a database read component and a database write component, or between an XML file input and a CSV output. Alternatively, we might use a data sorting component that takes sales order data from a file and sorts it by customer ID in ascending order.

In this chapter, we will look at:

- **Filtering data**: Removing or passing through specific records based on some attribute of the data
- **Sorting data**: Alpha and numeric sorts (singularly or in combination)
- **Summing and aggregating data**: Including finding minimum values, maximum values, and count of records as well as the commonplace sum of values
- **Normalizing and denormalizing data**: Grouping or un-grouping data
- **Finding and replacing data**: Looking for a particular string or set of characters in a data flow and replacing them with something else
- **Sampling specific rows from a data flow**: For example, passing through only the first or last row of a data flow

Don't be deceived by the simplicity of the processing components—they are extremely useful and will undoubtedly be used time and again as part of larger integration processes.

Filtering data

As we pass data through an integration process, we may often wish to filter it in some way. Data from source systems may be fine in terms of its format, but its content scope may be too broad for the receiving systems. For example, suppose we have an export of data from our financial system of all invoices due to our customers and we wish to send a list of the invoices to each customer; we wouldn't send the full list to all customers, but rather send a filtered list to each customer of only their own invoices.

We have seen in previous examples that the tMap component has filtering capabilities but the Studio provides a dedicated filtering component with some extra features for fine control (when there is no requirement for data mapping). We will look at three examples of how to use the filter component in your integration jobs:

- A straightforward filter
- The same filter, but also capturing the rejected records
- Finally, how to split a file based on filters

Simple filter

Let's start with a simple data filter process. Our source file is a list of European countries and their currencies—`currencies.csv` in the resources directory of this chapter. Take a quick look at the file. You will see that many European countries use the Euro as their currency; others have their own currency. Our job will filter the data input so that only those countries that have the Euro as their currency will appear in the output.

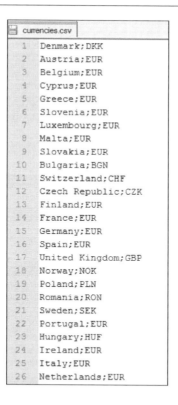

Follow along as we walk through the job:

1. Create a new directory under **Job Designs** and name it Chapter5.
   Within this, create a new job and call it Filtering1.

2. As we have done in the previous chapters, create a file delimited metadata
   for the currencies.csv file.

3. Click on the newly-created currencies metadata and drag-and-drop it onto
   the Job Designer. Select **tFileInputDelimited** from the pop-up window.

4. From the Palette, search for a **tFilterRow** component and a
   tFileOutputDelimited component and drop these onto the Job Designer.

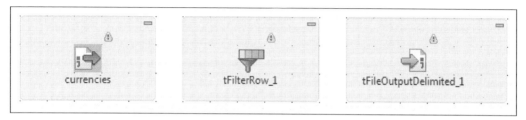

5. Let's now join the components together. From the currencies delimited input, right-click and select **Row | Main** and join it to the filter component. Right-click on the filter component, select **Row | Filter** and connect this to the delimited output component.

6. Click on the **tFilterRow** component, and in its **Component** tab we will configure the criteria we want to filter by. In the **Conditions** box, click on the + button—this will add some default values for the row.

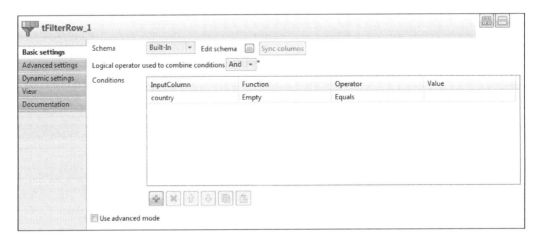

7. Change the **Input Column** value to **currencies**, leave the **Function** value as **Empty** and the **Operator** value as **Equals**, and add the value "EUR" (with quotes) into the **Value** field. As you will no doubt have guessed, this will filter the data set such that all records will have a currency of "EUR".

8. To complete the configuration, click on the delimited output component and change its **File Name** to currencies-out.csv in your output directory.

9. Go to the **Run** tab and click on **Run**. You will see that the job passes 26 rows to the filter component, but only 16 are passed through to the output component.

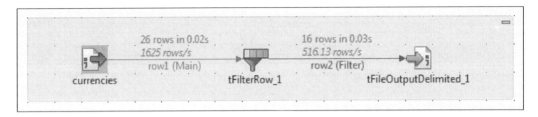

For a more interactive view of the data flow, go to the **Debug Run** tab and click on **Traces Debug**. You will see each row from the input file go into the `tFilterRow` component, but only those rows with a currency of "EUR" will flow out.

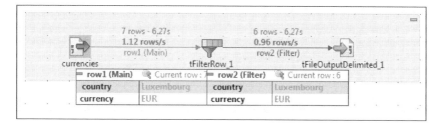

Take a look at the output file too. You can see that it only shows those countries whose currency is Euros, as shown in the following screenshot:

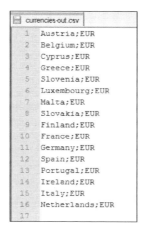

Filter and rejects

For our next example, we will use the simple filter job we created earlier as a start point. In the **Repository**, right-click on the **Filtering1** job and select **Duplicate**. In the pop-up window, change the name of the new job to `Filtering2` and click on **OK**. Double-click on this job to open in the Job Designer. You'll see all of the components and configurations we applied a moment ago. We are going to add to this job the log information about the rejected records. Follow the given steps:

1. Right-click on the delimited output component, select **Copy** and, right-clicking again, select **Paste**. This will put a copy of the component onto the Job Designer.

2. Change the **File Name** to `currency-rejects.csv` in your output directory.

3. From the filter component, right-click and select **Row | Reject** and drop the connector onto the new delimited output. Once the connection has been made you will notice that the new delimited output component has an error symbol against it (a white cross in a red circle at the top right of the component). Click on the **Edit schema** button of the **Component** tab and you will see that the reject input data stream has an additional schema field—an error message. We need to add this into the new delimited output component. The quickest way to do this is to click on **Sync columns** in the output component.

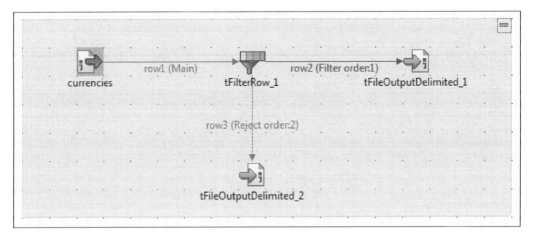

4. Now run the job. This time we will see 16 rows sent to the first delimited output component, as before, and 10 rows sent to the second delimited output component. Open the new rejects file and view the contents. You can see the rejected records with the reason why they were rejected—in this case, when comparing the currency to EUR, the comparison failed.

```
 currency-rejects.csv
 1   Denmark;DKK;currency.compareTo("EUR") == 0 faild
 2   Bulgaria;BGN;currency.compareTo("EUR") == 0 faild
 3   Switzerland;CHF;currency.compareTo("EUR") == 0 faild
 4   Czech Republic;CZK;currency.compareTo("EUR") == 0 faild
 5   United Kingdom;GBP;currency.compareTo("EUR") == 0 faild
 6   Norway;NOK;currency.compareTo("EUR") == 0 faild
 7   Poland;PLN;currency.compareTo("EUR") == 0 faild
 8   Romania;RON;currency.compareTo("EUR") == 0 faild
 9   Sweden;SEK;currency.compareTo("EUR") == 0 faild
10   Hungary;HUF;currency.compareTo("EUR") == 0 faild
```

Filter and split

For our final filtering example, we will split a file based on the filter criteria. As before, right-click on the **Filtering1** job in the **Repository** and select **Duplicate**. In the pop-up window, rename the job to `Filtering3` and click on **OK**. Double-click on **Filtering3** to open it.

1. Click on the **row1 (Main)** connector and, once highlighted, right-click and select **Delete**. This will disconnect the input component from the filter component.

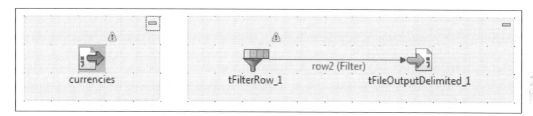

2. In the Palette, search for `replicate` and drop a `tReplicate` component onto the Job Designer. The `tReplicate` component duplicates the output it receives, allowing it to be passed to two or more components.

> Note that the data streams from a `tReplicate` component are not processed in parallel, but sequentially, in the order specified in the output connections.

3. Now click on the box containing the filter and delimited output components to highlight it. Right-click on this, select **Copy** and, right-clicking again, select **Paste**.

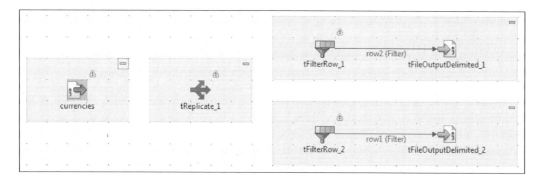

4. Join the currencies delimited input to the `tReplicate` component using **Row | Main**.

5. Again, using **Row | Main**, join the `tReplicate` component to each of the filter components.

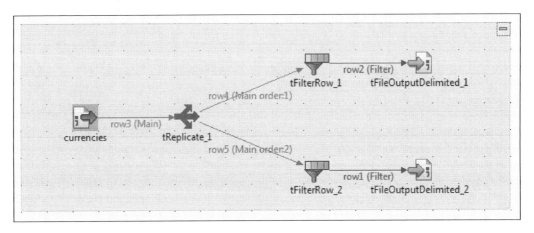

6. Click on the second filter component and change the **Operator** value in **Conditions** to **Not equal to**.

7. Change the second delimited output so that its **File Name** is different to the first delimited output component.

Run the job and you will see the replicate component send all 26 rows to both filter components, which then evaluate based on their own configurations, sending the Euro countries to one file and the non-Euro countries to the other.

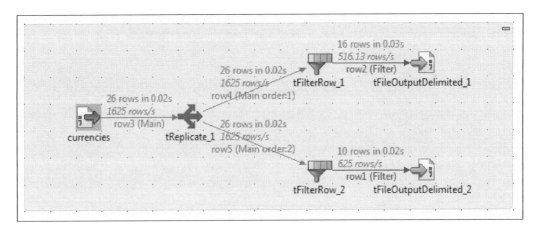

Sorting data

Our next data processing example will look at sorting data. Let's dive straight in:

1. Create a new job and name it `Sorting`.

2. We will use the currencies data file that we used previously in this example, so from the **Repository Metadata** drag the currencies delimited file onto the Job Designer. Select `tFileInputDelimited` from the pop-up window.

3. From the Palette, search for `delimited` and drop a `tFileOutputDelimited` component onto the Job Designer. Now do a search for `sort` and drop a `tSortRow` component between the two delimited components.

4. Right-click on the currencies delimited input and, using **Row | Main**, connect it to the sort component. Similarly, right-click on the sort component and use **Row | Main** to connect it to the delimited output component.

5. In the **Criteria** box of the `tSortRow` component, click on **+** to add a row—some default values will be shown. The criteria we enter here will determine how the output is sorted. Let's leave the **Schema column** value as `country`, but change the **sort num or alpha** value to `alpha` (as our file has text values, rather than numeric or date data). We can leave the **Order asc or desc?** value as `asc`.

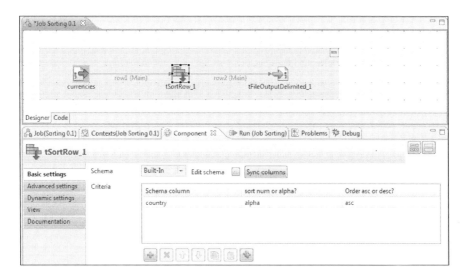

> **Order asc** configures the sort order to be in ascending order—
> alphabetically for text values and numerically for number values.
> **Order desc** sorts in descending order—highest to lowest for
> numbers and in reverse order alphabetically for text values.

6. Finally, configure the delimited output component. Change the **File Name**
   to `sorted-currencies.csv` in your `DataOut` directory.

OK! Let's run the job. When it is complete, check the output file—you should
see the data sorted by country, alphabetically in ascending order, as shown in
the following screenshot:

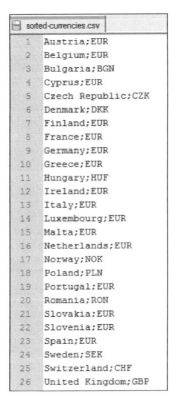

Now let's make a couple of changes to illustrate multiple sort criteria:

1. In the sort component, change the **Schema column** from `country`
   to `currency`.

2. Then, add a new row to the **Criteria** box and change its values to `country`,
   `alpha`, and `desc`.

The criteria we have configured will now sort the output by currency first, in ascending order and, where countries have the same currency, it will sort these rows by country in descending order, that is, alphabetically reversed.

3. Run the job again and check the output. You should now see the output as shown in the following screenshot:

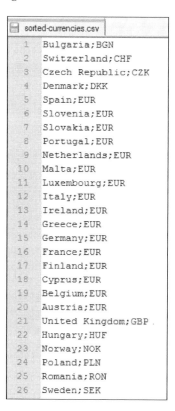

Aggregating data

An aggregation operation can often be thought of as summing some data items, but the Studio also uses aggregating functions to work out counts, minimum and maximum values, and average values, amongst other things. We will look at a simple data summation example.

The file we will work with is in the resources directory of this chapter and is named `invoices.csv`. It shows a number of invoices with the invoice number, customer name, and invoice amount. We want to extract the sum of the invoices for each customer.

1. Create a new job and name it `Aggregating`.

2. Create a **File delimited** metadata item for the `invoices.csv` file, following the steps we have used previously. Name column 0 as `invoice_number`, column 1 as `customer_name`, and column 2 as `invoice_value`. The Studio will choose a data type of **float** for the invoice value. It is better to use the data type **BigDecimal**, which preserves the two decimal places we expect with monetary values, so change this in the **Type** column of the final metadata configuration screen.

Description of the Schema							
Column	Key	Type	☑	N..	Date Pattern (Ctrl+S...	Length	Precision
invoice_number	☐	Integer	☑			4	0
customer_name	☐	String	☑			17	0
invoice_value	☐	BigDecimal	☑			8	2

3. Drag the invoices metadata item onto the Job Designer and select **tFileInputDelimited** from the pop-up window.

4. From the Palette, drop a delimited output component onto the Job Designer. Search for `aggregate` and drop a **tAggregateRow** component onto the Job Designer too.

5. We want the output file to be of the format:

   `[customer_name]; [total_invoiced_value]`

6. Add two fields, **customer_name_out** and **total_invoiced_value** to the output schema, setting the **total_invoiced_value** field to data type `BigDecimal`. Change the **File Name** to `customer_invoiced_total.csv` in the `DataOut` directory. Note that we have named the `customer_name` field differently in the output file to distinguish it from the `customer_name` field in the input file. The configuration of the aggregate component will be clearer as a result.

7. Right-click on the delimited input component, select **Row | Main,** and drop the connector onto the **tAggregateRow** component.

8. Right-click on the **tAggregateRow** component, select **Row | Main,** and join it to the delimited output component. Click on **OK** when prompted to get the schema of the target component.

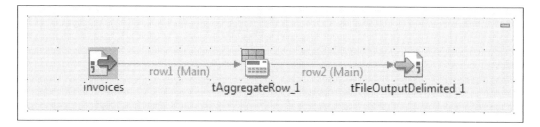

9. Finally, let's configure the **tAggregateRow** component. In the **Group by** box, click on the **+** button—some default values will appear. We want our data to be grouped by the output customer name, that is, the field **customer_name_ out**. This should already be selected for the **Output column** field, so leave this as it is. The **Input column position** is the input field that we want to map to the output field. Change this value to `customer_name`. The **Operations** box allows us to configure the aggregating functions we need. Click on the **+** button to add a row. Set **Output column** to `total_invoiced_value`, **Function** to `sum`, and **Input column position** to `invoice_amount`. Here, we have configured that the input column `invoice_amount` will get summed and mapped to the output column `total_invoiced_value`.

Run the job. You should see 30 rows get passed from the delimited input component to the aggregate component, but only five rows passed from the aggregate component to the delimited output.

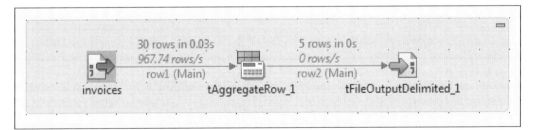

Take a look at the output file produced. You can see the five aggregated rows as shown in the following screenshot:

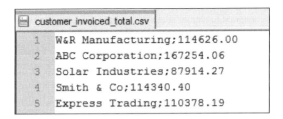

Normalizing and denormalizing data

Database normalization is the process whereby a database schema is designed to reduce data duplication and redundancy. If a database is not designed with normalization principles in mind, it can:

- Get overly large, due to duplicated data
- Make data maintenance difficult or give rise to data integrity issues if the same data values reside in multiple tables

While we are not directly concerned with database schema design in this chapter, our next two examples look at processing operations borne from the same principles as database normalization, so readers who aren't familiar with the concepts may wish to read some introductory material first. For a good primer on database normalization, go to `http://en.wikipedia.org/wiki/Database_normalization`.

Data normalization

Our first example shows how we can normalize data. Suppose we have a data file that has two fields: **product_id** and **categories**. A product can belong to more than one category and the category values are stored as a delimited list in the **categories** field. (The sample file `categories-to-normalise.csv` is in the resources directory of this chapter).

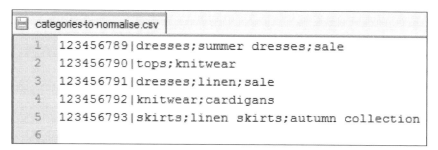

```
categories-to-normalise.csv
1   123456789|dresses;summer dresses;sale
2   123456790|tops;knitwear
3   123456791|dresses;linen;sale
4   123456792|knitwear;cardigans
5   123456793|skirts;linen skirts;autumn collection
6
```

In its current form, the data is not particularly easy to work with. For example, suppose that we wished to change the name of the `dresses` category to `evening dresses`. It is not as simple as updating the relevant cells in a spreadsheet. We would need to find those cells that contain the category `dresses`, identify the delimited value that is `dresses` (from a potentially unlimited list and in any order), and update accordingly, while leaving the other values unchanged. All rather complicated. It would be far easier to work with, if each category value was held as its own row, identified by the relevant product ID. The good news is that we can use the Studio to give us the normalized data we require.

The output we want to transform our input data to is shown as follows:

```
output.csv
1    123456789|dresses
2    123456789|summer dresses
3    123456789|sale
4    123456790|tops
5    123456790|knitwear
6    123456791|dresses
7    123456791|linen
8    123456791|sale
9    123456792|knitwear
10   123456792|cardigans
11   123456793|skirts
12   123456793|linen skirts
13   123456793|autumn collection
14
```

Let's create the job that does this:

1. Create a new job and name it `Normalize`.

2. Let's create a **File delimited** metadata component for our input file, `categories-to-normalize.csv`, as we have done previously. Note that the field separator in the file is |. Make sure that this is set in step 3 of the metadata wizard as, by default, the Studio will try to use ; as a field separator.

3. Now drag the new metadata component onto the Job Designer and select **tFileInputDelimited** from the pop-up window.

4. We need a normalize component, so search for `normalize` in the Palette and drop this onto the Job Designer.

5. We also need a delimited output file, so search for `delimited` in the Palette and add a `tFileOutputDelimited` component to the Job Designer.

6. Connect the components together—right-click on the input delimited component, select **Row | Main**, and drop the connector onto the `normalize` component. Connect from the `normalize` component to the delimited output using the same **Row | Main** method.

7. Going back to the `normalize` component, we need to specify how it normalizes. There are two key settings to consider—**Column to normalize** and **Item separator**. In our case, we want to normalize the categories, so select that from the drop-down list. Our categories are separated by a semi-colon, so enter ; in the **Item separator** box.

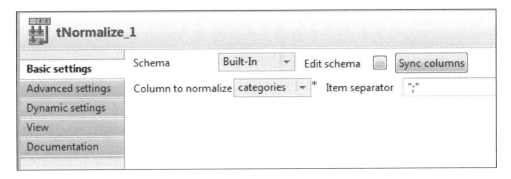

8. Finally, set the filename in the delimited output component to be `normalized-categories.csv` in your `DataOut` directory.

9. Let's run the job in **Traces Debug** mode. Click on the **Run** tab and then click on **Debug Run** in the panel below to access the trace mode. Click on the **Traces Debug** button to execute the job.

10. You will see the un-normalized data on the left-hand side of the trace and the normalized data on the right-hand side. Note that, because each input row is being converted into many output rows, the right-hand side of the trace only shows the first value for each input row.

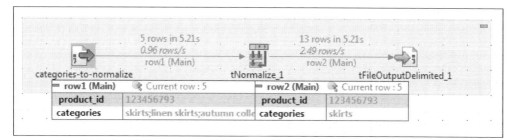

11. Let's also take a look at the output file. You can see that the input data has been fully normalized so that we have one row per `product_id`/ `category` combination.

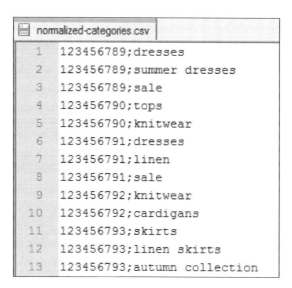

Data denormalization

Denormalization is, of course, the reverse process and is analogous to a "group by" in SQL. For the next exercise, create a denormalization job which reverses the data flows we built in the previous exercise. Use the `denormalize.csv` file (from the resources directory of this chapter) as the input data. You will need delimited input, denormalize, and delimited output components.

For comparison, there is a denormalize job in the job directory of this chapter.

Extracting delimited fields

As we have seen, some systems may store data in a denormalized form and, in the previous section, we saw how we could normalize the data. In essence, we were turning the data from column into a row. However, with some data, we may wish to change its normalized form not to rows, but to individual columns. For example, suppose a system stores its employee data with the following schema:

    [employee_id] | [name]

And the name field holds the first name and last name of the employee in the following format:

    [last_name], [first_name]

An example file is shown as follows:

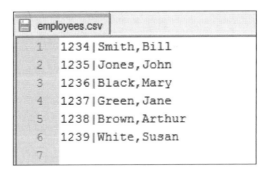

 Note that the schema does not have three fields, but that the second field contains the first and last name, separated by a comma.

Our objective in this example is to manipulate the data so that it maps to a three-field schema:

```
[employee_id] | [last_name] | [first_name]
```

Follow the walk-through given:

1. Create a new job and name it ExtractDelimitedFields.
2. Create a **File delimited** metadata item for our input file, employees.csv, in the normal manner. When you have created this, drag the metadata onto the Job Designer and select **tFileInputDelimited** from the pop-up window.
3. From the Palette, drop a delimited output component onto the Job Designer. Search for extractdelimited and drop a **tExtractDelimitedFields** component onto the Job Designer too. Place it in between the delimited input and the delimited output.

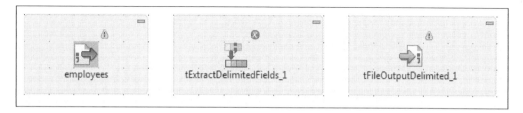

4. Connect the delimited input to the ExtractDelimitedFields component using the **Row | Main** connector.
5. We need the ExtractDelimitedFields component to have the final schema configuration that we require, specifically, employee_id, first_name, and last_name. So click on its **Edit schema** button to reveal the schema editor.

6. The left-hand side of the window will show the schema configured in the metadata and the right-hand side will be empty. Click on the **+** button of the right-hand side three times to add three new columns and name these `employee_id`, `first_name`, and `last_name`. Change the data type of the `employee_id` column to integer to match that in the delimited input file. Click on the **OK** button.

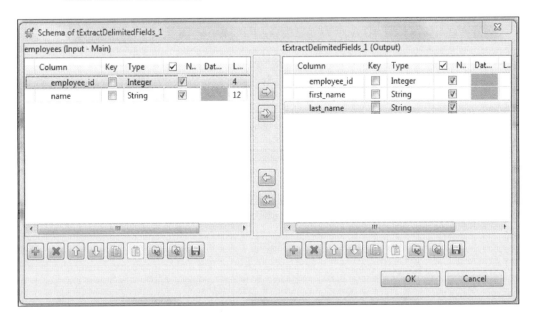

7. Now change the **Field to split** value to **name** — this is the field in the input stream that we wish to split. Make sure that the **Field separator** value is set to "**,**", as is used in our input file.

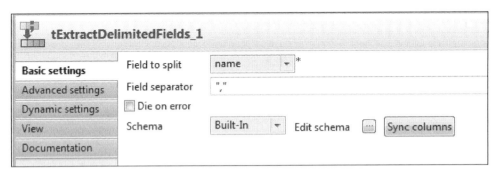

8. Finally, connect the `ExtractDelimitedFields` component to the delimited output component using **Row | Main** and change the **File Name** of the delimited output to `extract-delimited-fields.csv` in your `DataOut` directory.

OK! We are ready to run the job. Try this again in **Traces Debug** mode initially, and you will see the data transformed as the job runs.

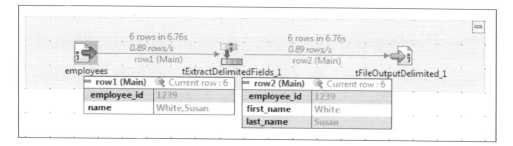

View the output file to verify the final result.

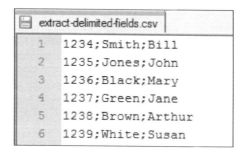

Perfect! Our `name` column splits as required.

 Note that the `tExtractDelimitedFields` component can only split one column from the original input source. If your input source had multiple columns to split in this manner, this could be achieved by chaining two or more `tExtractDelimitedFields` together.

Find and replace

We saw in *Chapter 3, Transforming Files*, in the StateLookup job example, that we can use the Studio to replace one value with another. In this example, we used a second reference data source and a tJoin component to take a value from the input file and replace it with the value held in the reference file (replacing the long-form of the state name with its two-character state code). This works really well if the replacement data is held in a reference file or database. However, sometimes we won't have this data stored elsewhere or the nature of the lookup is not as well structured as our state code example. In these instances, we can use a simple find and replace component to apply ad-hoc lookups. Let's see this technique in action.

In this job, we will take a list of two-character country codes and replace one of them with the full country name. Our input file is country-codes.csv in the resource directory of this chapter.

1. Create a new job and name it FindAndReplace.

2. Create a **File delimited** metadata item for our input file, country-codes. csv.

3. Search for replace in the Palette and drop a tReplace component onto the Job Designer. Also add a tLogRow component. We'll use the tLogRow component to view the output, but we could, of course, substitute this with a delimited output component. Drag the **country-codes** metadata onto the Job Designer and select **tFileInputDelimited** from the pop-up window.

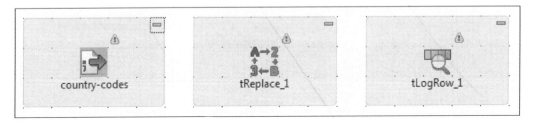

4. Connect the **country-codes** delimited input to the **tReplace** component using **Row | Main**. Then click on **Sync columns** in the **tReplace** component to copy the schema across.

5. Connect the **tReplace** component to the **tLogRow** component using the **Row | Main** connector.

6. Going back to the **tReplace**, click on its **Component** tab and, in the **Search/Replace** box, add a new row. Some default values will appear.

7. For this job, we want to replace the value AR with its full country name, ARGENTINA. Change the **Search** value to AR and the **Replace with** value to ARGENTINA.

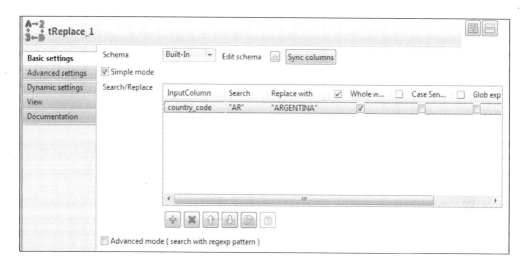

8. Run the job and you will see the following output in the console window:

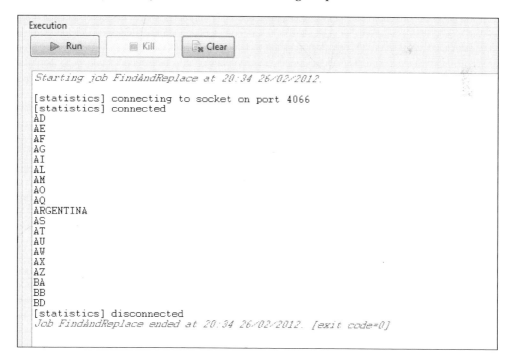

As you can see, the value of AR has been replaced with ARGENTINA, while all other values have been ignored.

For more complex scenarios, the Studio gives us the option to use regular expressions to match values. Readers not familiar with regular expressions can find a primer here:

```
http://en.wikipedia.org/wiki/Regular_expression
```

To enable the use of regular expressions, uncheck the **Simple mode** checkbox and click on **Advanced mode (search with regexp pattern)**. It is beyond the scope of this book to cover regular expressions in detail, but to illustrate a simple example, add a row to the Advanced mode and change the pattern value to A. (note that this is A dot). We are thus searching for any two-character strings that begin with A. Change the replace value to ZZ and run the job. You will see the following output:

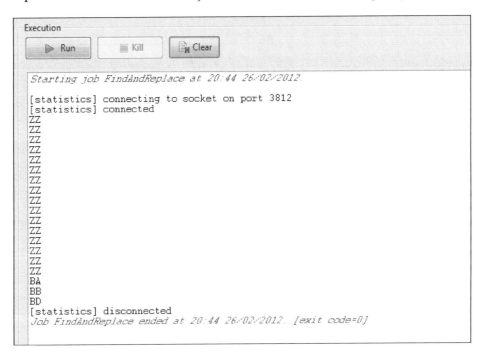

As expected, the country codes starting with A have been replaced with ZZ, while other codes have been ignored.

The **tReplace** component gives us some other configuration options.

The **Whole word** checkbox allows us to specify whether the string to find is a whole word or part of a word. If the **Whole word** checkbox is selected, then, if we were to replace A with Z on the following list:

```
A
AARDVARK
```

The output would be:

```
Z
AARDVARK
```

If the **Whole word** checkbox was not selected, the output would be:

```
Z
ZZRDVZRK
```

The **Case Sensitive** checkbox allows us to specify whether or not TOS matches on case as well as value.

Sampling rows

For our final example of processing techniques, we will look at how to extract specific rows from a data flow. For this technique, the Studio offers a tSampleRow component which filters rows according to their line numbers. We're going to use the same data as used in the previous example — country-codes.csv — and the job we create will be similar to the last example, so we'll reuse this and add some modifications.

1. In the repository, right-click on the **FindAndReplace** job and select **Duplicate**.

2. In the pop-up window, change the name to SampleRow and click on **OK**.

3. Double-click on the new job to open it and delete the tReplace component.

4. In the Palette, search for sample and drag a **tSampleRow** component onto the Job Designer, in between the delimited input and the tLogRow component.

5. Connect the component together using **Row | Main** in each case.

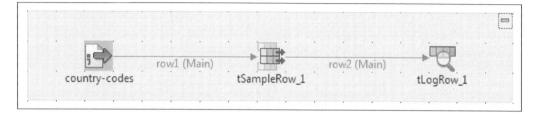

6. The **Basic Settings** tab shows some examples of how to configure the component. For our job, let's configure it to filter rows 5 to 10. In the **Range** box enter `5..10`.

7. Run the job and you will see the output in the console window.

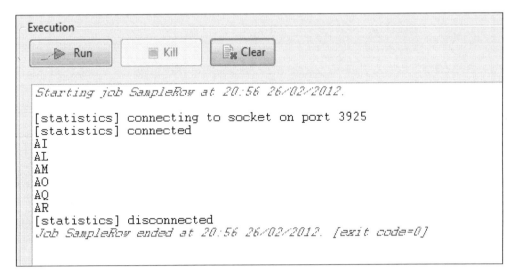

8. Try configuring the `tSampleRow` component to filter other rows, using the examples noted in the **Basic Settings** tab.

The `tSampleRow` component can be particularly useful when you want to get the first or last record from a data flow. For example, suppose we had a random list of employees with the date they joined your company, and you wanted to pass the name of the employee who had been with the company the longest. We could sort the data in ascending order based on the date he or she joined the company (using a `tSortRow` component) and then, using a `tSampleRow` component, select only the first row.

Summary

In this chapter, we explored the Studio processing components and how we can use them to modify the data flows between files, databases, and other start and end points through the use of filters, data sorts, and aggregations. We saw how we could group and un-group data with the Studio normalize and denormalize components. The Studio's `tReplace` component is a simple, but hugely useful addition to your toolkit and will undoubtedly find a place in many of your integration jobs. Finally, the ability to extract specific rows from a data flow through the `tSampleRow` component was reviewed and we will see examples later in the book where, when combined with a sorting component, this has some powerful applications.

When building integration jobs, you will commonly use the processing components in combination. For example, you might take a data flow from a database, filter out the records you want, then pass the data to a find and replace component, where you will substitute some values with others, finally passing onto an aggregating component to sum up the records. Before you move onto the next chapter, try to construct some jobs that combine a number of processing components.

In the next chapter, we will look at using the Studio to manage files—moving, renaming, copying, deleting, and FTPing.

6

Managing Files

We have seen in earlier chapters that files are often used as the medium in which data gets moved from one system to another. This could be a database extract that is written to a file in a specific format or a file that is converted from one format to another. In order to make your integration jobs complete and not rely on other automated or manual processes, the Studio offers the ability to program file operations beyond manipulating the file content. For example, we might wish to copy a file from one directory to another and once it has been moved to its final destination, delete the original file.

In this chapter we will:

- Develop integration tasks that copy, rename, and delete files
- Look at various tasks associated with archiving—specifically, time-stamping a file, zipping, and unzipping files
- Show how we can list the files in a directory and operate on them in turn
- Check for the existence of a file prior to attempting to process

When put together, these file operations will give you the tools to manage and manipulate the files produced or consumed by your integration jobs.

We will start by looking at "local" file operations—those files located on the computer that the Studio runs on. We will follow this by looking at **FTP** (**file transfer protocol**) operations. FTP allows us to work with remote files located on another computer.

Managing local files

In this section we will look at local file operations. We'll cover common operations that all computer users will be familiar with—copying, deleting, moving, renaming, and archiving files. We'll also look at some not-so-common techniques, such as timestamping files, checking for the existence of a file, and listing the files in a directory.

Copying files

For our first file job, let's look at a simple file copy process. We will create a job that looks in a specific directory for a file and copies it to another location.

Let's do some setup first (we can use this for all of the file examples). In your project directory, create a new folder and name it `FileManagement`. Within this folder, create two more folders and name them `Source` and `Target`. In the `Source` directory, drop a simple text file and name it `original.txt`. Now let's create our job:

1. Create a new folder in **Repository** and name it `Chapter6`.

2. Create a new job within the `Chapter6` directory and name it `FileCopy`.

3. In the Palette, search for `copy`. You should be able to locate a **tFileCopy** component. Drop this onto the Job Designer.

4. Click on its **Component** tab. Set the **File Name** field to point to the `original.txt` file in the `Source` directory.

5. Set the **Destination directory** field to direct to the `Target` directory.

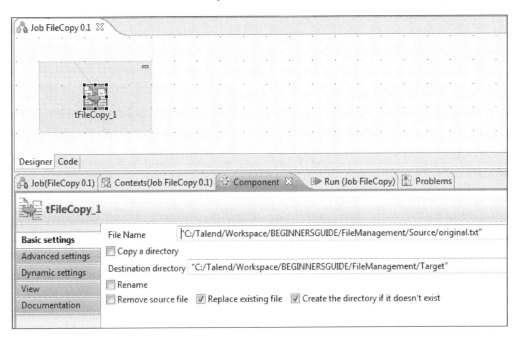

For now, let's leave everything else unchanged. Click on the **Run** tab and then click on the **Run** button. The job should complete pretty quickly and, because we only have a single component, there are now data flows to observe. Check your `Target` folder and you will see the `original.txt` file in there, as expected. Note that the file still remains in the `Source` folder, as we were simply copying the file.

Copying and removing files

Our next example is a variant of our first file management job. Previously, we copied a file from one folder to another, but often you will want to affect a file move. To use an analogy from desktop operating systems and programs, we want to do a cut and paste rather than a copy and paste. Open the `FileCopy` job and follow the given steps:

1. Remove the `original.txt` file from the `Target` directory, making sure it still exists in the `Source` directory.

2. In the **Basic settings** tab of the **tFileCopy** component, select the checkbox for **Remove source file**.

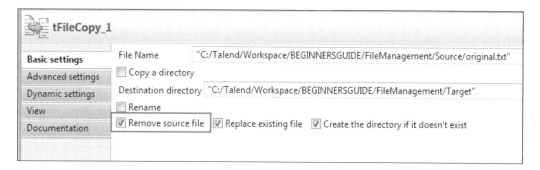

3. Now run the job. This time the `original.txt` file will be copied to the `Target` directory and then removed from the `Source` directory.

Renaming files

We can also use the **tFileCopy** component to rename files as we copy or move. Again, let's work with the FileCopy job we have created previously. Reset your Source and Target directories so that the original.txt file only exists in Source.

1. In the **Basic settings** tab, check the **Rename** checkbox. This will reveal a new parameter, **Destination filename**.

2. Change the default value of the **Destination filename** parameter to modified_name.txt.

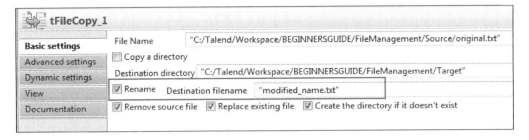

3. Run the job. The original file will be copied to the Target directory and renamed. The original file will also be removed from the Source directory.

Deleting files

It is really useful to be able to delete files. For example, once they have been transformed or processed into other systems. Our integration jobs should "clean up afterwards", rather than leaving lots of interim files cluttering up the directories. In this job example we'll delete a file from a directory. As with the other jobs so far in this chapter, this is a single-component job.

1. Create a new job and name it FileDelete.

2. In your workspace directory, FileManagement/Source, create a new text file and name it file-to-delete.txt.

3. From the Palette, search for filedelete and drag a **tFileDelete** component onto the Job Designer.

4. Click on its **Component** tab to configure it. Change the **File Name** parameter to be the path to the file you created earlier in step 2.

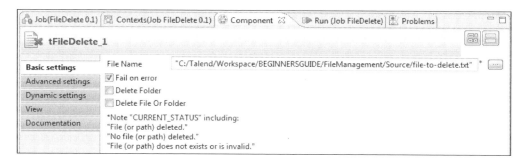

5. Run the job. After it is complete, go to your `Source` directory and the file will no longer be there.

Note that the file does not get moved to the recycle bin on your computer, but is deleted immediately.

Timestamping a file

Sometimes in real life use, integration jobs, like any software, can fail or give an error. Server issues, previously unencountered bugs, or a host of other things can cause a job to behave in an unexpected manner, and when this happens, manual intervention may be needed to investigate the issue or recover the job that failed. A useful trick to try to incorporate into your jobs is to save files once they have been consumed or processed, in case you need to re-process them again at some point or, indeed, just for investigation and debugging purposes should something go wrong. A common way to save files is to rename them using a date/timestamp. By doing this you can easily identify when files were processed by the job. Follow the given steps to achieve this:

1. Create a new job and call it `FileTimestamp`.
2. Create a file in the `Source` directory named `timestamp.txt`. The job is going to move this to the `Target` directory, adding a time-stamp to the file as it processes.
3. From the Palette, search for `filecopy` and drop a **tFileCopy** component onto the Job Designer.
4. Click on its **Component** tab and change the **File Name** parameter to point to the `timestamp.txt` file we created in the `Source` directory.
5. Change the **Destination Directory** to direct to your `Target` directory.

6. Check the **Rename** checkbox and change the **Destination filename** parameter to `"timestamp"+TalendDate.getDate("yyyyMMddhhmmss")+".txt"`.

7. The previous code snippet concatenates the fixed file name, `"timestamp"`, with the current date/time as generated by the Studio's `getDate` function at runtime. The file extension `".txt"` is added to the end too.

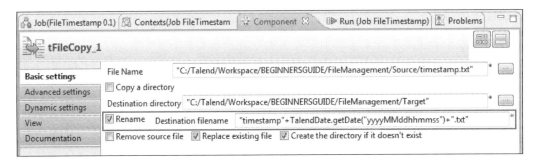

Run the job and you will see a new version of the original file drop into the `Target` directory, complete with timestamp. Run the job again and you will see another file in `Target` with a different timestamp applied.

Depending on your requirements you can configure different format timestamps. For example, if you are only going to be processing one file a day, you could dispense with the hours, minutes, and second elements of the timestamp and simply set the output format to `"yyyyMMdd"`. Alternatively, to make the timestamp more readable, you could separate its elements with hyphens— `"yyyy-MM-dd"`, for example.

You can find more information about Java date formats at `http://docs.oracle.com/javase/6/docs/api/java/text/SimpleDateFormat.html`.

Listing files in a directory

Our next example job will show how to list all of the files (or all the files matching a specific naming pattern) in a directory. Where might we use such a process? Suppose our target system had a data "drop-off" directory, where all integration files from multiple sources were placed before being picked up to be processed. As an example, this drop-off directory might contain four product catalogue XML files, three CSV files containing inventory data, and 50 order XML files detailing what had been ordered by the customers. We might want to build a catalogue import process that picks up the four catalogue files, processes them by mapping to a different format, and then moves them to the catalogue import directory. The nature of the processing means we have to deal with each file individually, but we want a single execution of the process to pick up all available files at that point in time. This is where our file listing process comes in very handy and, as you might expect, the Studio has a component to help us with this task. Follow the given steps:

1. Let's start by preparing the directory and files we want to list. Copy the FileList directory from the resource files of this chapter to the FileManagement directory we created earlier. The FileList directory contains six XML files.

2. Create a new job and name it FileList.

3. Search for Filelist in the Palette and drop a **tFileList** component onto the Job Designer.

4. Additionally, search for logrow and drop a **tLogRow** component onto the designer too.

We will use the **tFileList** component to read all of the filenames in the directory and pass this through to the **tLogRow** component. In order to do this, we need to connect the **tFileList** and **tLogRow**. The **tFileList** component works in an iterative manner—it reads each filename and passes it onwards before getting the next filename. Its connector type is **Iterative**, rather than the more common **Main** connector. However, we cannot connect an iterative component to the **tLogRow** component, so we need to introduce another component that will act as an intermediary between the two.

5. Search for iteratetoflow in the Palette and drop a **tIterateToFlow** component onto the Job Designer. This bridges the gap between an iterate component and a flow component.

6. Click on the **tFileList** component and then click on its **Component** tab. Change the directory value so that it points to the FileList directory we created in step 1.

7. Click on the **+** button to add a new row to the **File** section. Change the value to "*.xml". This configures the component to search for any files with an XML extension.

8. Right-click on the **tFileList** component, select **Row | Iterate**, and drop the resulting connector onto the **tIterateToFlow** component.

9. The **tIterateToFlow** component requires a schema and, as the tFileList component does not have a schema, it cannot propagate this to the iterate-to-flow component when we join them. Instead we will have to create the schema directly. Click on the **tIterateToFlow** component and then on its **Component** tab. Click on the **Edit** schema button and, in the pop-up schema editor, click on the **+** button to add a row and then rename the column value to filename. Click on **OK** to close the window.

10. A new row will be added to the Mapping table. We need to edit its value, so click in the Value column, delete the setting that exists, and press *Ctrl* + space bar

11. to access the global variables list.

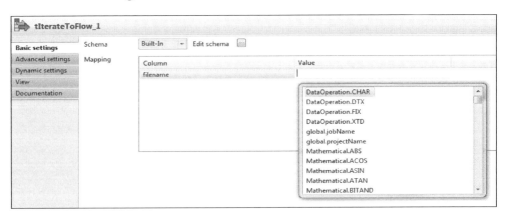

12. Scroll through the global variable drop-down list and select **"tFileList_1_ CURRENT_FILE"**. This will add the required parameter to the `Value` column.

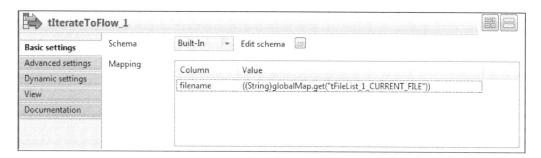

13. Right-click on the **tIterateToFlow** component, select **Row | Main**, and connect this to the **tLogRow** component.

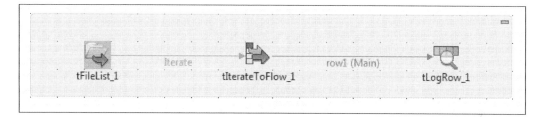

14. Let's run the job. It may run too quickly to be visible to the human eye, but the **tFileList** component will read the name of the first file it finds, pass this forward to the **tIterateToFlow** component, go back and read the second file, and so on. As the `iterate-to-flow` component receives its data, it will pass this onto **tLogRow** as row data. You will see the following output in the `tLogRow` component:

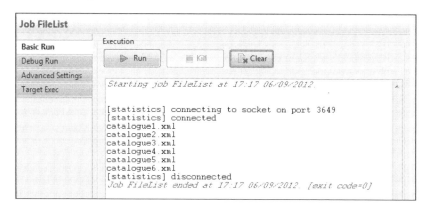

Now that we have cracked the basics of the file list component, let's extend the example to a real-life situation. Let's suppose we have a number of text files in our input directory, all conforming to the same schema. In the resources directory of this chapter, you will find five files named `fileconcat1.txt`, `fileconcat2.txt`, and so on. Each of these has a "random" number of rows. Copy these files into the `Source` directory of your workspace. The aim of our job is to pick up each file in turn and write its output to a new file, thereby concatenating all of the original files. Let's see how we do this:

1. Create a new job and name it `FileConcat`.

2. For this job we will need a file list component, a delimited file output component, and a delimited file input component. As we will see in a minute, the delimited input component will be a "placeholder" for each of the input files in turn.

3. Find the components in the Palette and drop them onto the Job Designer.

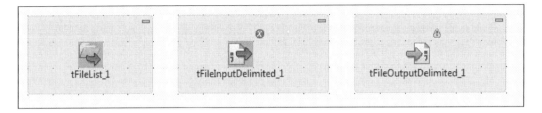

4. Click on the file list component and change its **Directory** value to point to the `Source` directory.

5. In the **Files** box, add a row and change the **Filemask** value to `"*.txt"`.

6. Right-click on the file list component and select **Row | Iterate**. Drop the connector onto the delimited input component.

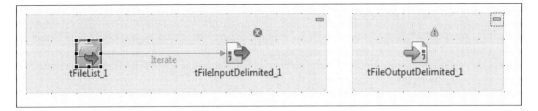

7. Select the delimited input component and edit its schema so that it has a single field `rowdata` of data type `String`.

8. We need to modify the **File name/Stream** value, but in this case it is not a fixed file we are looking for but a different file with each iteration of the file list component. TOS gives us an easy way to add such variables into the component definitions. First, though, click on the **File name/Stream** box and clear the default value.

9. In the bottom-left corner of the Studio you should see a window named **Outline**. If you cannot see the **Outline** window, select **Window | Show View** from the menu bar and type `outline` into the pop-up search box. You will see the **Outline** view in the search results—double click on this to open it.

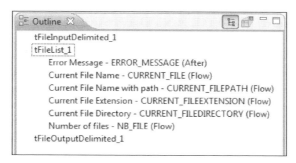

10. Now that we can see the **Outline** window, expand the **tFileList** item to see the variables available in it. The variables are different depending upon the component selected. In the case of a file list component, the variables are mostly attributes of the *current file being processed*. We are interested in the filename for each iteration, so click on the variable **Current File Name with path** and drag it to the **File name/Stream** box in the **Component** tab of the delimited input component.

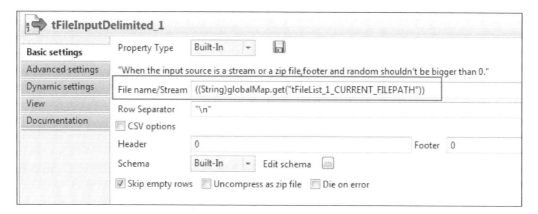

11. You can see that the Studio completes the parameter value with a **globalMap** variable—in this case, **tFileList_1_CURRENT_FILEPATH**, which denotes the current filename and its directory path.

12. Now right-click on the delimited input, select **Row | Main**, and drop the connector onto the delimited output.

13. Change the **File Name** of the delimited output component to `fileconcat-out.txt` in our target directory and check the **Append** checkbox, so that the Studio adds the data from each iteration to the bottom of each file. If **Append** is not checked, then the Studio will overwrite the data on each iteration and all that will be left will be the data from the final iteration.

14. Run the job and check the output file in the target directory. You will see a single file with the contents of the five original files in it. Note that the Studio shows the number of iterations of the file list component that have been executed, but does not show the number of lines written to the output file, as we are used to seeing in non-iterative jobs.

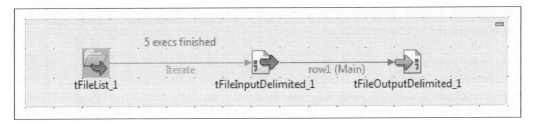

Checking for files

Let's look at how we can check for the existence of a file before we undertake an operation on it. Perhaps the first question is "Why do we need to check if a file exists?"

To illustrate why, open the `FileDelete` job that we created earlier. If you look at its component configuration, you will see that it will delete a file named `file-to-delete.txt` in the `Source` directory. Go to this directory using your computer's file explorer and delete this file manually. Now try to run the `FileDelete` job. You will get an error when the job executes:

```
Starting job FileDelete at 21:16 12/03/2012.

[statistics] connecting to socket on port 3394
[statistics] connected
Exception in component tFileDelete_1
java.lang.RuntimeException: File does not exists or is invalid.
    at beginnersguide.filedelete_0_1.FileDelete.tFileDelete_1Process(FileDelete.java:292)
    at beginnersguide.filedelete_0_1.FileDelete.runJobInTOS(FileDelete.java:504)
    at beginnersguide.filedelete_0_1.FileDelete.main(FileDelete.java:372)
[statistics] disconnected
Job FileDelete ended at 21:16 12/03/2012. [exit code=1]
```

The assumption behind a delete component (or a copy, rename, or other file operation process) is that the file does, in fact, exist and so the component can do its work. When the Studio finds that the file does not exist, an error is produced. Obviously, such an error is not desirable. In this particular case nothing too untoward happens—the job simply errors and exits—but it is better if we can avoid unnecessary errors.

What we should really do here is check if the file exists and, if it does, then delete it. If it does not exist, then the delete command should not be invoked. Let's see how we can put this logic together:

1. Create a new job and name it `FileExist`.

2. Search for `fileexist` in the Palette and drop a **tFileExist** component onto the Job Designer. Then search for `filedelete` and place a **tFileDelete** component onto the designer too.

3. In our `Source` directory, create a file named `file-exist.txt` and configure **File Name** of the **tFileDelete** component to point to this.

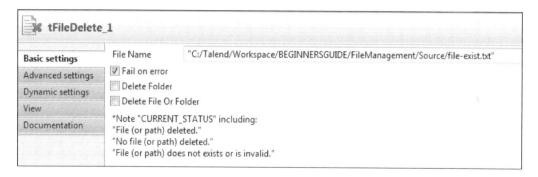

4. Now click on the **tFileExist** component and set its **File name/Stream** parameter to be the same file in the `Source` directory.

5. Right-click on the **tFileExist** component, select **Trigger | Run if**, and drop the connector onto the **tFileDelete** component. The connecting line between the two components is labeled **If**.

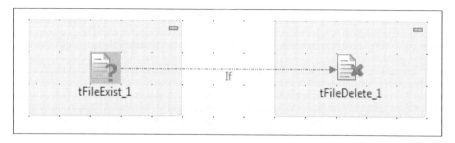

6. When our job runs the first component will execute, but the second component, **tFileDelete**, will only run if some conditions are satisfied. We need to configure the `if` conditions.

7. Click on **If** and, in the **Component** tab, a **Condition** box will appear.

8. In the **Outline** window (in the bottom-left corner of the Studio), expand the **tFileExist** component. You will see three attributes there. The **Exists** attribute is highlighted in red in the following screenshot:

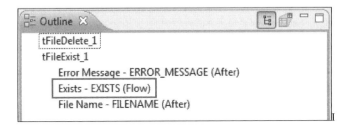

9. Click on the **Exists** attribute and drag it into the **Conditions** box of the **Component** tab.

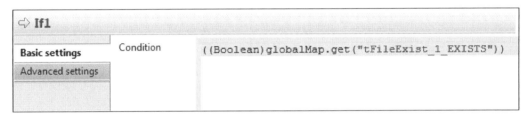

10. As before, a global-map variable is written to the configuration.

11. The logic of our job is as follows:

    i. Run the **tFileExist** component.

    ii. If the file named in **tFileExist** actually exists, run the **tFileDelete** component.

       Note that if the file does not exist, the job will exit.

We can check if the job works as expected by running it twice. The file we want to delete is in the `Source` directory, so we would expect both components to run on the first execution (and for the file to be deleted). When the `if` condition is evaluated, the result will show in the Job Designer view. In this case, the `if` condition was true—the file did exist.

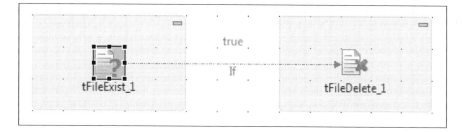

Now try to run the job again. We know that the file we are checking for does not exist, as it was deleted on the last execution.

This time, the `if` condition evaluates to false, and the delete component does not get invoked. You can also see in the console window that the Studio did not log any errors. Much better!

Sometimes we may want to verify that a file does *not* exist before we invoke another component. We can achieve this in a similar way to checking for the existence of a file, as shown earlier. Drag the **Exists** variable into the **Conditions** box and prefix the statement with `!` — the Java operator for "not":

```
!((Boolean)globalMap.get("tFileExist_1_EXISTS"))
```

Archiving and unarchiving files

Integration jobs often produce or consume lots of files, so the ability to archive (or zip) files can help save on disk space or help speed up an FTP process. Let's create a simple job that looks for files in a specific directory and zips up those that it finds. To set it up, copy the five `filearchive` text files from the resource directory of this chapter into your `Source` directory. Then:

1. Create a new job and name it `FileArchive`.

2. Search for `Filearchive` in the Palette and drag a **tFileArchive** component onto the Job Designer.

3. In its **Component** tab, set the **Directory** parameter to the `Source` directory. Note that, by default, the archive component will look at the files in the named directory *and* any of its subdirectories. If you do not want this behavior, uncheck the **Subdirectories** checkbox.

4. Set the **Archive file** parameter to `archive.zip` in your `Target` directory.

5. We could simply archive all files in our `Source` directory by leaving the **All Files** checkbox checked, but in this case we will be more specific, so uncheck the **All Files** checkbox.

6.   The **Files** box will be revealed. Add a new row to this by clicking on the + button and change the **Filemask** value to `filearchive*.txt`. This will select all of the files matching this name format.

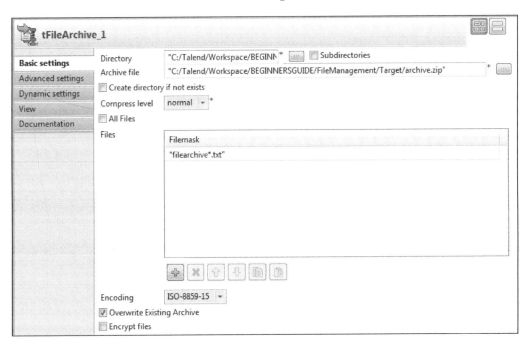

7.   Let's leave the other parameters unchanged and run the job. Check the `Target` directory and you will see the newly created archive file.

As an exercise, create a job that takes an archive file and unzips its contents to a directory. A sample job for this task can be found in the resources directory of this chapter.

FTP file operations

Integration jobs often connect different systems residing on different servers; so the Studio's FTP components will frequently play a part in your developments. The Studio supports many FTP actions — for example, Get, Put, Delete, Rename, File List, File Exist, and so on — and we'll look at how to use some of these in this section.

Readers may find it useful to have an FTP client installed on their computers to follow this section of the chapter and to check that files have been FTP'd correctly. There are many free FTP clients available for download on the Internet. FileZilla is recommended and can be downloaded from `http://filezilla-project.org/`.

FTP Metadata

We will start by defining an FTP connection in our repository metadata. As we saw previously with our database connection, it is really useful to be able to define a connection that can be used repeatedly. Follow the given steps:

1. In the **Repository**, expand the **Metadata** section, right-click on the **FTP** icon, and select **Create FTP**.

2. Enter FTP_CONNECTION in the **Name** box and enter values in the **Purpose** and **Description** boxes if you wish. Click on **Next**.

3. Enter your FTP username, password, host, and port into the appropriate boxes.

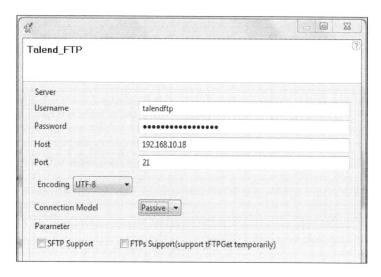

4. Click on **Finish**.

Now that the connection is set up, we can create some FTP jobs.

FTP Put

The FTP Put component takes a file (or files) from your local machine and FTPs them to a remote computer. Create a new job named FTPPut and follow the given steps:

1. Click on the FTP connection you created in the **Repository Metadata** and drag it onto the Job Designer.

2. Select **tFTPPut** in the pop-up window and click on **OK**.

3. Click on the **FTP Put** component in the Job Designer. You will see that a lot of its configuration values are already set, courtesy of the metadata FTP connection. We will need to configure the **Local Directory**, **Remote Directory**, and **Files** settings.

4. Change the **Local directory** field to be the directory on your computer where the files you want to transfer reside.

5. Change the **Remote Directory** to be the directory on the remote server where you are going to transfer to.

6. Click on the **+** button in the **Files** box to add a row. Change the **Filemask** and **New name** values to be that of the file you are transferring. Note that the Studio gives the option to change the filename as part of the transfer, but we will ignore this for now.

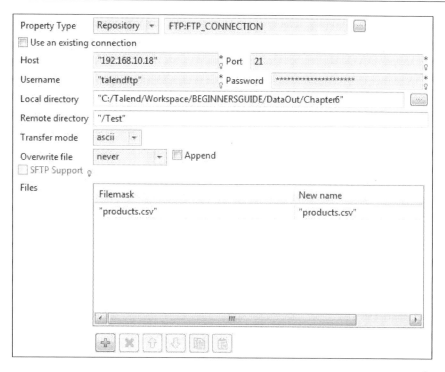

7. This is all we need to configure for a basic FTP Put job, so let's run the job. You will find that the file is transferred to the remote server successfully, leaving the original file in the local directory.

FTP Get

Now let's create a job that does the opposite of FTP Put—transfers a file from a remote server to your local computer.

The job configuration process is very similar, except that when you select your FTP component from the pop-up window after dragging the FTP connection onto the Job Designer, select **tFTPGet** rather than **tFTPPut**.

Have a go at configuring this job now. When you have finished, the **tFTPGet** component should look something like the following screenshot:

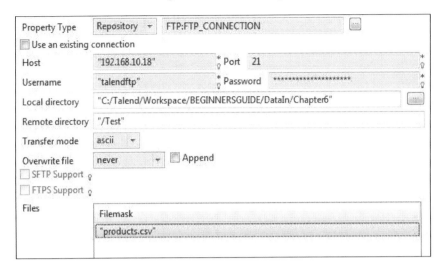

 Note that the Studio does not give the option to change the filename with the FTP Get component.

Run your job and you will see the file transfer back to your local directory (again, leaving the original on the remote server).

There is a sample FTP Get job in the resources directory of this chapter for you to refer to.

FTP File Exist

We saw earlier in the chapter how the Studio can check for the existence of a file in a directory before it processes it. It offers a similar FTP component that allows you to check for the existence of a file on a remote server.

Following the *file exists* example earlier in the chapter, create a job that checks for a file on your FTP server and, if it exists, *gets* the file to your local machine.

You will need the following components: tFTPFileExist, tFTPFileGet, and a Run If connector.

There is a sample job in the resources directory of this chapter for you to refer to.

FTP File List and Rename

Our next job will use two FTP components to list the files in a remote directory and rename them with a timestamp. Follow the given steps:

1. Create a new job and name it `FTPListAndRename`.

2. Drag the **FTP_CONNECTION** connection from the **Repository Metadata** onto the Job Designer. Select a **tFTPFileList** component from the pop-up window.

3. We also need an FTP file rename component, so drag another **FTP_CONNECTION** component onto the Job Designer and select **tFTPRename** from the pop-up window this time.

Our job now has two different components, but both have the same name.

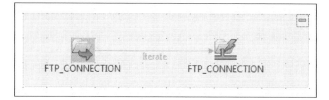

To make your job clearer to read and understand, you can rename each component to show its purpose. By double-clicking on the text name of each component, you can put it into "edit mode" and rename it appropriately. Here, we have renamed components to `FTPFileList` and `FTPFileRename`.

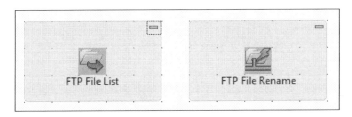

4. Configure the file list component by changing the **Remote directory** value to /Test and the **Filemask** value to *.* (this is a wildcard entry and will list every filename with any extension).

5. Connect the file list component to the file rename component by right-clicking on the file list, selecting **Row | Iterate**, and dropping the connector onto the file rename component.

6. Now let's configure the file rename component. Change the **Remote directory** value to /Test.

7. Click on the **+** button of the **File** box to add a new row.

8. In the **Filemask** column, press *Ctrl* + space bar to access the global variables. Select **FTP File List.CURRENT_FILE** from the drop-down list.

9. In the **New name** column, press *Ctrl* + space bar again and scroll to find **TalendDate.getDate**. Select this to add it to the **New name** column. Modify the default value to be as follows:

```
TalendDate.getDate("YYMMDD")
```

10. Place your cursor at the end of the getDate variable and press *Ctrl* + space bar again. Select **FTP File List.CURRENT_FILE** from the drop-down list.

11. Place your cursor between the two variables that have been added and type the following line:

```
+"_"+
```

12. Your **New name** expression should now be as follows:

```
TalendDate.getDate("YYMMDD")+"_"+((String)globalMap.get
    ("tFTPFileList_1_CURRENT_FILE"))
```

13. This will change the filename so that it is prefixed with the current date. The two elements of the new filename, the current date and the old filename, will be separated with an underscore.

Run the job to test the process. You will find that the remote files are renamed with the timestamp, as configured.

Deleting files on an FTP server

Our final FTP example shows how to delete files on an FTP server. This is a routine that you might typically use at the end of a processing job as part of a clean-up process, possibly after the files have been archived for safekeeping. There are at least two ways to approach this problem: the first is brute-force, the second is more controlled.

In the first method you could simply use a tFTPDelete component and, applying a file mask to pick out the files to be deleted, simply delete what is there. The second method uses a tFileList component to specify what should be deleted. In this example, we will use the file list method and add in a renaming component too.

The desired flow of functionality is as follows:

1. List the files on an FTP server.
2. Time-stamp and move the files to a processed directory.
3. Delete the original source files.

Follow the given steps:

1. Create a new job and name it FTPFileDelete.
2. Using the FTP **Metadata** in the **Repository**, create three components on the job designer—tFTPFileList, tFTPRename, and tFTPDelete.
3. Connect the three components using iterate connectors.

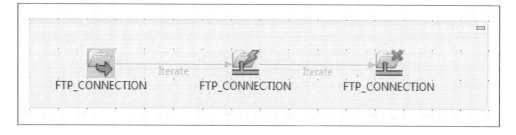

4. Configure the file list component to look for CSV files on the remote server directory, using the **Filemask** parameter.

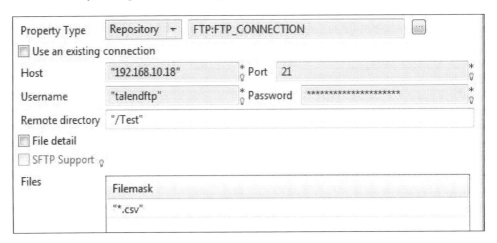

5. Now click on the rename component. We are going to use this to move the file to a new directory and add a timestamp to the filename.

6. Configure the **Remote** directory and then place your cursor in the **Filemask** column of the **Files** box. Click *Ctrl* + space bar to show a list of global variables we can use in this job.

7. Find and select **FTP_CONNECTION.CURRENT_FILE**. This accesses the current file from the **tFileList** iteration.

8. In the **New name** column, add the following code:

```
"/Test/Processed/"+TalendDate.getDate("yyyyMMdd")+
    "_"+((String)globalMap.get
    ("tFTPFileList_1_CURRENT_FILE"))
```

9. This does a number of things. It, again, uses the current filename but prefixes this with the current date (`TalendDate.getDate("yyyyMMdd")`) and an underscore (`"_"`). We also specify that the file path is `"/Test/Processed/"` and so the Studio will move it to the `Processed` subdirectory as part of this file rename process. Note that you need to create the `Processed` directory on the remote server first—the Studio does not create it on the fly.

10. Finally, click on the **tFTPDelete** component and configure its **Remote directory** and **Files** parameters. The **Files/Filemask** parameter should again be set to the `CURRENT_FILE` variable.

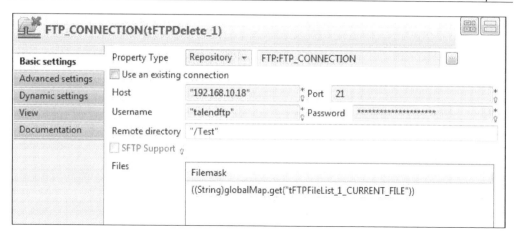

11. Run the job and you should see the file move from the `"/Test"` directory to `"/Test/Processed"` with the addition of a timestamp, as specified.

Summary

Managing files is a very important part of the integration development process. Because files are so widely used in integration jobs, we need to have strategies to effectively deal with them and, even though file management is the less "glamorous" part of the integration job—compared to XML mapping or database extraction, for example—its importance cannot be overstated. Moving files in a logical manner, renaming and archiving appropriately, and checking for the existence of a file before attempting to do anything with it is simply good practice. Without these techniques your integration jobs will only be partially complete; so it is highly recommended that readers spend time planning their developments to incorporate these elements.

In chapters 3 to 6, we have spent time looking at specific components and the integration techniques associated with them. Our example integration jobs were focused and relatively simple, but, in the real world, integration jobs are much more complex, incorporating many different components. *Chapter 7, Job Orchestration*, introduces us to more complex jobs with multiple components, subjobs, and job flow control.

7
Job Orchestration

In the previous chapters, we have looked at examples of integration jobs that had a single purpose and were composed of small numbers of components, maybe two or three together. The purpose of these examples was to explain how different components work and are configured; but, in real-life situations, our integration jobs are likely to be made up of 10, 20, or more components, as we use Talend integration jobs to control the full end-to-end process, from file management to data processing tasks; from file mapping to database operations.

In this chapter, we will learn about job orchestration and how we can use subjobs, iterate connections, and flow components to control the logical flow of our jobs.

We will learn the following topics in this chapter:

- Breaking the overall integration job into discrete tasks using subjobs
- Defining flow logic within our jobs so that certain tasks are invoked only if specific conditions apply
- Providing checkpoints where we can trap errors or failures
- Using iterate and loop concepts to cycle through a number of executions of a specific task
- Splitting and merging dataflows

What is a subjob

A subjob is a subset of the components in a job. A subjob can be viewed as a grouping of components that undertake a discrete part of the overall integration job. An example might be the components that map an XML file to a CSV file, using a **tFileInputXML** component, a **tMap component**, and a **tFileInputDelimited** component.

Subjobs can be easily identified, as the Studio groups the components of subjob within a gray box.

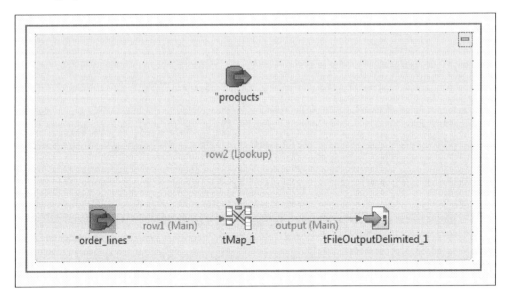

Some subjobs may consist of only a single Talend component, while other subjobs may have many components. A Talend job consists of one or more subjobs.

A simple subjob

We will begin with a simple subjob example. Our integration scenario is as follows:

- We want to extract data from a database to a delimited file
- We need to zip the file to archive it

We will use the same database that we used for the integration examples in *Chapter 4, Working with Databases*. Let's build the subjob by performing the following steps:

1. Create a new job and name it SimpleSubjob.
2. We will extract data from the **order_lines** table, so expand the **DEMO_DB 0.1** metadata connection (in the **Repository** window) to reveal the **Table Schemas**.

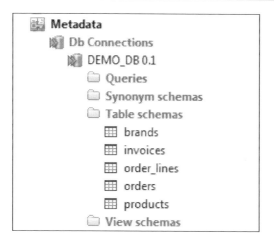

3. Click on the **order_lines** table and drag it onto the Job Designer. Select **tMySQLInput** from the pop-up window.

4. Search for `delimited` in the **Palette** window and drop a **tFileOutputDelimited** component onto the Job Designer.

5. Connect the two components by right-clicking on the MySQL Input component, selecting **Row | Main,** and dropping the resulting connector onto the delimited output component. We have formed our first subjob!

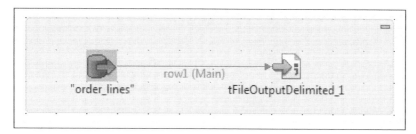

6. Configure the delimited output component by changing the **File Name field** to `order-lines.csv` in your `DataOut` directory.

7. We can run this integration now to check if it works.

8. Our next step is to configure the archiving/zipping tasks. Search for `archive` in the **Palette** window and drop a **tFileArchive** component onto the designer.

9. Set the **Directory** field to be the directory the archive component will zip up. In our case, this will be `C:\Talend\Workspace\GETTINGSTARTED\DataOut\Chapter7`. Note that there is a **Subdirectories** checkbox that optionally allows you to include (if checked) or exclude (if not checked) subdirectories and their files.

10. Set the **Archive file** field to be the name of the archive file that will be created by the process. We'll set this to `C:/Talend/Workspace/GETTINGSTARTED/DataOut/Chapter7/order-lines.zip`.

11. We can specify that only certain files are archived by unchecking the **All Files** checkbox and setting appropriate file mask parameters, but we will leave the **All Files** checkbox ticked for now. The configuration settings for the archive component are shown in the following screenshot:

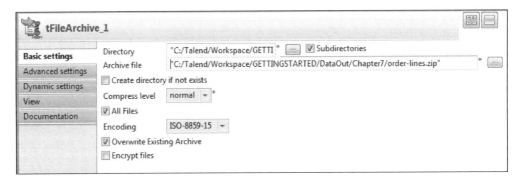

12. Your job will now look like the following screenshot:

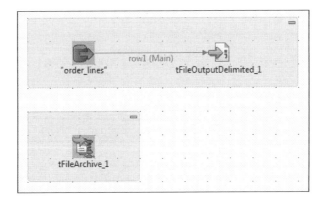

13. So, we now have two subjobs; the first extracts the data from the database and writes it to a delimited file, and the second zips the delimited file. We now need to connect these two subjobs in a logical way so that the desired results are achieved. In this case, we want the database extract to happen first, followed by the file-zipping task.

14. Right-click on the **order_lines** component, select **Trigger | On Subjob OK**, and drop the connector onto the **tFileArchive** component.

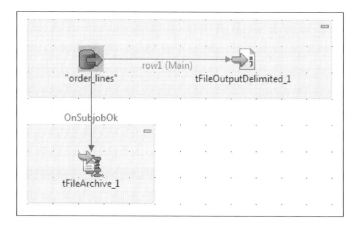

Although the subjob connector has been linked from the first component in the first subjob, note that Talend treats this as, *when the whole of the first subjob completes (without error), execute the second subjob*. The **On Subjob** triggers can only be set from the first component in a subjob and, if you right-click on the delimited output component, you will see that **On Subjob OK** or **On Subjob Error** is not available in its menus. Note that, without the **OnSubjobOK** trigger, the two subjobs—the extract to file and the archive—would run in an arbitrary and unpredictable order. This could mean that the archive might attempt to execute before the extract file has been written and so not achieve the results we require.

15. Now run the job. As expected, the delimited file is created and this is then zipped in the same directory.

On Subjob Error

Let's extend our first example by illustrating how a job can be made to take different execution paths based on what happens during the running of the job.

In the previous example we configured an **OnSubjobOK** example, but what if the subjob did not work as expected? The Studio also offers another subjob connector—**OnSubjobError**—for this situation. Let's modify the job to show this; perform the following steps:

1. Search for message in the **Palette** window and drop a **tMsgBox** component onto the designer.

2. We can accept most of the default settings for this component, but change the **Message** parameter to Something Went Wrong!!.

3. Right-click on the **order_lines** component, select **Trigger | On Subjob Error,** and drop the connector onto the message box component.

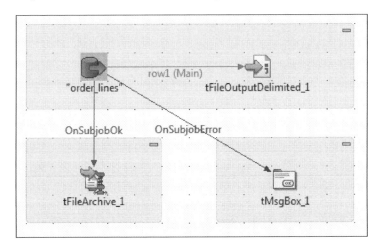

If we run the job now, it will work in exactly the same way as before. The database query will run, the data will be extracted to a file, and the file will be zipped.

However, let's change the **order_lines** configuration to force an error condition. Change the **Query** value so that it refers to a database table that does not exist.

```
"select id, order_id, product_id, quantity from order_linesx"
```

Note the addition of x at the end of the order_lines query. This configures the database query component to read from table order_linesx, which does not exist and, so, this component will error when the job runs. Now re-run the job and the message box will appear.

Click on **OK**. The message box will close and the job will end (without completing its task).

In real-life situations we won't know in advance where a job might show an error, so we can make the message box component a little more useful by making it show the error message returned by the job. In previous job examples, we have used components that use global variables available from the **Outline** window in the bottom left-hand side corner of the Studio. Expand this section now to reveal the global variables for **order_lines** and delimited output components. You will see that each component offers an error message variable.

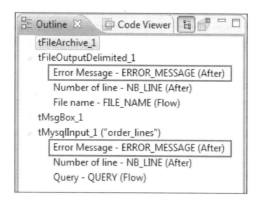

Click on each error message in turn and drag it into the **Message** text box of the message box component. Separate the two variables with a + sign.

Run the job again and you will see a new message from the message box component, as shown in the following screenshot:

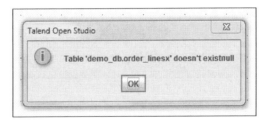

This now shows the error from the **order_lines** component, **Table 'demo_db.order_linesx' does not exist**, along with the error message from the delimited component—in this case it's returning null because the delimited component did not show any error. We can make this even more usable by amending the Message configuration. Edit the configuration so that it is as follows:

```
"Something went wrong | "+"Order Lines: "+((String)globalMap.
get("tMysqlInput_1_ERROR_MESSAGE"))+" | DelimitedOutput: "+((String)
globalMap.get("tFileOutputDelimited_1_ERROR_MESSAGE"))
```

This formats the error and makes it more readable. Now we get the message shown in the following screenshot:

Our first two examples show the principles of subjobs and illustrate how we can use subjobs to invoke different flows based on specific criteria, in this case, subjob success or failure. We will now move on to consider component-level conditions.

On Component OK

As we saw in the two previous examples, the Studio allows us to define flow conditions when a subjob, or a group of components, completes or shows errors. When we define an **On Subjob Complete** condition, *all* of the components in the subjob must complete before the next subjob is triggered.

However, we may sometimes require another subjob to commence as soon as it is able (when a specific component within a subjob is complete), rather than waiting until all of the components are complete. To achieve this, we can use the Studio's **On Component OK** condition.

The job illustrated in the following screenshot shows an **On Component OK** in use:

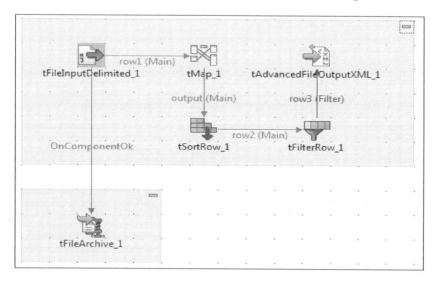

In this example a delimited file is read, transformed by a **tMap** component, sorted, filtered, and then written to an XML file. The input file is also archived once it has been read. Crucially, the archiving process happens as soon as the delimited file has been read. If, instead, the connection to the archive component had been **On Subjob OK**, the archive would not have happened until the XML file had been written to the disk.

For simple jobs that run quickly, the impact is negligible, indeed, even hard to see when the job is run. For processes that run for a longer time, however, where an input has to be read and processed, then passed on for a second round of processing, the ability to use **On Component OK** could make the overall running length of the job substantially shorter. This is because both subjobs now run in parallel rather than back-to-back, as they would if we had used **On Subjob OK**.

The **On Component OK** trigger is configured in much the same way as **On Subjob OK** is. Right-click on the initial component and select **Trigger | On Component OK**. We saw previously that **On Subjob OK** is always connected from the first component in a subjob. **On Component OK** gives more options and can be connected from any other valid component within a subjob.

Our previous example is shown in the next screenshot in a modified form, where the **On Component OK** connection is made from the **tSortRow** component so that, now, the archiving process happens once the sorting has finished.

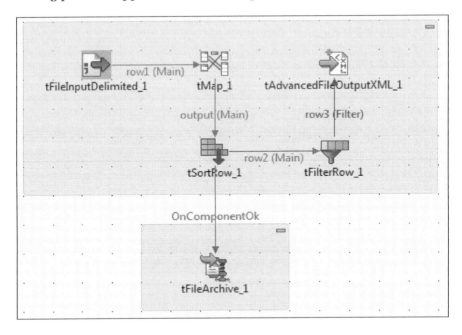

As with subjob connectors, the Studio also offers an **On Component Error** connector.

Run If

In *Chapter 6, Managing Files*, we created a job that checked for the existence of a file before it tried to process the file (good coding practice!). This used a **Run If** connector and readers who have already worked through this example will be familiar with its purpose and configuration.

Run If triggers a subjob or component when a defined condition is met, the existence (or non-existence) of a file, if the number of rows returned is greater than 100, and countless other conditions.

A **Run If** connection is made by right-clicking on the source component, selecting **Trigger | Run If**, and dropping the connector onto the target component. Click on the connector and enter a condition expression, in Java, into the **Condition** box.

Condition expressions can be dragged from components in the **Outline** tab to the **Condition** box.

Alternatively, pressing *Ctrl* + Space bar when your cursor is in the **Condition** box will display a list of global and context variables that can be used as condition expressions.

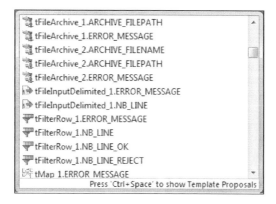

Jobs as subjobs

Talend Open Studio allows developers to use jobs within jobs. This is a great technique to use if you have tasks that can be used over and over again in many integration jobs. Over time, developers can build up a library of standard tasks, and componentizing in this way makes your development quicker and easier and promotes reuse of code, which is always good practice.

For example, suppose you have developed an FTP job that lists the files in a directory, connects to a remote FTP server, and transfers the files before deleting the source files. This FTP job can be designed generically so that it can be used for similar purposes in other jobs. Let's see what this might look like.

Our first job is the generic FTP job as shown in the following screenshot:

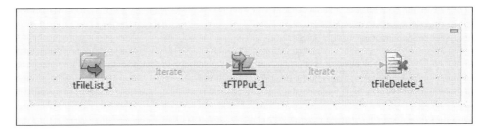

Our second job takes a delimited file, processes the data using a **tMap component,** and then writes the data to an XML file.

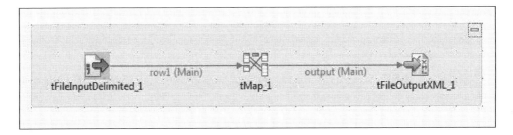

We can now enhance this job by bringing in the generic FTP job. In the **Repository window,** click on the generic FTP job and drag it to the Job Designer of the data transform job. Right-click on the delimited input component, select **Trigger | On Subjob OK,** and drop the connector onto the generic FTP job.

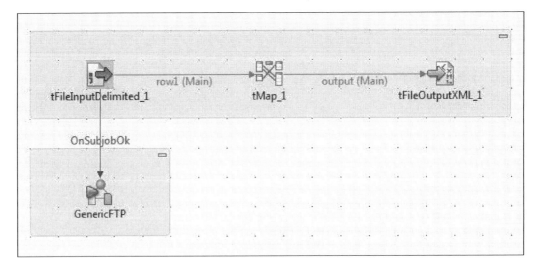

Now, on execution, the transformation will happen, followed by the FTP task.

For one-off jobs, it is sometimes difficult to see how you can componentize or refactor tasks into self-contained jobs (and it is often a little more work to do so, even if you can see it). However, componentization is a very valuable technique and will pay dividends in better productivity and better coding if developers take opportunities to use it whenever they can.

Iterating and looping

Looping and iterating structures are common to most programming languages and Talend Open Studio is no different. In this section, we will look at ways to use the Studio to implement loops and iterations and further automate your integration jobs through these repeating functions.

Iterate connections

In *Chapter 6*, *Managing Files*, we looked at the **tFileList** component and saw an example of how to iterate the flow between components, in this case iterating through the files in a directory and passing these filename values onwards one by one. The Studio offers an Iterate flow option from its start components, that is, those that can commence a subjob or flow, often in addition to a **Main** flow. Let's illustrate another example of an iterate flow now.

In this scenario, we have a delimited input file and we want to transform its output in some way. The input file contains e-mail addresses in one of its columns and we also want to send an e-mail to each e-mail address. We can approach this problem in a number of ways. An easy solution would be to read the input file twice, with one subjob undertaking the data transformation and another subjob handling the process of sending e-mails. This is illustrated in the following screenshot:

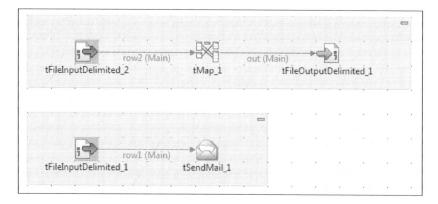

This method will work perfectly well, but it is not the most elegant way to construct such a job. It is also not the most efficient, because the input file will be loaded and processed twice. A better way to build this job is to attach both processing functions, the data transformation and the process of sending e-mails, to the same delimited input component. However, the Studio does not allow us to have two **Main** connections from a component. So, let's take a look at the **Iterate** connection.

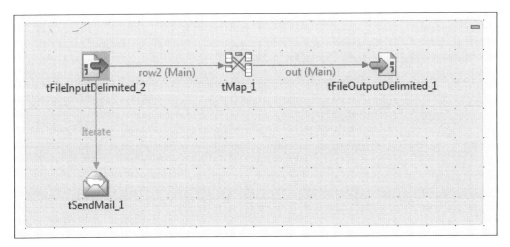

As shown in the previous screenshot, the delimited input connects to the data transformation process in the normal manner, but also connects to the send e-mail component using an **Iterate** connector. Now, as each row is processed from the input file, it is passed to the data transformation process *and* the send e-mail process.

ForEach loop

Talend's ForEach component allows us to loop through a set of values and pass these onto the next component using an iterate link. Let's look at an example in practice.

Suppose we have a database table that records invoice values by region. The table is shown in the following screenshot:

region_id	value
▶ region1	573.44
region1	145.54
region1	417.84
region1	203.89
region1	301.14
region1	340.04
region1	495.64
region1	515.09
region1	398.39
region2	262.24
region2	437.29
region2	320.59
region2	242.79
region2	184.44
region2	164.99
region2	612.34
region2	476.19
region2	281.69
region3	359.49
region3	378.94
region3	592.89
region3	534.54
region3	223.34
region3	456.74
region3	553.99

Our task is to produce three file extracts from the database, one for each region. A simple way to approach this problem would be to have three **tMySQLInput** components, each with a slightly different query, and each extracting to a different file.

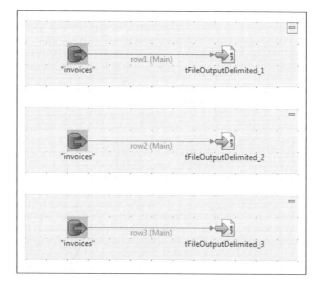

This would work okay, but if, for example, the table structure changed at some point in the future, you would need to change each **tMySQLInput** component to comply, which might lead to errors or bugs if the changes are not properly propagated to all components.

A more elegant solution would be to use a ForEach loop to connect to a single **tMySQLInput component** and a single delimited output. Perform the following steps to build this job:

1. Create a new job and name it `ForEach`.

2. In the **Palette** window, search for `foreach` and drop a **tForeach** component onto the Job Designer.

3. Click on its **Component** tab and, in **Basic settings**, click on the **+** button three times to add three new rows. Change the row values to `region1`, `region2`, and `region3`.

4. From the **Metadata** section in the **Repository** window, expand the **DEMO_ DB 0.1** database connection to reveal the **Table schemas** section and drag an **invoices** table component onto the Job Designer. Select **tMySQLInput** from the pop-up window.

5. Right-click on the ForEach component, select **Row | Iterate**, and drop the connector onto the **invoices** component.

6. We now need to modify the **Query field**. We want our query to be dynamic each time it runs, so we modify the query so that it retrieves different data based on the region. The query that currently exists in the invoices component is as follows:

    ```
    "SELECT `invoices`.`region_id`, `invoices`.`value` FROM
    `invoices`"
    ```

    We need to amend this to add a dynamic region value on each iteration.

7. From the **Outline** window in the bottom left-hand side corner of the Studio, expand the **tForeach** component and select the **Current Value field**. Drag this over to the **Query** window. Now modify the query so that it becomes as follows:

    ```
    "SELECT `invoices`.`region_id`, `invoices`.`value` FROM
    `invoices` where `invoices`.`region_id` = '"+((String)globalMap.
    get("tForeach_1_CURRENT_VALUE"))+"';"
    ```

> Note the use of single quotes around `"+((String)globalMap.`
> `get("tForeach_1_CURRENT_VALUE"))+"`. This is required because the region value is a string and SQL requires string values to be in single quotes.

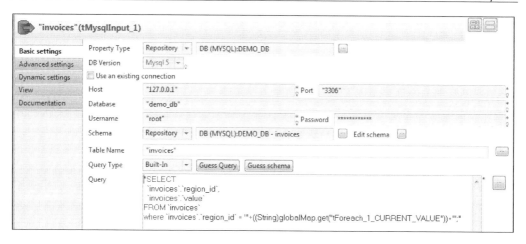

8. Now, each time the ForEach component runs, it passes each region value in turn to the MySQL input component, which uses the region value with the query. Finally, let's add a delimited output component to the Job Designer and connect this to the MySQL input component.

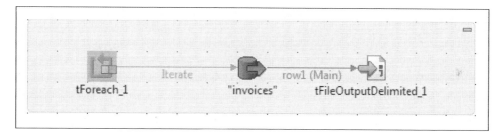

9. Change the **File Name** field of the delimited component to the following:

```
"C:/Talend/Workspace/BEGINNERSGUIDE/DataOut/
Chapter7/"+((String)globalMap.get("tForeach_1_CURRENT_
VALUE"))+"invoices.csv"
```

Again, we have used ForEach CURRENT_VALUE in the output filename.

Run the job to see the output. As expected, three files are produced, each with data from a single region.

To make the job truly dynamic, we could enhance it further and remove the hardcoding of region values in the ForEach component. Follow these additional steps:

1. Drag a **DEMO_DB 0.1** connection metadata, from the **Metadata** section in the **Repository** window, onto the Job Designer. Select **tMySQLInput** from the pop-up window. We're going to use this new component to dynamically retrieve all of the region values in our **invoices** table and pass these through to the ForEach component.

2. Click on the **DEMO_DB** component and, in its **Component** tab, add the following SQL statement to the **Query** box:

   ```
   "select distinct region_id from invoices"
   ```

3. Click on the **Guess Schema** button and the Studio will automatically retrieve the schema based on the query.

4. We now need to turn the output from the new component into an iteration, so that this can be passed onto the ForEach component. To achieve this we will make use of Talend's Flow To Iterate component, which takes each row of input data and iterates it to subsequent components. Search for `flowtoiterate` in the **Palette** window and drop a **tFlowToIterate** component onto the Job Designer.

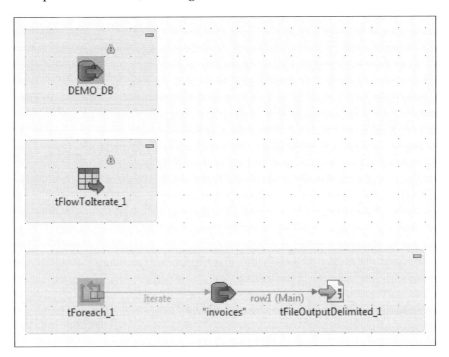

5. Right-click on the **DEMO_DB** component and, selecting **Row | Main**, connect it to the **tFlowToIterate** component.

6. Right-click on the Flow To Iterate component, select **Row | Iterate**, and connect it to the **tForEach** component.

7. Our final configuration changes the **tForEach** component so that it uses the iterated region ID values. Click on its **Component** tab and delete the region values that we previously configured. Click on the **+** button to add a new row and delete the default value that appears.

8. With your cursor in the new row of the **Value** table, press *Ctrl + Space bar* to access the global variables. You will find **tFlowToIterate_1.region_id** in the list. Double-click on this and the following value will be entered into your row:

   ```
   ((String)globalMap.get("row2.region_id"))
   ```

9. Your job should now look like the following screenshot:

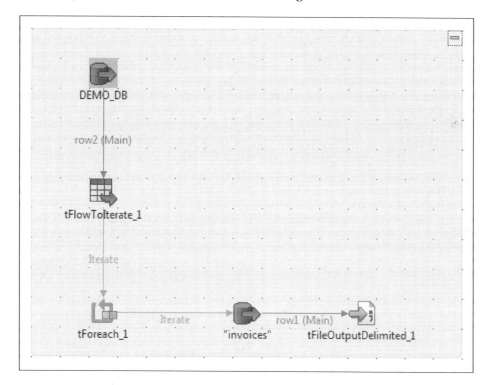

Let's review what's happening here. The **DEMO_DB** component executes first and retrieves the list of region IDs from the **invoices** table (in this case, **region_1**, **region_2**, and **region_3**). These values are passed onto the Flow To Iterate component, which, one by one, passes them to the ForEach component, via the global variable (`(String)globalMap.get("row2.region_id")`). For each iteration of the region ID value, the ForEach component passes the current region ID value to the invoice MySQL input component, which inserts the value into its query. Finally, on each iteration, the results of the query are written to the delimited output file, where, again, the current region ID value is used in the filename.

Run the job to see this process in action. The advantage of this new version of the job over the original version is that it is future proof, at least with regard to the number of regions in the organization. If new regions are added to the database table, they will automatically be included in the job, producing as many output files as there are regions.

Loop "n" times

We may also want a process to execute a certain number of times, and we can use Talend's **tLoop** component for this purpose. Import the `Loop2` job from the `Resources` directory. Let's walk step-by-step through its structure.

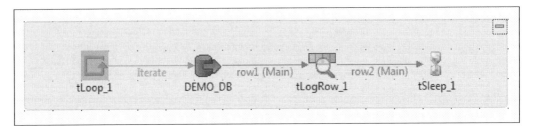

This job has four components:

- A **tLoop** component, which we use to set the number of times that a process will execute
- A **tMySQLInput** component configured using our **DEMO_DB 0.1** connection in the **Metadata** section of the **Repository** window
- A **tLogRow** component, to show the output of the query
- A **tSleep** component, which we use to determine the wait period between each execution of the process

We might use such a job if, for example, we wanted to report on-sales data from our database every hour. In reality, the job would not write to a **tLogRow** component, but might write to a file or, perhaps send an e-mail, but for convenience, we'll use the console display component.

Click on the **tLoop** component to view its configuration:

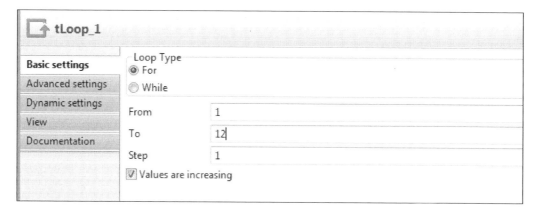

In this case, we have configured it to use a **For** type of loop, specifically, loop from **1** to **12** with an increment step of one each time. As you can see, we can also configure a **While** loop.

The **tMySQLInput** component has a simple query that extracts the sum of the invoice values from the **invoices** table.

Our final component, the **tSleep** component, configures the pause (in seconds) between each execution of the loop. To run the query every hour, this should be set to 3600, but set the **Pause (in seconds)** value to 10 and run the job. You will see the first execution take place and write the output of the query to the console screen. The job will then wait for 10 seconds before executing again, and it continues this pattern until 12 executions have taken place. Note that in our example the query output is the same each time as the **invoices** table is not being updated between executions, but our example scenario in a live system would show different values every hour.

Infinite loop

We can take the looping concept a step further by introducing an infinite loop for those jobs that you want to run forever. Open the job InfiniteLoop from the Resources directory. Its job design is shown in the following screenshot:

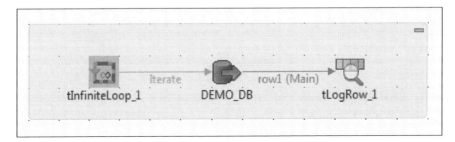

The infinite loop component replaces the **tLoop** component and the **tSleep** component and all that needs to be configured here is the gap (in milliseconds, not seconds!) between each execution. Set this value to 5000 milliseconds, that is five seconds, and kick off the job. This will keep running until you kill the job.

Duplicating and merging dataflows

Our final section in this chapter will look at how we can duplicate and merge dataflows. Duplicating dataflows is particularly useful as it allows us to undertake different processing on the same data without having to read a file twice or query a database twice. Merging dataflows allows us to take data from different sources and rationalize it into a single dataflow.

Duplicating data

Open the job DuplicatingData from the Resources directory.

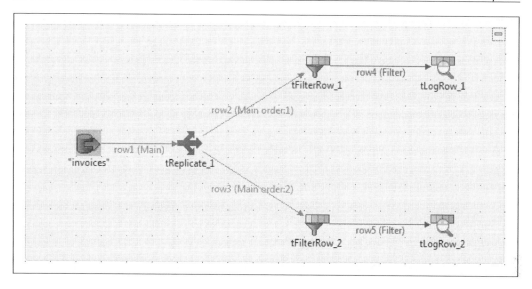

It starts with a simple database query. The dataflow from this is replicated using a **tReplicate** component and the same dataflow is subsequently passed to two processing streams. In this case the processing is very simple, a filter on each dataflow to filter for rows from **region1** or **region3** respectively. As noted previously, the processing on each dataflow could be completely different, for example, one flow being extracted to a CSV file while the other transformed and imported into a different database.

> The **tReplicate** component can have any number of flows coming out of it, not just two.

Merging data

Most businesses and organizations have multiple different systems that they require to function and some of these systems will hold data about the same entities, such as customers, products, employees, and so on. It is an ongoing business challenge to keep all of this data synchronized and *one version of the truth* is a common goal for the IT Department. Talend's **tUnite** component can help to merge data from different systems to support this often unreachable goal.

A simple job illustrating this is shown in the following screenshot:

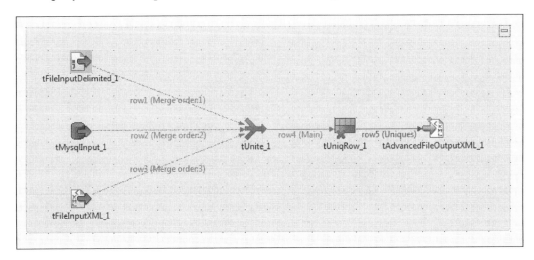

In this example, let's suppose we have three sources of customer data: a delimited file from our e-commerce system, a database extract from our finance system, and an XML file from the marketing department. We want to merge these files and create an XML file that can be passed onto our central **Customer Relationship Management (CRM)** system.

The dataflows from each input component are merged in the **tUnite** component and then passed onto a Unique Row component to remove any duplicate records. The *de-duped* data is then passed onto an XML output component for mapping to the expected format.

Note that the **tUnite** component expects all of its input dataflows to have the same schema. What would you do if this was not the case? Perhaps you might define the schema for the **tUnite** component to be the superset of fields from the three inputs and use the **tMap** components between the three inputs and the **tUnite** component to make the inputs merge together (even if some of the values are empty).

Summary

Understanding Talend's orchestration components is the key to being able to develop complex integration jobs. By controlling dataflows, adding logic between components or groups of components, and looping and iterating through tasks, jobs will expand from simple *one-trick ponies* to complete end-to-end processes, giving you, the integration developer, many more opportunities to construct robust and coherent integrations.

Chapter 8, Managing Jobs, introduces the concept of Context Variables and allows us to configure, within a single job, parameters for different environments, development, test, and production, for example.

8
Managing Jobs

We have spent a lot of time looking at how to build integration jobs using the Studio and some of the different components available to developers for achieving specific tasks. However, a key part of the development process focuses not on the job functionality itself, but on managing the code that is produced by a development project.

In this chapter, we will learn how to manage our job code using the Studio. Specifically, we will look at the following topics:

- Code versioning and how we can use the Studio to manage iterations of the same job
- Exporting and importing jobs from the Studio for collaboration purposes or to back up
- Exporting jobs for standalone execution
- Scheduling jobs for automated execution

Job versions

Mostly software development is an iterative process. Within a project, developers will iterate through a develop and test cycle until the software is ready to be put into production use. We can also think of an iterative process across projects; release 1 is deployed and is used for a period of time, but some enhancements or amendments are needed, so another project is undertaken and, at the end of this, release 2 is deployed into the wild. This process may go on for many years!

In order to support these iterative processes, the software is versioned to keep track of the code and components that constitute a given release. While the Studio does not contain a full-featured version control system, it does have some features which allow developers to manage software versions.

As we have been developing jobs in the previous chapters, you may have noticed that the Studio adds a version number to the end of the job name that we define. You can see this in the **Repository** view of jobs.

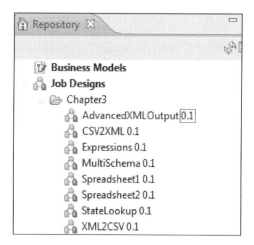

As highlighted in the image in the previous screenshot, **0.1** is added as a suffix to every job name by default. This is the Studio version number for the job. If you browse to the directory that holds the job code (in this case it is in `C:\Talend\Workspace\BEGINNERSGUIDE\process\Chapter3`), you can see that the Studio creates some artifacts that correspond to our job design.

We can create a new version of this job by right-clicking on the job in the **Repository** view and selecting **Open another version**. This will open the job version pop-up window.

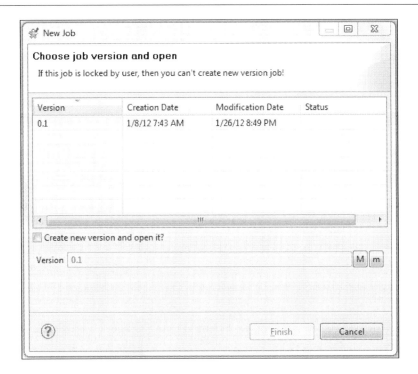

As shown in the previous screenshot, only version 0.1 exists right now. If we select **Version** 0.1 and click on **Finish**, the job will open in the normal manner. If we want to create a new version, tick the checkbox labeled **Create a new version and open it?** and click the **m** or **M** button to increment the version number.

The **m** button increments the minor version number, that is 0.1, 0.2, 0.3, and so on. The **M** button increments the major version, that is 1.0, 2.0, 3.0, and so on. There is no absolute convention on how to use version numbers in software development, but it is worth defining a strategy that makes sense to you. For example, you could use simple minor increments for the iterative development process within a project, followed by major increments to denote a certified release for production use. For readers who would like to read more about this topic, visit http://en.wikipedia.org/wiki/Software_versioning for an introduction to this subject.

For our example, click on the new version checkbox, increment the minor version number by clicking the **m** button, and click on **Finish**. This opens a new version 0.2. Notice that the **Repository** view now shows the job with its new version also.

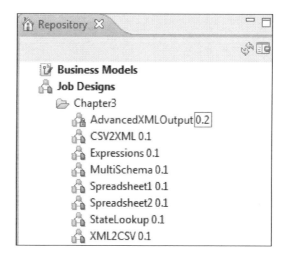

Notice too that the Studio has created a new set of artifacts for the new version, as shown in the following screenshot:

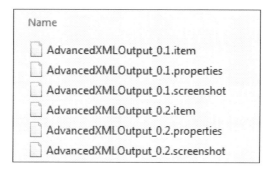

Close version 0.2 in the job designer and right-click on the job, again select **Open another version**. Now you can see version 0.1 and version 0.2 in the pop-up window.

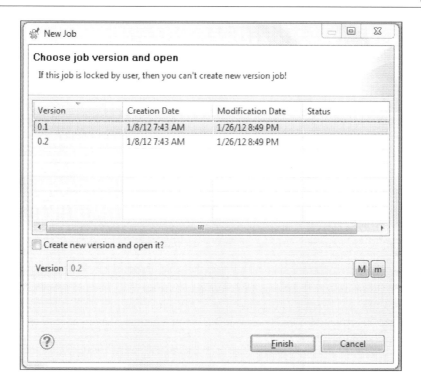

From here, you can open either version or create a new version (incrementing the major or minor version number as described previously).

Some key points to note are as follows:

- New versions are created from the latest version only. You cannot create a new version from a version older than the current latest version. In our previous example, if we create version 0.3, it will be a copy of version 0.2. There is not a direct method to create a new version based on version 0.1.

- Should you want to revert back to an older version (for example, version 0.3 based on version 0.1) you can create a new version, delete all of its components, open version 0.1, and copy and paste the components from version 0.1 into version 0.3.

- Only the latest version of a job can be edited. All other older versions are *read only*. Older versions can still be executed, but their configuration is now fixed.

Exporting and importing jobs

The Studio offers a number of different ways to export and import the jobs you create and each approach has a different purpose behind it. In this section we will look at the different methods of importing and exporting jobs and also look at why you might choose one method over another.

Exporting jobs

As we have seen in the section about job versions, the Studio creates file artifacts when you create a job design and stores these on your local computer's filesystem. When you run a job within the Studio, the artifacts, which represent the job configuration, are compiled into Java code before being executed. This development setup and process may be sufficient for some readers, particularly where there is only one developer creating jobs and/or the jobs can be run manually from the studio tool.

When this is not the case, it is useful to be able to export jobs from the Studio tool for two primary reasons:

1. You want to collaborate with other developers and need some way to make the jobs available to them. You may wish to simply give them the job artifacts that are created or you may be checking them into a sophisticated source control application. Either way, the job files need to be in a form where they can be moved from the creator's computer to another location.

2. You want to run the jobs automatically, without using the studio tool, either on your computer or, more likely, on a different computer.

Depending upon your needs you will export the jobs from the Studio in different ways.

Exporting a project

You may wish to export a complete project (the full contents of the repository). Follow these steps to do this:

1. Click on the **Export Talend projects** toolbar button above the **Repository** window, highlighted in red in the next screenshot:

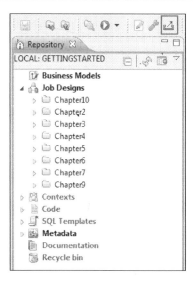

2. You will be presented with the **Export Talend projects in archive file** pop-up window.

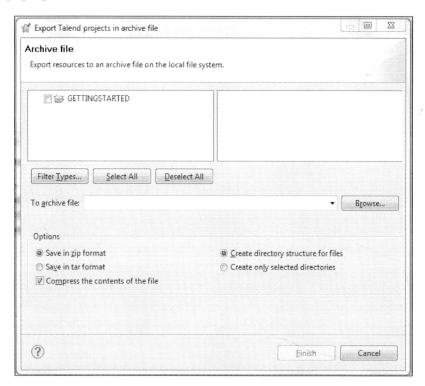

3. The pop-up window shows the list of projects in your workspace. In our example, we see the project named **GETTINGSTARTED**.

4. Click on the project to highlight it. You will see two files selected in the right-hand window, as shown in the following screenshot:

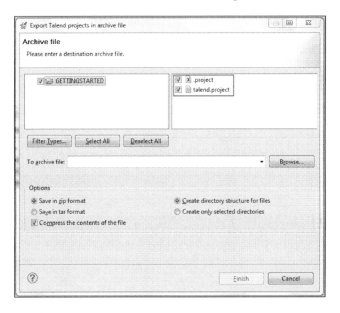

5. Click on the **Browse...** button and browse the directory where you want to save the project export. Give the archive (zip) file a suitable name. In this example, we have used the filepath `C:\Talend\Exports\GETTINGSTARTED.zip`.

6. Finally, click on **Finish** to run the export process.

The export archive that is created through this process can be imported back into the Studio by using the **Import...** function on the Studio start-up screen. See the section, *Importing a project*, later in this chapter for details on how to do this.

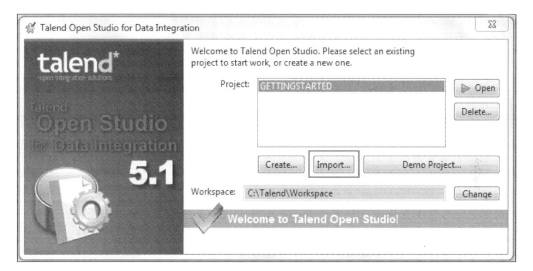

Exporting a job

Sometimes you may only need to export a single job, rather than a whole project. Again, follow these steps:

1. In the **Repository** window, expand the **Job Design** section and select a job to export.

2. Right-click on the job and select **Export items**. The **Export items** pop-up window will appear.

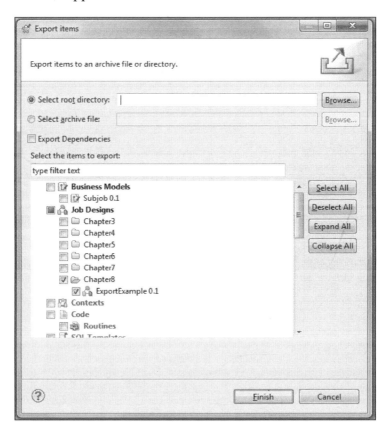

3. The job that you chose to work with will be pre-selected, but you also have the option to select additional jobs at this point if you wish. For now, we will work with the single job we selected.

4. You can choose to export the job as a set of files in a directory or a set of files in a zipped archive. We will export the job as a set of files in a directory, so make sure that **Select root directory** is selected and click on **Browse** to select an export directory.

5. We can also, optionally, decide to export any dependencies of the job. This might include FTP or database connections stored as metadata and used in the job, code snippets, or other dependent items in the **Repository** window. Check the **Export Dependencies** box if this is required.

6. Click on **Finish** to run the export process.

Again, have a look at the files that are extracted. This time only the *process* directory of our project file structure is exported, containing the three standard job artifacts we observed earlier.

> Note that more directories and files would be created if **Export Dependencies** had been checked and there were dependent items to export.

Exporting a job for execution

The export project and export job processes we have looked at allow developers to take files out of the Studio in an organized manner and make them available for use by other developers, checked into source control systems, or simply placed on a filesystem for backup purposes. The final type of export we will look at exports a job in a format such that it can be executed outside of the Studio. In this type of export, the Studio compiles the code into a standalone executable format and packages up all of the necessary files to support this. This allows developers to run the jobs on other computers or schedule them to run at certain times. Perform the following steps:

1. Choose a job from the **Repository** window and right-click on it, selecting **Export Job**. The **Export Jobs** pop-up window will appear.

2. Click on the **Browse** button to select a directory and archive the file to export to.

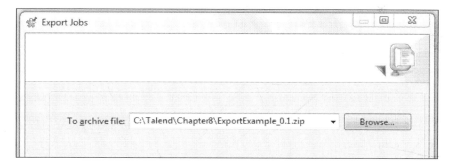

3. If your job has multiple versions, you can select which one is exported or, indeed, you can choose to export all versions if you wish. Select from the **Job Version** drop-down box to make your choice.

4. We need to choose the specific format of the job export. Click on the **Export Type** drop-down menu to see the options. The export offers a number of web services and **Enterprise Service Bus (ESB)** options and you may choose to use these if appropriate to your environment. However, we'll choose **Autonomous Job**. This provides a standalone code package that can be executed directly from your computer.

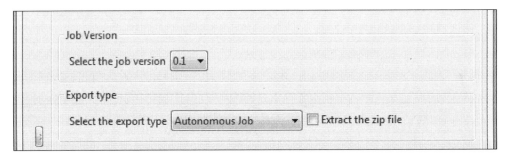

5. We are also going to modify the **Shell launcher** option. The export process creates a .bat file (for Windows) or a .sh file (for Linux/Unix) that can be used to execute the job in a standalone manner. Choose the option appropriate for your operating system. (In this case we will select **All** to show what is exported, but you would normally choose just one of the options.)

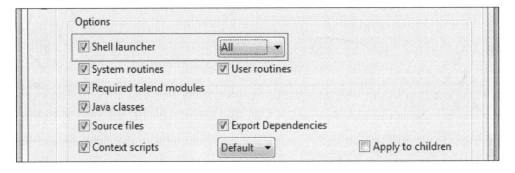

6. Let's leave all of the other options as the selected defaults and click on **Finish**.

7. Go to your export directory and you will find a zipped archive file there. Unzip the archive.

8. The resulting directory contains a set of files that completely encapsulate the job, including the shell scripts (.bat and .sh) that allow you to execute the job.

9. Double-click on your unzipped directory and you will see two further directories; a `lib` directory and a directory named the same as your job name. Click on the job name directory and you will see a number of files and directories, including a `run.bat` and `run.sh` file.

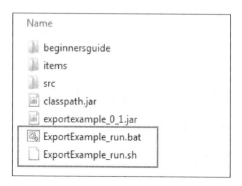

10. Windows users can use the `.bat` file and either double-click on it to execute it or use the Command Window to execute the file from the Windows shell. Linux and Unix users can use Terminal to browse to the directory containing the `.sh` script and use the following command to execute:

```
sh [file name].sh
```

The export directory is completely independent of the Studio, so you can copy the files to another computer and execute the job from there (this assumes that the new computer is able to access databases, FTP servers, or other file locations configured within the job).

Try this out now. If you are using a Windows operating system, double-click on the `.bat` file and a Command Window will open as the job runs. When the job is complete, the window will close. If you are using Linux or Unix, execute the `.sh` script as described previously. Check your output directories to validate that the job has worked successfully.

Importing jobs

Now that we have successfully exported jobs and projects, let's look at how we import them into the Studio.

Importing a project

There are two ways in which developers can import a project into the Studio. One is from the Studio startup screen and the other is from within the Studio itself. Let's start with the startup screen by following these steps:

1. Start up the Studio and on the logon screen, click on **Import**.

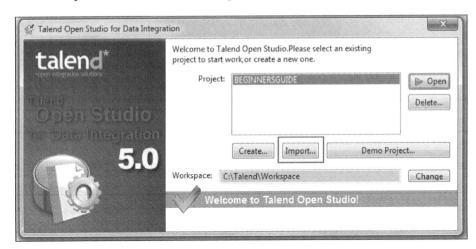

2. Enter a new project name and click on the **Browse** button of **Select root directory** to browse to your previously exported project files.

3. Click on **Finish** and the project files will import into the new project.

4. When the import is complete, you'll be presented with the logon screen again, but this time our newly imported project will be available in the list of projects.

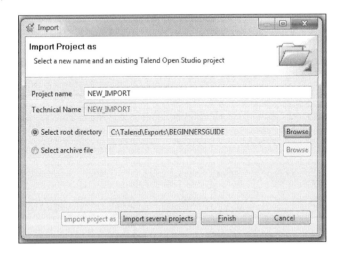

Select your new project and click on **Open**. If your project export is contained in an archive file, you can choose the second option **Select archive** file, rather than **Select root directory**.

Importing a job

Follow these steps to import an individual job from an export:

1. In the **Repository** window, right-click on **Job Designs** and select
    Import items.

2. Click on the **Browse** button of **Select root directory** and browse to the
    directory where your job export is stored.

3. Click on **OK** and the job will appear in the **Items List** window.

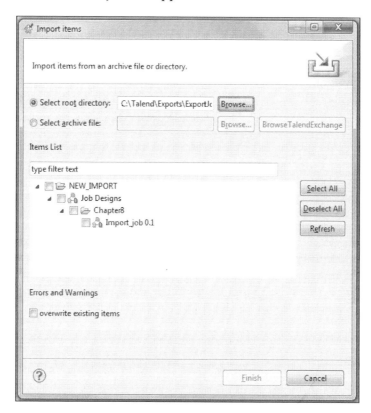

4. In the **Items List** window, check the box next to the job that you want
    to import.

5. Click on **Finish**. Your job will now appear in the **Repository** window and can be edited or executed as normal. If it doesn't appear immediately, click on the refresh icon in the top right-hand side corner of the **Repository** window.

Scheduling jobs

Once a job has been developed and tested, it can be deployed into production use. Most integration jobs tend to run on some sort of schedule-every day, every hour, every Monday at 9 a.m., and so on.

The Studio does not offer a built-in scheduling tool, but through the job export options we can package up all of the code required to run a job outside of the Studio. As noted previously, this package includes a shell script to execute the job under either Windows or Linux/Unix. The shell scripts can be scheduled using your operating system's native tools, Windows Task Scheduler or, on Linux, Cron, or there are many scheduling tools, both open source and proprietary, that can be used to schedule the shell scripts.

Summary

Managing jobs is not nearly as exciting or rewarding as building jobs, but understanding the processes around version control, exporting and importing jobs from the Studio, job execution, and scheduling will be critical to all serious users and developers. Building the disciplines of version control into your development process will improve organization and quality and will allow developers to collaborate or handover integration jobs with minimum fuss. Readers who are new to formal source control processes are encouraged to read further on this subject and to use the tools built into the Studio, versioning, exporting, and importing, to make their development processes as robust as possible.

In the next chapter, we will learn how we can make integration jobs flexible by utilizing global variables built into the Studio environment. We'll also look at context variables, which allow us to run the same job with a different context; for example, executed once with variables that relate to a test environment and executed again, but this time with variables that relate to a production environment. The use of global and context variables makes our jobs more flexible and less hardcoded, a significant benefit to developers.

9
Global Variables and Contexts

In any kind of programming, variables are simply placeholders for values that are used in the execution of a program. The values in the variables might change on different executions. For example, the `day_of_week` variable might hold the value of `Tuesday` today, but `Wednesday` tomorrow. Variable values might also change within a single execution. For example, we might use a variable to hold the running total of invoices processed. As each invoice is processed, the value held in the variable will change.

The use of variables allows our jobs to be dynamic and not have hardcoded values in them.

In this chapter, we will learn about:

- **Studio global variables**: The variables that the Studio makes available through the components we use in our integration jobs
- **User defined global variables**: Ad-hoc variables that can be configured in your jobs
- **Job contexts**: The variables we can create to execute jobs with different parameters for different environments or scenarios

Global variables

We have seen the use of global variables in some of the job examples covered in earlier chapters of the book, but this section will deal with the subject in more detail, showing how we can use the component global variables generated automatically by the Studio. For the more adventurous or experienced developer, we will also explore how to create and use your own global variables.

Studio global variables

Global variables, in the Studio context, are variables that are available to all components, modules, or functions within a job. As we develop jobs in the Studio, global variables are made available depending upon the components used. Let's illustrate this with a simple job.

1. Import the job named `GlobalVariables` from the resource directory of this chapter and click through the various components in it. The job contains a file list, delimited input, **tMap**, and delimited output components. Note that not all of the parameters are configured at this point. We'll address this as we work through the following jobs:

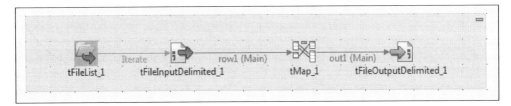

2. Take a look at the **Outline** tab in the bottom-left corner of the Studio. Expand some of the items and you will see some global variables for the components added to your job. We can use these global variables in our job configurations to make the jobs dynamic.

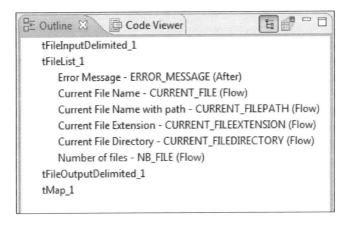

3. Click on the delimited input component. We need to configure the **File name/Stream** parameter. In the **Outline** window, expand the `tFileList` component and click on **Current File Name with path** in the **Outline** window. Drag this to the **File name/Stream** box of the delimited input component.

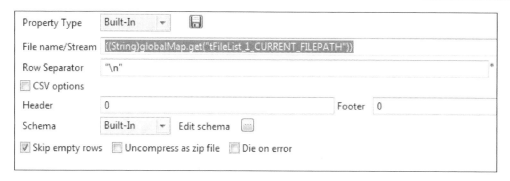

4. You will see the following value added to the textbox:

```
((String)globalMap.get("tFileList_1_CURRENT_FILEPATH"))
```

This global variable passes the value of the current file (and its path) through the delimited input component. Note that the file list and its connection to the delimited input are iterative, so, on each iteration, the delimited file input is reading the "current" file.

5. When the job is executed, our current file is read and passed through the tMap component. It is then written to a delimited output file. We can also use a global variable here.

6. Click on the delimited output component. We want to configure the **File Name** parameter so that processed files are output to a new directory and the filename is modified to reflect that it has been processed. In the **File Name** field, enter the following value (including quotes):

```
"C:/Talend/Workspace/BEGINNERSGUIDE/DataOut/Chapter9/processed_"
```

This is the "fixed" element of the path and filename for each processed file.

7. Now drag-and-drop the **Current File Name** global variable from the **Outline** window into the **File Name** box. Add a + sign between the fixed path and the global variable to join the two elements together. Your final parameter value should be:

```
"C:/Talend/Workspace/BEGINNERSGUIDE/DataOut/Chapter9/
processed_"+((String)globalMap.get("tFileList_1_CURRENT_FILE"))
```

8. Run the job—the files will be picked up in turn and written to the output directory, prefixing the filename with processed_.

User defined global variables

The global variables that the Studio provides in the components are, generally, adequate for most integration jobs and provide variables that are specific and relevant to the components being used. However, there will be occasions when you want to use a variable across a component that is not provided by the Studio. Examples might include:

- "Fixed" values that you need to access in your integration job—client = "Acme Corporation" or tax_rate = 20%, for example

- Variables that you create from standard Java functions—day, month, year values, for example

- Variables that you set based on the data accessed by the integration job

Fortunately, the Studio makes it easy for us to create our own global variables. We'll look at a couple of ways to do this now.

In the first example, we'll use the Studio's globalMap.put function to set the variable value.

1. Right-click on the **GlobalVariables** job we have just created and select **Duplicate**. In the **Input new name** pop-up window, change the name to CreateGlobalVariable.

2. Open the job and drop a **tJava** component onto the Job Designer. We're going to use this to set up a global variable and then use the value assigned to this in our job.

3. Click on the **tJava** component and enter the following code into the **Code** window:

```
String datestamp=TalendDate.getDate("YYYYMMDD");
globalMap.put("dateStamp",datestamp);
```

4. This code sets a variable, datestamp, with the year, month, and day values of the current date. The variable is then set as a global variable, dateStamp, that makes it available to other components.

5. Connect the **tJava** component to the original subjob using an **On Subjob OK** connection.

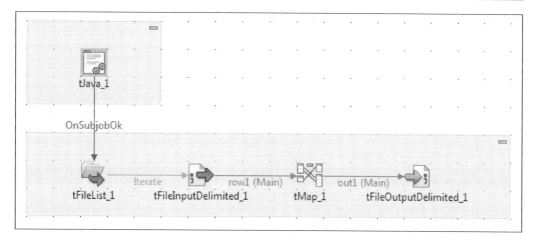

6. Click on the delimited output component and change its filename to be:

    ```
    "C:/Talend/Workspace/BEGINNERSGUIDE/DataOut/Chapter9/"+(String)
    globalMap.get("dateStamp")+"_"+((String)globalMap.
    get("tFileList_1_CURRENT_FILE"))
    ```

7. We are using the `globalMap.get` command on our new global variable
    `dateStamp` to get the global variable value into the filename.

8. Run the job and check the output. You should see three files created in
    the output directory prefixed with the year, month, and day values.

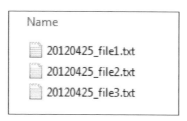

In the next example, we will use a Studio component specifically designed for setting
global variables—the `tSetGlobalVar` component.

We want the job to read a directory of files (with timestamped filenames) and pick out the oldest file for processing. In your `DataIn\Chapter9` directory, set up five new files, each with the filename of pattern `file_yyyymmdd.txt`. The files are shown as follows:

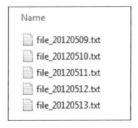

Now follow the given steps:

1. Create a new job and name it `GlobalVariablesComponent`.

2. From the Palette, drop the following components onto the Job Designer: **tFileList, tIterateToFlow, tSampleRow, tSetGlobalVar**, and **tFileCopy**.

3. Set the **tFileList** component to read the `DataIn\Chapter9` directory and set the **Filemask** to `"*.txt"`.

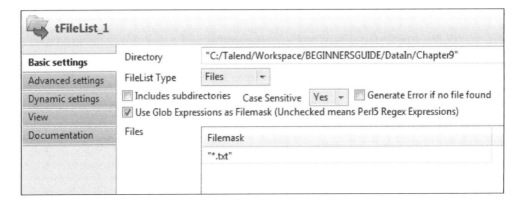

4. Ensure that the **Order by** value is set to **By file name** and the **Order action** value is set to **ASC**. This sorts the file list output data by filename in ascending order and in our scenario puts the oldest file as the first data element to be the output.

5. Connect the file list component to the **tIterateToFlow** component using an iterate connector. (The **tIterateToFlow** component transforms an iterated list into a data flow that can be processed).

6. Set the schema of the **tIterateToFlow** component. Add a single schema row and name it `filename`. In the **Mapping** table, `filename` will appear in the **Column** column. Delete the value in the **Value** column and press *Ctrl +* space bar to access the list of global variables. Find **tFileList_1.CURRENT_ FILEPATH** and select this to save it into the **Value** column.

7. Connect the **tIterateToFlow** component to the sample row component using a **Main** connector.

8. Click on **Sync Columns** on the sample row component to sync the schema from the **tIterateToFlow** component. In the **Range** box, delete the default value and enter 1. This will allow us to access the first row provided by the **tIterateToFlow** component. As we noted earlier, the first row represents the filename of the oldest file.

9. Connect the **tSampleRow** component to the **tSetGlobalVariable** component using the **Row | Main** connector.

10. Now click on the **tSetGlobalVariable** component. Click on the + button to add a row to the **Variables** table. Set the **Key** value to `"myFile"` and the **Value** value to `row2.filename`. Here we are setting the variable `"myFile"` to have the value of the filename passed from the sample row component. (Note that the **tSampleRow** output is `row2` and the schema field we are passing is `filename`, hence **Value** is set to `row2.filename`.)

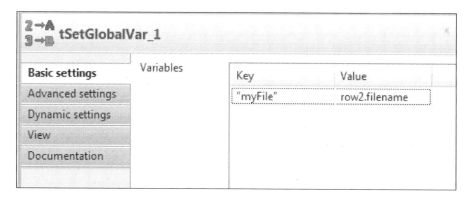

11. Click on the **tFileList** component and connect this to the **tFileCopy** component using an **OnSubjobOK** connector.

12. In the **tFileCopy** component set the **File Name** to be:

```
(String)globalMap.get("myFile")
```

13. This accesses the variable `myFile` that we have previously set. Set the **Destination directory** value to:

    ```
    "C:/Talend/Workspace/BEGINNERSGUIDE/DataOut/Chapter9"
    ```

14. Now run the job. The files will be listed in ascending order and the data will be passed through the sample row component. The first value is selected and passed to the set global variable component where it is set against our defined variable. Finally, the file copy component uses this variable value to pick the file to copy to the destination directory.

The ability to create our own global variables offers tremendous flexibility and almost any data item associated with your job can be turned into a useful global variable.

Contexts

The Studio commonly utilizes another type of variable – a context variable. Context variables allow jobs to be executed in different ways, with different parameters.

A classic example of this is when we develop a job and want to run it in different environments – development, test, and production, for example. Let us suppose that our job has to connect to a database, and, as is common, the connection details for development, test, and production databases are different. We could create three copies of the job, each one with different connection details configured, but this duplicates code and makes job maintenance more difficult. Far better would be to create a single job and allow it to run with different connection details depending upon the database you want to target at any given time. The Studio context solves this problem.

Contexts are user-defined variables that can be invoked at runtime and there are three ways that we can implement context variables – embedded variables, repository variables, or external variables. We will create three jobs that illustrate each scenario.

Embedded context variables

Embedded context variables are (as the name suggests) embedded in the job you are developing and are configured much like any other component parameters in the window below the Job Designer. Follow the example given next. In this case, we will show how to access different file locations with different contexts, which is exactly what might happen when we run jobs for a "test" context or a "production" context.

1. Create a new job and name it `EmbeddedContext`.

2. From the **Palette**, drop the delimited input, **tMap**, and delimited output components onto the Job Designer.

3. Create a simple schema in the delimited input component—a single field called `data` will suffice—and set up the same schema in the delimited output component. Join the components together as shown in the following screenshot:

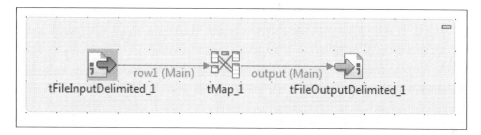

4. Let's now create the directory structure to reflect our test and production scenario. Create the following directories:
   - `C:\Talend\Workspace\Context\Source`
   - `C:\Talend\Workspace\Context\Test`
   - `C:\Talend\Workspace\Context\Production`

5. Place a simple, one field file in the `Source` directory (there's a sample file in the resource directory of this chapter named `context.txt`).

6. Change the **File name/Stream** parameter of the input component to `C:/Talend/Workspace/Context/Source/context.txt`.

7. Open the **tMap** component and map **row1** to **output**.

8. Now let's work on the contexts. Click on the **Contexts** tab of the panel below the Job Designer. Click on the **+** button at the bottom of this window to add a new context variable row and change its name to `destination_directory`.

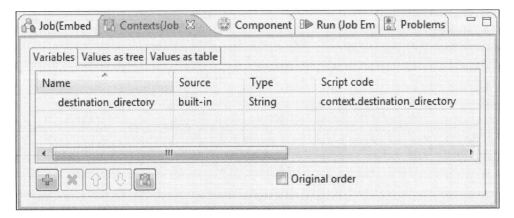

9. Now click on the **Value as table** tab. Click on the icon in the top right-hand corner of this window — this allows us to configure different contexts.

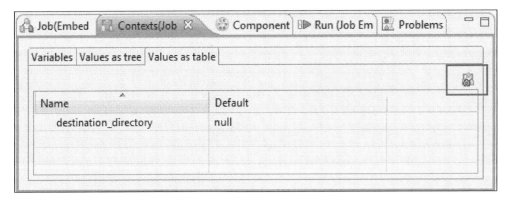

10. The pop-up window that appears will show a default context (called **Default**) — we will add two new contexts to this. Click on the **New** button and enter **Test** in the pop-up window. Click on **OK**. Repeat this and create a **Production** context.

11. We don't need the **Default** context, so click on the checkbox next to the **Test** context (to make it the default context for the job) and then click on **Default** and the **Remove** button to delete it. You should now be left with two contexts, **Test** and **Production**.

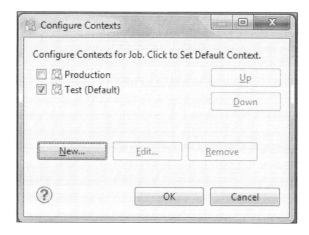

12. Click on **OK** to close the window.

13. Returning to the **Value as table** window, you can now see two new columns—**Production** and Test—added to the window. We can now enter variable values for each of these contexts.

14. Click in the **Production** column on the line for our variable `destination_ directory`. Enter the path to our production directory — `C:/Talend/ Workspace/Context/Production/`. Note the trailing forward slash at the end.

15. Similarly, click in the **Test** column and enter the path to our test directory — `C:/Talend/Workspace/Context/Test/`.

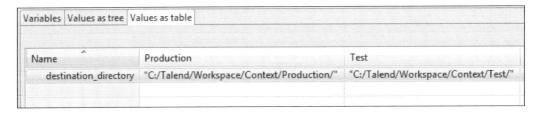

Name	Production	Test
destination_directory	"C:/Talend/Workspace/Context/Production/"	"C:/Talend/Workspace/Context/Test/"

16. Our final setup task is to reference our variable in the appropriate component. Click on the delimited output component and delete the default value in the **File Name** parameter. With your cursor in the **File Name** box, press *Ctrl* + space bar and a list of variables and functions will appear. You will find **context.destination_directory** in this list. Select this to apply it to the **File Name** parameter. We need to append the output filename to the end of the context variable, so add a suitable filename as shown in the following screenshot, using + to concatenate this with the directory name:

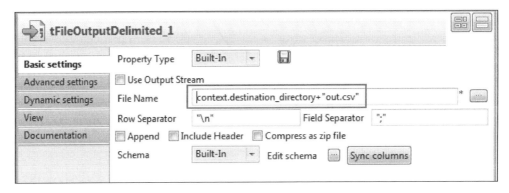

17. We can now run the job. However, the execution process is slightly different to what we have seen before. This time, we need to select the execution context before we start the job. Go to the **Run** tab and in the right-hand column, you will see a drop-down list which displays the different context variables we have configured.

18. Select **Test** from the drop-down list to run the job with a **Test** context. Now click on the **Run** button and you will see the output file write to the **Test** directory.

19. Change the context drop-down to **Production** and run the job again. As expected, the output file will write to the **Production** directory this time.

Repository context variables

As we have seen with other metadata items, contexts can be stored in the Studio repository, allowing them to be centrally maintained, available to other developers and reused on other jobs. If you plan to use a set of context variables in more than one job, it makes sense to add them to the repository, rather than embed them directly in the job. Let's walk through setting up contexts in the repository.

1. Create a new job and name it `RepositoryContext`.

2. We will use the job from the embedded context example for this illustration, so open the embedded context job and copy and paste the three components into the `Repositorycontext` job.

3. In **Repository**, right-click on **Contexts** and select **Create context group**.

4. Name your context group `RepositoryContext1` in the pop-up window and click on **Next**.

5. You will now see a window that is similar to the **Context** tab of the Job Designer. Click on the **+** button to add a new row and change the **Name** value to destination_file_path.

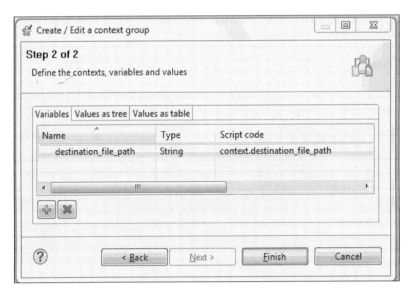

6. Click on the **Values as table** tab, and then click on the **Configure Contexts** button in the top right-hand corner.

7. As before, create a **Test** and a **Production** context, set **Test** to be the default context, and delete the **Default** context.

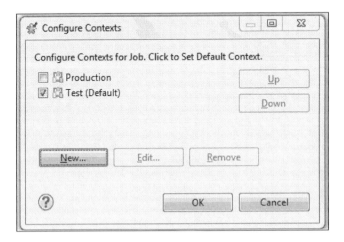

8. Click on **OK** to save to **Contexts**.

9. We now have **Production** and **Test** columns in the **Value as table** window. Configure the path to the **Production** and **Test** directories by adding the following to the `destination_file_path` row in the **Production** and **Test** columns respectively:

     ○ `C:/Talend/Workspace/Context/Production/out.txt`

     ○ `C:/Talend/Workspace/Context/Test/out.txt`

10. Click on **Finish**.

11. Having created the context group in the **Repository**, we now need to add it to the job. Click on the **Context** tab below the Job Designer and click on the **Select Context Variables** button.

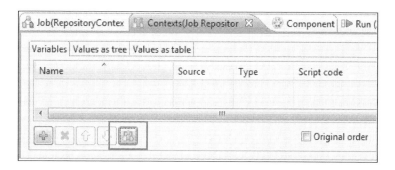

12. The pop-up window will show all of the contexts held in the **Repository** — in our case just **RepositoryContext1**. Expand this context group and check the **destination_file_path** variable.

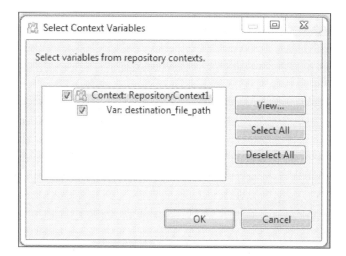

13. Select **OK**.

14. You will be presented with another pop-up — **Add Context Group**. The pop-up requests that you add the non-existent context group into the job. This adds the **Test** and **Production** context groups that we created earlier. Ensure that the **Context: RepositoryContext** checkbox is checked and click on **OK**.

15. Finally, click on the delimited output component, delete the value in the **File Name** parameter, and placing your cursor in the parameter box, press *Ctrl* + space bar. All of the global variables will be revealed in a drop-down box. Select **context.destination_file_path** from the list.

As before, we can run the job from the **Run** tab, selecting the context, either **Test** or **Production**, that we wish to run and the output file will be produced in the appropriate directory.

External context variables

External context variables are variables held in a file and loaded into the Studio job at runtime. Follow the given steps to create the example job:

1. Create a new job and name it ExternalContextVariable.

2. Open the RepositoryContext job. We can use the same components from the RepositoryContext job in the ExternalContextVariable job, so select all three components and copy and paste them into the external context job.

3. In the **Palette**, search for properties and drop a **tFileInputProperties** component onto the Job Designer.

4. Now search for contextload and drop a **tContextLoad** component onto the Job Designer.

5. The **tFileInputProperties** and **tContextLoad** components have predefined schemas and each row of the properties files is represented by a key/value pair. Join the properties file to the context load using the **Row | Main** connector.

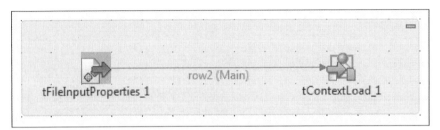

6. As we noted at the start of this section, the context parameters are held in an external file, so let's create that file now. To match the schema of the components noted previously, the `properties` file is simply a number of rows, each with a key/value pair. The key and value are separated by the "equals" sign ("="). Let's suppose the context we want to configure is for our production environment. In our `properties` file, we can create a row with a variable name and the value we want that variable to hold for a given context. In this example the row will hold the values:

   `file_path=C:/Talend/Workspace/Context/Production/out.txt`

7. Add this to the file and save the file as `externalcontext_prod.properties`.

8. In the **Configuration** tab of the input properties component, change its **File Name** parameter to point to the new properties file. In this case the parameter will be set to `C:/Talend/Workspace/Context/externalcontext_prod.properties`.

9. From the properties input file, right-click and select **Trigger | On Subjob OK** and place the connector onto the delimited input file.

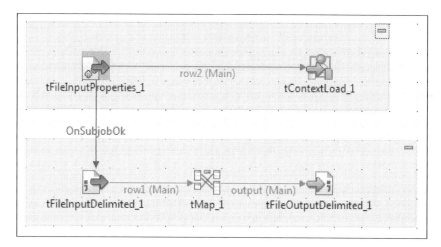

10. Go to the **Contexts** tab below the Job Designer and click on the + button to add a new variable. We want to add in a row for the variable we created in our context properties file, so change the name to `file_path`.

11. Click on the **Component** tab of the delimited output component and change its **File Name** parameter to `context.file_path`.

12. We have now made the connection between the variable (and its context value) in the `properties` file, a context variable in the job, and the use of that context variable in a component, in this case the delimited output component. Run the job to check if it works as expected.

If you change the variable value in the `properties` file or create a new `properties` file and configure the job to use this, a different context will be loaded and different outputs or actions will be executed.

Complex context variables

In the examples shown in this chapter we have seen the use of a single context variable in the Studio job. In real life, the context variables will probably be far more complex, with the need to configure many variables to meet the requirements of the job. For example, we may wish to set up FTP and database connection details as context variables in order to run the job against the production FTP and database, or the test FTP and database. If we were using an external context file, the values in it might be something as shown in the following screenshot:

```
 1   ftp_host=192.168.10.12
 2   ftp_user=ftpuser
 3   ftp_password=P4ssword!
 4   ftp_port=21
 5   mysql_host=192.168.34.54
 6   mysql_user=reader
 7   mysql_password=r34d0nly!
 8   mysql_port=3306
 9   mysql_database=reporting
10
```

The principles of more complex context variables are exactly the same as we saw in the examples, whether embedded, repository, or external.

Using embedded, repository, and external contexts

Now that we have seen how to configure the different types of context variables, the obvious question to ask is "When should I use embedded contexts (or repository contexts or external contexts)?"

Embedded contexts, by their nature, are not available outside of the job in question, so it makes sense to only use these if you are unlikely to need the context values in another setting.

Repository contexts are available to all jobs in the project, so it makes sense to use the repository to store these variables if you have many jobs that can utilize the contexts you have set up. Repository contexts are also useful in a collaborative development environment where you may have two or more developers working on integration jobs. It is a good development practice to put as much configuration as possible into the repository so that others can make use of it, thereby increasing developer productivity and ease of maintenance for your integration jobs.

External contexts are very useful if you have a very controlled deployment process and where, for example, the development and deployment processes are carried out by different teams. If a job has gone through a strict development and test process, you may not want your deployment team to reopen a job in order to modify its execution context. However unlikely, it is possible that the job configuration may be accidentally altered, invalidating the job and the testing you have completed on it. In these circumstances, the use of an external file to hold the context variables means that the job itself can be deployed without any changes from the test environment and all that needs to be changed is the context variable values in the properties file. External contexts may also be used when the details of the production environments—usernames, passwords, and so on—are not published to the development teams for system security reasons. Externalizing contexts in this manner allows developers to work with the integration jobs and deployers to work with the context files without the need for either party to know anything about the other's work.

Summary

As you become more experienced with the Studio, you will find that you see more and more opportunities to use context variables. Grab these opportunities with both hands! We have explored contexts by using the traditional "test/production" scenario, but it equally exists for "client A/client B/client C", "subsidiary A/subsidiary B/subsidiary C", and many other situations. Contexts make your jobs more flexible and allow you to reuse jobs repeatedly, with only minor changes reflected in context variables.

Our next chapter, *Chapter 10, Worked Examples*, will take what we have learnt from chapters 3 to 9 and put it all together in some real-life examples of integration jobs. The jobs are more complex and end-to-end in nature and will show how the Studio can manage the full integration process for you.

10
Worked Examples

This chapter builds on the knowledge we have gained in the previous chapters and illustrates a number of real-life integration scenarios. You will see that the examples use techniques from different chapters and combine file manipulations with database queries, subjobs with file management, for example, to create full end-to-end integration jobs.

You will hopefully have learned now that the Studio is incredibly flexible, and one result of this is that there is often more than one way to approach a task and develop a suitable job that satisfies the integration requirement. Keep this in mind as we walk through the scenarios in this chapter and see if you can come up with different configurations that achieve the same end.

First let's set the scene. Delightful Dresses is a fashion retailer and it operates an e-commerce website to sell its products online. It sources some of its merchandise directly and has an **Enterprise Resource Planning (ERP)** application to support this and other key business processes. It also sources merchandise from two third-party suppliers, Fabulous Fashions, and Runway Collections. Merchandise from the third-party supplier is displayed on the website, along with its own merchandise, and the third parties fulfill the orders placed for their products, with Delightful Dresses fulfilling their own products through the ERP system. (In industry terminology, the third parties are also known as drop-shippers).

Our task is to integrate the various systems so that the e-commerce website can operate. The website requires:

- Product data
- Inventory data

The website also sends out information to show what orders have been placed and what needs to be fulfilled. It also expects the fulfillment systems to update it with order statuses once the merchandise has been dispatched.

In addition to these tasks, we will also look at some other scenarios where the Studio can help automate and streamline manual processes. Specifically, we will create jobs that will perform the following tasks:

- E-mailing daily sales data to the Delightful Dresses management team
- Automating product visibility on the e-commerce website

Product catalog

Our first worked example will look at the product data required to display products on the website. Product content is the data that is displayed on the website, for example; product names, product descriptions, prices, and product attributes. It also includes data that is not displayed, but is required for the proper functioning of a website: SKU IDs and categorization data. We will start by looking at the conditions related to the product's catalog import and derive the integration job requirements from there.

1. The website has a standard catalog import format-an XML file. All product data coming into the website platform must be presented in the standard catalog import format.

2. The website has a file import process. A file named `catalog.xml` is placed onto the website's server in a directory named `/imports/catalog`. The import process runs on an hourly cycle and checks for an appropriately named file in this directory. If a file is present, the process picks up the file, imports it, and then moves the original file to a `completed` directory, `/imports/catalog/completed`.

3. We have four sources of data to integrate into the product catalog process. Firstly, we have data from the retailer's ERP system. This is supplied in XML format and it broadly contains the same sort of data as required by the website. It will need to be transformed into the product catalog import format.

4. Secondly, we have data from one of the retailer's suppliers, Fabulous Fashions. This is supplied in a delimited file format. This data, again, is similar to that required by the website, but there are two issues that we would like to deal with. The product data from this source has a **color** field, but the data in it contains abbreviations rather than color names that we might want to display on a website. For example, it contains the colors **BLK** and **WHT**, instead of **Black** and **White**. Additionally, the supplier does most of its business in Europe, and so its product sizes are set to the European standards. However, our website is for the North American market, where size standards are different. The product data from the supplier contains

sizes such as 36, 38, 40, and so on. We will need to transform these into the North American equivalents.

5. Thirdly and fourthly, we have product data from another of the retailer's suppliers, Runway Collections Ltd. This supplier's product data comes in two files, one containing the main product's content: names, descriptions, and so on, and the other containing SKUs and prices only (this allows the supplier to send price changes without having to send all of the product data). To make this integration even more interesting, there's no guarantee that a product file and a price file will arrive at the same time, and, even if they do, they might contain data for different products and SKUs. This presents a challenge for us. There's a constraint on the website such that it can accept products without prices, but not prices without products, so we'll need to figure out how we can work around this issue.

6. All three data sources described previously can send multiple datafiles per day and there's no fixed time for each of the files to be sent. Further more, the source systems will FTP the data onto the server hosting the Studio and the website into some nominated directories.

7. There is no connection between the three systems supplying the data and it is possible that they may use the same product and SKU IDs, so we'll need some way of making the SKUs unique across the website platform.

8. The datafiles are presented with filenames of a similar format, namely:

   `[data_source]_[yyyyMMddhhmmss].[file_extension]`

   Examples of filenames are:

   ○ `erp_20120930120000.xml`
   ○ `fabulous_fashions_20120930142524.csv`

Our next task is to pick out the key information from the previous scenarios and use this to define the high-level job requirements.

1. The scenario described previously is quite complex, and it often makes sense to break down complex requirements into smaller, simpler requirements. An obvious way to do this here is to define four separate jobs, one for each data source, rather than trying to combine the requirements into one mega job. Sometimes this will not be appropriate, but in this case, we'll go with this approach.

2. The website has a standard import process and it requires a file named `catalog.xml`. As we have four data sources feeding into this process at an undefined schedule, we need some way of checking that a file has not already been presented to the website import process before we try to present another, otherwise files will be overwritten.

3. The data from Fabulous Fashions needs to be modified and enriched as it is transformed. We will need to incorporate some lookup files into the process to facilitate this.

4. The data from Runway Collections is more challenging. As we can present product data without prices, we can deal with the first file they present. However, on its own, we cannot present the price-only datafile as this does not have enough content in it to form a valid import file. We can get around this by looking up the missing product content data from the website platform and using this, along with the SKU/price data from the second file to create a valid catalog import file. There are also some timing issues we should aim to deal with. If a product's content file and a price file get presented to us at approximately the same time, and we try to process the price-only file first, it may be that some of the SKUs in this file may not exist in the website platform (and, hence, we cannot incorporate the lookup files described previously). However, if the product content file was processed *before* the price file, then the website platform should have all of the relevant data for us to do the lookup process successfully. Even with such timing and dependency checks, we should anticipate that the price-only file sometimes presents SKUs that do not exist in the website platform. In this case, it would be nice to deal with these effectively, perhaps by writing unknown SKUs to a `rejects` file.

5. As there might be a chance of getting the same SKU code from different data sources, we need to modify the data so that duplicate SKUs are not presented to the website platform. We will do this by prefixing each SKU with an identifier which denotes the data source.

Data import from the ERP system

Let's start by looking at the data import from the retailer's ERP system. The illustration in the following screenshot shows the full job. We will look at each section of the job in turn.

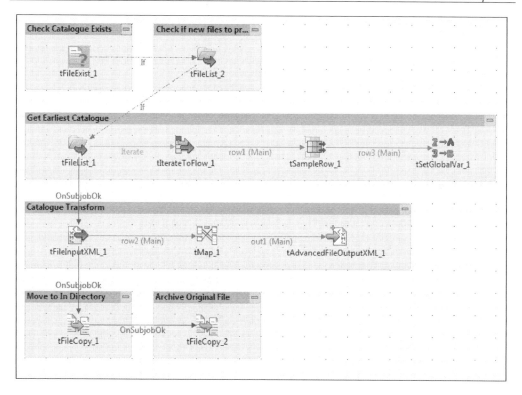

 Note that we have added a title to each section of the job to aid readability and understanding. To add a title, simply click on a subjob box (the outer box containing all of the components); in the **Component** tab, you will see a checkbox named **Show subjob title**. Click on the checkbox and add your title into the textbox that is revealed.

The first subjob checks whether or not a catalog file already exists in the website's import directory, using a **tFileExist** component. If it does exist, we don't want to create a new file and, in doing so, overwrite the file that is waiting to import. Our job logic, then, will check whether a file already exists. If it does exist, then the job will end; if it doesn't exist, the job will proceed. This flow logic is achieved using an **If** connector between the file exist component and the next subjob. We have used the global variable to facilitate this.

```
((Boolean)globalMap.get("tFileExist_1_EXISTS"))
```

Note that in the **If** flow, the global variable is prefixed by ! to indicate does *not* exist.

The second subjob checks if a file is waiting to be processed. Here we use a **tFileList** component and in the **If** connector to the next subjob, we use the component's global variable **Number of Files**. This file list component counts the number of files matching a given file mask. We want to check that there is, indeed, a file to process, so the code we use on the **If** connector is as follows:

```
((Integer)globalMap.get("tFileList_2_NB_FILE"))> 0
```

Therefore, if the number of files matching our filename mask is greater than zero, that is there's one or more files, then the job will proceed. If there isn't, it will exit gracefully. It is worth putting these checking components into your integration jobs. If you don't have them, then the job would still work if a file is present, but would error somewhere during the job if a file is not present. In our configuration, the job will not error irrespective of whether or not a file is present.

The next subjob looks for the earliest file sent by the ERP system. We noted earlier that the source systems can send multiple files per day and the schedule is not predefined. Therefore, we should anticipate that the ERP system might send two or more files in quick succession. Moreover, because we have four data sources and these run independently, there is no guarantee that a file from a particular source will have been processed by the time the next file from the same source arrives. The files need to be loaded in the *earliest first* order so that the integrity of the source ERP system is maintained.

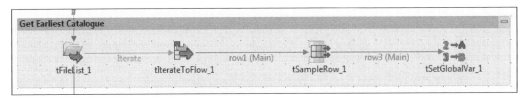

The subjob lists the files in the directory that the ERP sends files to, and this data is iterated to the rest of the subjob through an Iterate To Flow component. The file list component is configured so that the files are iterated in filename ascending order (which for us, given the filename convention described earlier in the chapter, presents the earliest file first). The Iterate To Flow component turns the iterative data into a series of rows. From the row flow, we get the first row of data (the earliest filename) using a **tSampleRow** component. This single row of data is then sent to a set global variable component, where the earliest filename is set into a variable that we can then use throughout the job.

Now that we know which is the first file we need to deal with, we can implement an XML transformation using a **tMap** component as shown in the following screenshot:

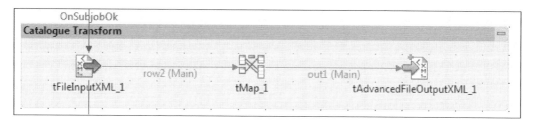

We'll use this step of the process to make our SKU IDs unique across all suppliers. In the **tMap** component, we prefix the SKU ID with a unique identifier to denote it as originating in the ERP system. In this case, we have used the following convention:

```
"erp_"+row.sku
```

Finally, having created our output file, we'll move this to the website's import directory and then archive the original file presented by the ERP system. It is always a good practice to archive the original source file in case there are errors in processing, which means you might need to reprocess a file. Note that with both of the **tFileCopy** components, we have checked the **Remove Source File** checkbox. In the first component, this will remove the temporary copy of the catalog we have created after it has been copied to the website's import directory, and this cleanup exercise is common to many jobs. In the second **tFileCopy** component, it will remove the original source file once it has been copied to the archive directory, so that the file does not get processed again.

Data import from Fabric Fashions

The import job for the data from Fabric Fashions follows a similar pattern for data from the ERP system. The overall job schematic is shown in the following screenshot:

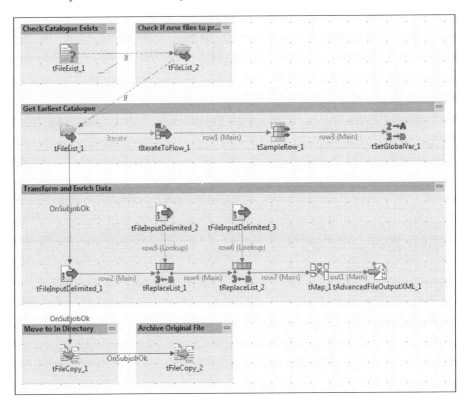

The first three subjobs are exactly the same as the previous job and undertake the following operations:

- Check if a catalog file exists in the website import directory. If yes, then exit, if no then proceed
- Check if there are new files to process from Fabric Fashions. If no, then exit, if yes then proceed
- Find the earliest catalog from Fabric Fashions

The fourth subjob is where the main processing takes place. This is shown in the following screenshot:

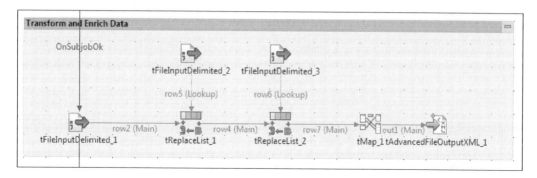

Here, the job reads a delimited input file and two find and replace components that deal with the color and size substitution. So BLK becomes Black and Size 36 becomes Size 4, for example. In both cases, the lookup files are simple old value-new value pairs.

 Note that we could have dealt with the color and size substitutions within a single find and replace component. However, the processing cost of having two components instead of one is negligible and it makes the job easier to understand and maintain if unrelated data is kept separate.

Once the substitutions are completed, we use a **tMap** component to make the SKU ID unique across all suppliers. We'll use a similar convention to that used in the previous job. It is as follows:

```
"fab_"+row7.sku
```

Finally, the dataset is written to an XML file in the required format.

We then move the newly created catalog file to the website import directory and archive the original source file from Fabulous Fashions for safekeeping.

Data import from Runway Collections

We will need two integration jobs for data from Runway Collections. The first is an import of the core product data: names, descriptions, attributes, and so on. The second job deals with the price data, which can change on a much more frequent basis, so it is sent separately.

The first job is very similar to the job dealing with the data from Fabric Fashions, as shown in the following screenshot:

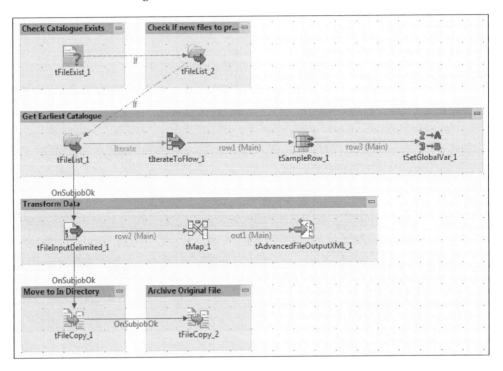

As before, we have the file check components, followed by a subjob which gets the earliest catalog file available for processing. The transform subjob reads a delimited file and passes this to a **tMap** component, where the SKU ID is, as previously, made unique. We'll do this by adding the following:

```
"run_"+row2.SKU
```

Once data has passed through the **tMap** component, it is written to an XML file. Finally, we move the file to the import directory and archive the source data.

The second job is a little more involved. Take a look at the overall schematic in the following screenshot:

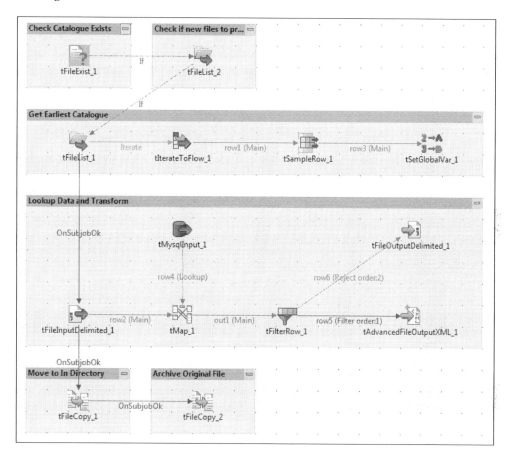

Again, the same subjobs start the processing. The main subjob, **Lookup Data and Transform**, retrieves data from the website's database to enable the job to build a valid catalog. The initial delimited input file consists only of the SKU ID and price data of the form:

1234567;45.00

1234568;45.00

1234569;45.00

1234570;45.00

1234571;45.00

1234572;65.00

1234573;65.00

```
1234574;65.00
1234575;65.00
1234576;65.00
1234577;50.00
1234578;50.00
1234579;50.00
1234580;50.00
1234581;50.00
```

The data from the database consists of the SKU ID (prefixed with its unique identifier `fab_`), the name, the size, the description, and so on.

```
fab_1234567;Blue Dress;8
fab_1234568;Blue Dress;10
fab_1234569;Blue Dress;12
fab_1234570;Blue Dress;14
fab_1234571;Blue Dress;16
fab_1234572;Green Skirt;8
fab_1234573;Green Skirt;10
fab_1234574;Green Skirt;12
fab_1234575;Green Skirt;14
fab_1234576;Green Skirt;16
```

When these two dataflows are joined together in the **tMap** component, the resulting data set is as follows:

```
fab_1234567;45.00;Blue Dress;8
fab_1234568;45.00;Blue Dress;10
fab_1234569;45.00;Blue Dress;12
fab_1234570;45.00;Blue Dress;14
fab_1234571;45.00;Blue Dress;16
fab_1234572;65.00;Green Skirt;8
fab_1234573;65.00;Green Skirt;10
fab_1234574;65.00;Green Skirt;12
fab_1234575;65.00;Green Skirt;14
fab_1234576;65.00;Green Skirt;16
fab_1234577;50.00;;
fab_1234578;50.00;;
fab_1234579;50.00;;
```

```
fab_1234580;50.00;;
fab_1234581;50.00;;
```

We then use a **tFilter** component to pass on the records with a full set of data, those records with an SKU ID, a price, a name, and a size. This data is transformed into an XML catalog for the website. Those records without a name or a size are rejected by the **tFilter** component and written to a delimited file. This rejected file is, again, an example of good integration practice. While we cannot immediately use this data on the website platform, it has value in that it can be interrogated in a separate process to identify those pricing records which don't have the required information, thus saving Delightful Dresses time and money.

Product inventory data

Now that we have products on the website, we need to think about inventory data, specifically, which products are in stock and can be purchased by customers of the website. Again, let's detail the key points of the scenario we have to deal with:

1. Inventory data can come from the same three sources as our product data: the retailer's ERP system, Fabric Fashions, and Runway Collections.

2. The three systems present their data in the following formats: ERP presents in XML; Fabric Fashions presents in a delimited file; Runway Collections presents in a delimited file.

3. Inventory data can be presented to the website system many times per day from these sources. All files will be date/time-stamped so that we know the order in which they arrived.

4. The website system, however, only processes inventory data once per day (at midnight). It requires a file in the XML format.

5. As the inventory data references the product catalog data, we will face the same issue about uniqueness of SKU IDs across all data sources.

From this, we can note the important high-level requirements for the integration job.

1. We can develop a single job that aggregates the data from all sources into a single file to be presented to the website system.

2. Files from the source systems will build up over the day and we will process them all in one go, prior to the website inventory run at midnight.

3. We need to allow for the possibility that a SKU might be in more than one file across the course of a day. This suggests that the inventory level for that SKU has been updated during the day and we should look at the latest data and ignore any earlier data.

4. We'll need to prefix the SKU IDs, as we did in the catalog imports, to maintain SKU ID uniqueness across the system.

Let's walk through the job we have created. The job schematic is shown in the following screenshot:

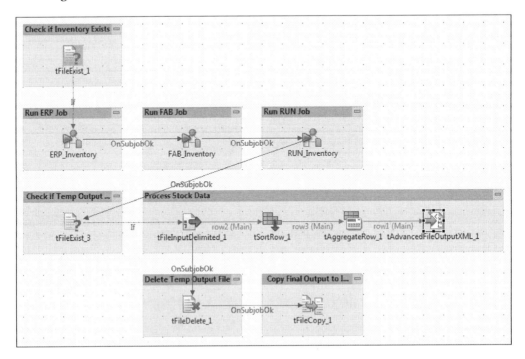

Before we walk through the individual elements in detail, note that the job contains three other jobs: ERP_Inventory, FAB_Inventory, and RUN_Inventory. We'll talk about these three jobs in detail shortly.

The job starts in a similar manner to the catalog jobs, by checking whether or not there is an inventory file already waiting to be processed by the website platform:

This check uses a **tFileExist** component to look for an inventory file in the website's inventory processing directory. This component uses an **If** connector to join with the rest of the job, using the following code:

```
!((Boolean)globalMap.get("tFileExist_1_EXISTS"))
```

This **If** connector allows the job to proceed if the inventory file does not exist in the website processing directory.

The next screenshot shows three individual jobs, one for each data source:

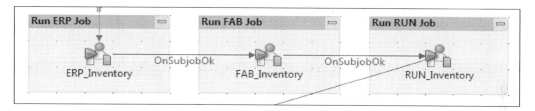

 The obvious question at this point is why would we use jobs within a job instead of simply using the components contained within these embedded jobs? The reason, in this case, is that the embedded jobs were composed of subjobs themselves and, in order to get the job flow and logic correct, these subjobs had to be encapsulated in a component that would always run in its entirety. If the individual components had simply been included in the master job, it would not have been possible to construct the flow logic and have it run in a consistent way on every execution, no matter what the conditions. Deciding when to take this approach is a matter of experimentation and experience. If you cannot achieve the flow you need with regular components and subjobs, try encapsulating the relevant components into an embedded job.

Open the `ERP_Inventory` job to see the details inside:

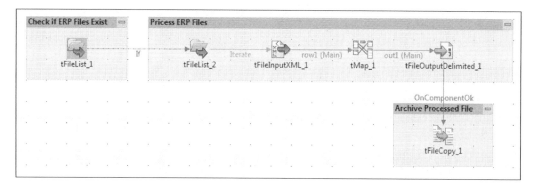

This job has three steps. Firstly, it checks to see if there are any files from the ERP system to process. The subjob will throw a `file not found` error if this step is omitted, so always check for files before trying to process them.

The second step iterates through all of the ERP files that exist, mapping them to a delimited output format. Crucially, the delimited output file is configured to **Append**, so that on each iteration, the new data is appended to the bottom of the file, rather than replacing any existing data.

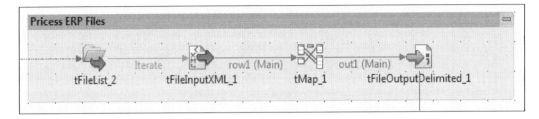

We'll see later that the other data source subjobs also write to the same file, appending as they go.

Note that in the **tMap** component, we capture the filename of the current file and write this into the delimited output file. We'll use this later to remove all but the latest record for an SKU where more than one inventory record exists.

Finally, on each iteration, the original source file is moved to an `archived` directory.

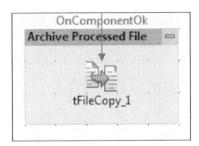

The other subjobs, FAB_Inventory and RUN_Inventory, follow a similar pattern as that of ERP_Inventory, so take a moment to open the sample jobs to familiarize yourself with the configurations.

The next step in the job checks to see if there is an output from the three subjobs:

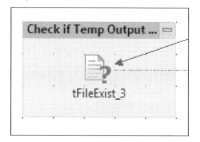

This is required because it is possible that an output is not produced on every execution of the job, perhaps because there were no data source files at that point in time. Without this check, the next step of the job would show an error if an output file is not present.

Next, the main processing section of the job runs as shown in the following screenshot:

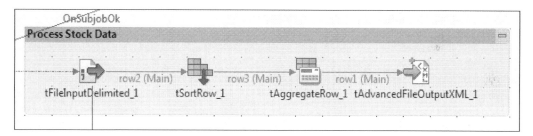

In this subjob, the delimited output from the three subjobs is read (remember that on each subjob the output file is appended). After that, it is sorted by an SKU ID and filename in ascending order. The **tAggregateRow** component then acts upon this data stream, grouping by SKU and passing through the last records of the filename and stock values. This deals with the issue noted earlier, that an SKU ID might appear in more than one file and we need to take the last record for a given SKU and discard the earlier records. The data is then written to an XML format as required by the website platform.

The final step in the job deletes the appended output file and then moves the XML file to the import directory of the website platform:

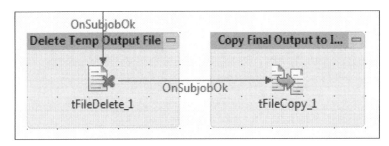

Order file processing

Now that we have product and inventory data on our website, we can start to take orders. The key points for this process are noted as follows:

1. Customers visit the website and place orders for merchandise.

2. The orders are stored in the website system and, on an hourly basis, all new orders are extracted to an XML file. Order extract files are time-stamped to make the filename unique and so that we can determine which is the newest or oldest file. A sample of the order extract is as follows:

```
<?xml version="1.0" encoding="UTF-8"?>

<ORDERS>
  <ORDER ID="10" ORDER_DATE="06/06/12">
    <DELIVERY_ADDRESS>
      <TITLE>Mr</TITLE>
      <FIRST_NAME>James</FIRST_NAME>
      <LAST_NAME>Smith</LAST_NAME>
      <ADDRESS1>123 North Street</ADDRESS1>
      <ADDRESS2>Greenhills</ADDRESS2>
      <CITY>London</CITY>
      <POSTCODE>W1 2RD</POSTCODE>
      <COUNTRY>UK</COUNTRY>
    </DELIVERY_ADDRESS>
    <ORDER_LINE ID="99" SKU="run_99998" SKU_NAME="Red Dress"
QUANTITY="1" PRICE="39.99"/>
    <ORDER_LINE ID="100" SKU="fab_99997" SKU_NAME="Green Skirt"
QUANTITY="1" PRICE="49.99"/>
    <ORDER_LINE ID="101" SKU="del_12345" SKU_NAME="Standard
Delivery" QUANTITY="1" PRICE="4.95"/>
  </ORDER>
</ORDERS>
```

3. The order file contains some basic order information such as the order ID and the order date, the delivery address details, and a number of order lines, showing the items that have been purchased.

4. The order extract file is output to /orders/out and there is also a /orders/out/collected directory to store extracted files that have been subsequently collected.

5. SKUs from all suppliers are available to buy from the website, so a typical order might contain SKUs from Fabric Fashion *and* Runway Collections *and* the retailer's own merchandise.

6. In addition to the merchandise items, an order also contains an order line to denote the delivery product: next day delivery, 3-5 day delivery, and so on. The delivery SKU appears only once in the order, so we need to ensure that all suppliers receive this data so that the appropriate delivery option can be chosen.

The high-level requirements for the job are as follows:

1. We should assume that there will be multiple order files to collect at any given point in time. We can reduce the chance of this happening by having the order processing job run more frequently than the order export from the website system, for example, every half an hour, compared to the hourly export of orders from the website. However, there may be times when there are two or more exports waiting to be processed, so we should develop our job to cope with this situation. It would make sense to process the oldest file first in this situation.

2. An order can contain SKUs from multiple suppliers. We do not want to send Fabric Fashions data to Runway Collections or ERP data to Fabric Fashions, for example, so we need to develop some method for splitting the data based on the SKUs in an order.

3. In our previously developed catalog job, we added a prefix to each SKU to make it unique within the website system. However, these prefixed SKUs now appear in the order file and they will not be recognized by the suppliers' systems. We will need to strip out the prefix to return the SKU ID to its original state.

Let's look at the overall job schematic.

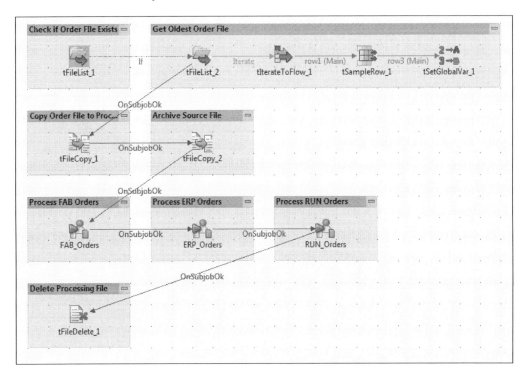

As you can immediately note, this job, like our inventory job, has other jobs within it. We'll look at the detail of these subjobs shortly, but first, let's walk through the flow and logic of the main job.

Our first step is to check whether or not order files exist and are ready to be processed, using a **tFileList** component.

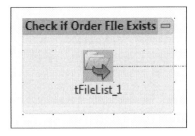

The **tFileList** component has an **If** connector to the next subjob with the condition that the number of files found is greater than zero (that is, there is at least one order file to process).

The next part of the job finds the oldest file to process, using the same methodology that we have employed in our previous jobs:

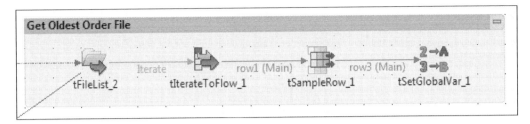

The job then copies the oldest file to a processing directory and archives the same file to the /orders/out/collected directory for safekeeping.

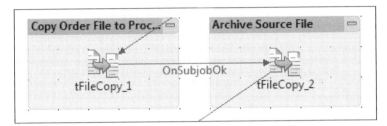

The file that was copied to the processing directory is now pushed through three different subjobs, one for each supplier, that extracts the relevant data required by each. (We will look at the detail of these jobs shortly.)

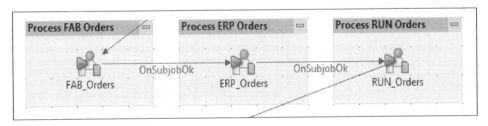

Finally, the processing file is deleted:

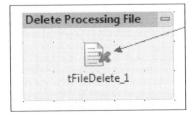

The three processing subjobs shown previously all work in the same way, with slight configuration variations for each supplier. We'll look at the subjob that processed orders for Fabulous Fashions. There are two parts to the subjob; the first is the main processing section, followed by a file copy component that moves the output to a directory where it can be picked up by the appropriate downstream system.

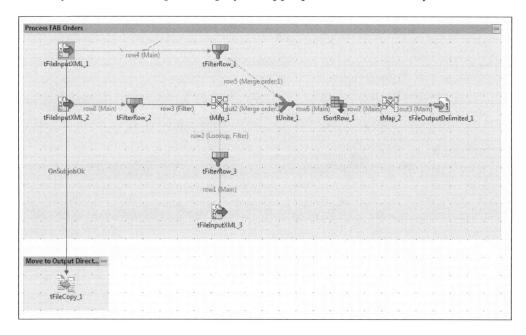

The first flow of the job is shown in the following screenshot:

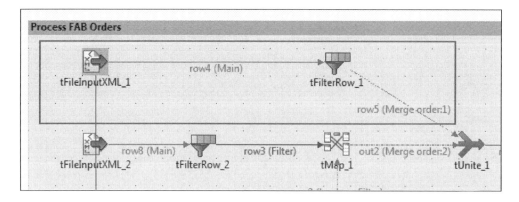

This flow extracts the order lines and filters them by the SKU prefix, which in this example is set to fab_. This ensures that only the Fabulous Fashions merchandise items are passed through.

We also need to extract the delivery SKUs, but cannot simply send all of the delivery SKUs to Fabulous Fashions, because not all orders will contain Fabulous Fashion items and so, not all delivery SKUs will be relevant to Fabulous Fashions. In the second flow of the subjob, we extract all of the order lines and filter them so that only the delivery lines are passed through **tFilterRow_3** as shown in the following screenshot:

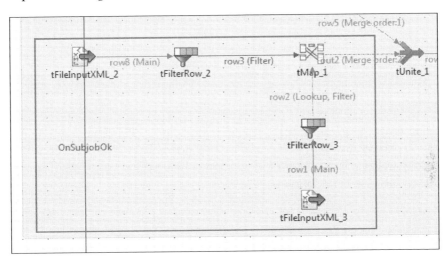

We then join this dataflow with a lookup dataflow which only contains order lines for Fabulous Fashions SKUs. The lookup flow is, in fact, an exact copy of the first flow described earlier. In the **tMap** component, we join the two flows on Order ID, so the data flow emerging from the **tMap** component is all of the delivery SKUs that appear in orders that also contained at least one FAB SKU.

> Why do we have the same flow duplicated in a job? In this case, the first flow of FAB order lines and the lookup flow of the same. The reason is that the Studio won't allow you to replicate a dataflow to different points in another dataflow, which is what would be required if we were to achieve this with a single dataflow of FAB order lines. In order to get the desired result, we need to undertake two separate and identical reads of the input file.

In the final part of the subjob, the dataflows of FAB merchandise SKUs and FAB delivery SKUs are merged back into a single flow:

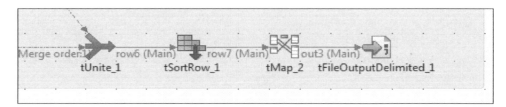

The data is sorted so that it is in the order ID, line ID sequence, passed through a **tMap** component to strip out the SKU prefix, and written to a delimited file.

After this integration, our supplier systems now have order data and they can now dispatch orders to customers. Our next integration will look at a typical next step in the process, the supplier/fulfillment systems advise which items from the original order have actually been shipped.

Order status updates

Once the orders have been processed by the suppliers, they will send back an order status update to the website system, confirming fulfillment. Here are the key features of this process:

1. The suppliers FTP files to a directory on the website server. All suppliers follow the same format and the filenames' convention is [supplier code]_shipped_[timestamp].csv, for example fab_shipped_201206060900.csv.

2. The suppliers can supply these files many times per day on a schedule that is not predetermined.

3. Once processed, the output file needs to be moved to the website's order status import directory.

4. The file required by the website is in XML format and is to be named orderstatus_update.xml.

5. The website has a constraint that an item cannot be shipped more times than it was ordered. If data is presented to the website that attempts to ship an order line that has already been shipped, the import process to the website will fail, requiring manual intervention. For standard merchandise items, this is unlikely to happen as we can assume that the supplier system has sufficient control to prevent double-shipping. However, we need to develop a control for this scenario for two reasons; firstly, because, although the supplier systems might also not allow double shipping, a file from a supplier might get presented twice in an error; and secondly, in splitting the order to our different suppliers, we have sent each supplier a notification of the delivery SKU. As a result, the delivery SKU will always be presented more than once on orders that contained items from multiple suppliers.

This is a key consideration for us in this job. To deal with this, we'll do two things:

  ○ As we process the data, we'll look up the current shipping status within the website application. Any order items presented from a supplier that are already shipped in the website database will be ignored.

  ○ Before we create a new order status update file for the website based on data from the suppliers, we'll check that the website is not already processing a previous order status update file. Without this check, we could find ourselves in a situation where order line ID, 12345, is waiting to be processed by the website, when the same data is presented, in error, from a supplier datafile. If we check the database at this point, the order item will not have been shipped, so it will be passed through to a new order status update file. However, simply checking the database does not tell us that the same data is in a file waiting to be processed. If we wait until the first file has been processed by the website, we can be sure that the database status is correct and up-to-date.

The following screenshot shows the overall job schema:

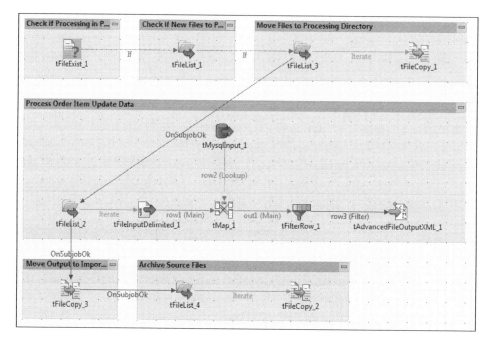

The first step of the job checks for files to decide whether or not the job should continue.

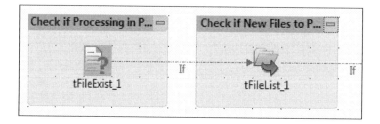

The first component checks if there is a file in the website's import directory waiting to be processed. If the file does not exist, then the job proceeds to the second component, which checks if there are new files from the suppliers to process. If there are new files, the job proceeds.

The next step copies new files to a working directory:

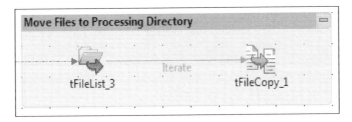

The main processing part of the job runs next:

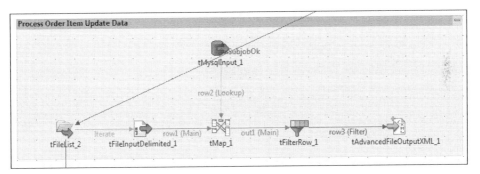

The subjob iterates through the files in the working directory and passes the data through a **tMap** component, where it applies a lookup on data from the website database. In the **tMap** component, we use data from the file and data from the website database to determine if a status update in the file can be allowed to progress or not. The logic uses three pieces of data from each order line: the quantity ordered (from the database), the quantity already shipped (from the database), and the quantity to ship (from the supplier file). If the *quantity ordered – quantity shipped – quantity to ship* is greater than or equal to zero, then we set an **allow** flag to Y; otherwise, the **allow** flag is set to N. The data then passes through to a **tFilterRow** component where we let through the lines with an **allow** flag of Y and ignore those with an **allow** flag of N.

The data is written out to an XML file in the format required by the website. Note that, as we are using an iterate process for the file processing, the XML output component is set to **Append**; that is, successive iterations are written to the same file.

The final stage of the job is about cleanup and archiving:

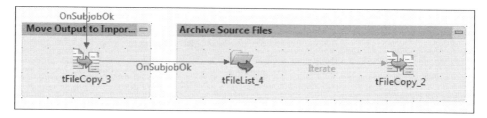

The first subjob moves the processing output file to the website import directory. The final subjob lists all of the original source files in the processing directory and moves them to an archive directory for safekeeping.

Automating processes

The jobs we have described in this chapter so far are typical integration jobs, mapping, and transforming data to comply with an integration specification from standalone systems. However, we can also use the Studio to automate processes that would often be undertaken manually. Let's look at a couple of examples.

E-mailing daily sales

The management of Delightful Dresses wants to know the value of sales from the website on a daily basis. This might be done manually by an employee running a report, downloading it onto their computer, and then e-mailing it to an e-mail group. There are a specific set of steps to follow and they don't vary from day to day, an ideal process to automate.

This can be achieved directly in the Studio and the high-level job schematic is shown in the following screenshot:

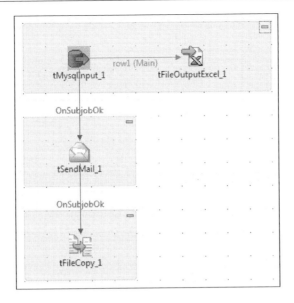

As you can observe, the job is relatively simple. Perform the following steps:

1. The Studio runs a SQL query against the website database.
2. The data output is written to an Excel file.
3. The file is attached to an e-mail and distributed.
4. The file is archived for safe-keeping.

We have made the process more dynamic and user-friendly by using global variables to note the date of execution. For example, the e-mail subject in the **tSendMail** component is configured as follows:

```
"Website Daily Sales for "+TalendDate.getDate("DD-MM-CCYY")
```

This puts the current date into the e-mail's subject line, along with a static piece of text, so that recipients know exactly what the e-mail is about.

One can easily imagine this technique being used for a whole suite of reports, as shown in the following screenshot:

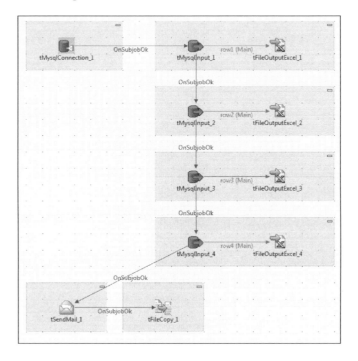

Despite the number of business intelligence tools available to organizations these days, the quality and timeliness of reporting data is often poor. While the Studio is not designed to be a reporting tool, a simple technique such as this can offer acceptable results with little time investment.

Automating product visibility

On the website platform, administrators will use the back office interface to make products available for sale or remove from sale when they are no longer available. The manual process is time-consuming, requiring administrators to log in to the back office, find products that are in stock, but not visible, and set their visibility flag to `true`. The removal process is similar; find products that are out of stock and set their visibility flag to `false`. It would not be a great hardship to do this manually if there were only a small number of affected products on a daily basis. However, large websites have a constantly changing inventory and new products are added all the time, so it might be a significant task to do this manually involving hundreds of products on a daily basis. This is a great opportunity to automate!

An example job for this process is shown in the following screenshot:

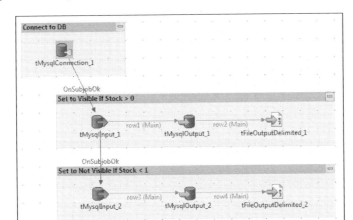

The job makes a connection to the database, then updates those SKUs with positive stock. It sets the visibility status of SKUs from `false` to `true`. There follows a second update, which sets SKUs to "not visible" if they have zero (or negative) stock and where they are currently set to "visible". In both cases, we also write the rows updated in the database out to a file, so that we have a record of what was updated on any given execution. This is really important for post-execution troubleshooting, so always remember to include these Audit Log components.

Summary

The worked examples in the chapter have brought together the theory from previous chapters into practice in a real-life integration scenario. As has been illustrated in these jobs, it is not just the data transformations or database extractions that are important, it is vital that we think about the elements of the job outside of this. File archiving after processing, deleting temporary files, checking for the existence of files before processing, and choosing which file to process first are, among other things, a hugely important part of an end-to-end integration job. It is worth taking the time to sketch out the end-to-end process before you start to develop, so that you consider all of the important factors and constraints.

Getting the end-to-end process correct is often a matter of experience, but if you are new to integration development, don't be put off. Practice (and lots of testing) makes you perfect!

The next chapter will be useful to beginners and experienced developers alike, noting many useful resources to help you with your learning and development.

A
Installing Sample Jobs and Data

The jobs that are created in this book can be downloaded and imported into your Studio environment. Additionally, there are some sample input data files and a database that can be copied for use in the examples. Follow the setup steps given next to install the jobs and data.

Downloading job and data files

In order to download the job and data files, visit the support page of the Packt website at `http://www.packtpub.com/support`, select the name of the book from the drop-down list, and enter your e-mail address. The code download link will be e-mailed to you and the necessary files can be downloaded by clicking on the link.

Once you have downloaded the job package, unzip it and open it. Inside, you will find three directories—`SampleDataFiles`, `DBBackup`, and `ExampleJobs`. Inside each of these subdirectories are the files you need to install.

Sample data files

Within the `SampleDataFiles` directory is a further set of directories containing sample input files. They have been organized chapterwise for easy reference.

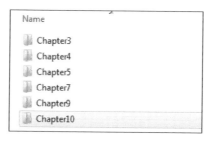

Once you have created your workspace directory and a new project, create a `DataIn` directory within the project and copy the chapter directories (shown previously) into the `DataIn` directory.

As an example, if your workspace was created in `C:\Talend\Workspace` and you created a project named `DEMOPROJECT`, your `DataIn` directory would exist alongside the files and directories created by the Studio when a project is created, as shown in the following screenshot:

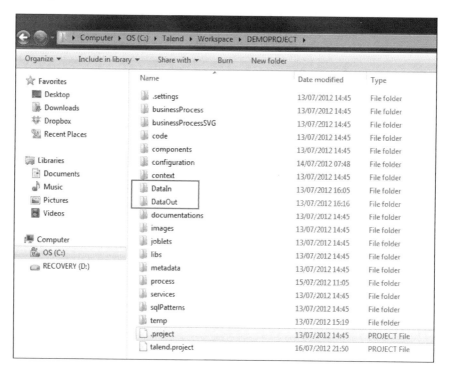

Note that we have also created a `DataOut` directory for files that will be produced by our jobs.

Sample database

The job package contains a MySQL database backup file. Restoring this will create a database with a number of populated tables that will be used by some of the jobs we create. To restore the backup, open MySQL Workbench and click on **Manage Import/ Export,** as shown in the following screenshot:

On the Admin screen, click on **Data Import/Restore** in the left-hand pane and then browse to the DBBackup directory on your computer.

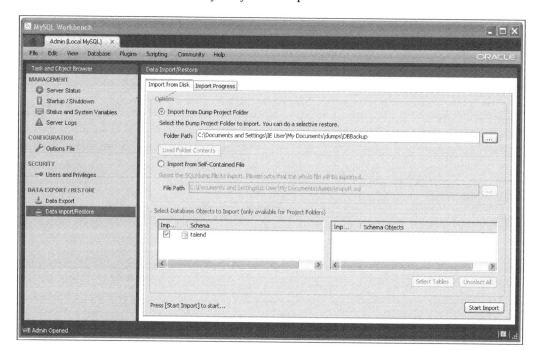

The schema in the DBBackup directory will be shown in the bottom-left pane of the main window.

Now click on **Start Import**. The database will be created in your local MySQL instance.

Sample jobs

To import the sample jobs, start up the Studio and on the start-up screen, click on **Advanced...** as shown in the following screenshot:

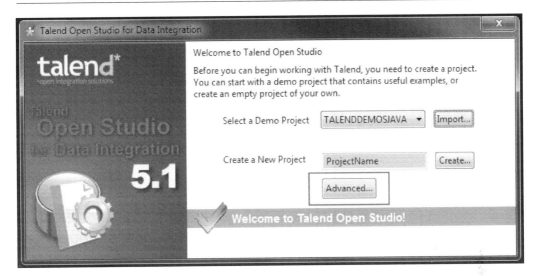

Once on the Advanced screen, click on the **Import...** button as shown in the following screenshot:

On the **Import** window, enter a project name, such as GETTINGSTARTEDTOS, and using the **Select root directory** field, browse to the ExampleJobs directory. Select the project folder within the ExampleJobs directory, namely GETTINGSTARTEDTOS.

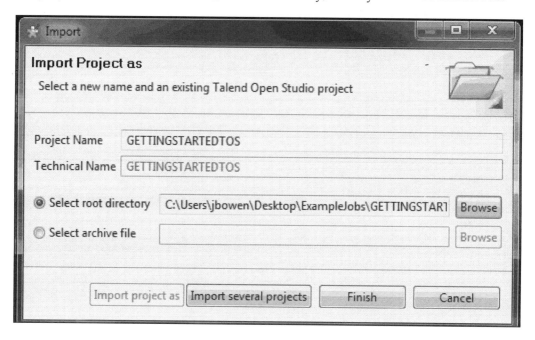

Finally, click on **Finish** to import the projects into your workspace. Once the import is complete, you will see the new project in the projects list on the start-up screen. Select the project and click on **Open** to open the imported project.

B
Resources

The aim of this book is to give you an introduction to the Studio and its concepts, to start you on the path to developing integration jobs with ease. However, as your knowledge builds and your experience develops, you will want to know more about what the Studio can do for you. Fortunately, there are some fantastic resources available for developers of all skill levels.

In this appendix, we'll walk through some of the key additional resources you may use from time to time. Readers are very much encouraged to use them. We'll look at:

- The TalendForge Community forum
- The official Talend documentation
- Webinars and tutorials
- The Talend Exchange, where you can download open source components not included as standard in the Studio

Talend documentation

Talend provides excellent documentation and readers are encouraged to download and use this as they learn about developing with the Studio.

Talend provides:

- A prerequisites guide—the hardware and software requirements you will need to run the Studio
- A software installation guide
- A user guide, which introduces the concepts and principles of the studio tool
- A component reference guide, which provides information on each of the components in the Palette, with configuration guides and explanations of all of the configuration parameters

The component reference guide is particularly useful and is often a "go-to" document when developing jobs. It provides example uses for most of the components and illustrates how these examples are set up, giving developers a set of mini-tutorials to use for components that they are less familiar with.

Talend documentation can be downloaded from `http://www.talend.com/download/data-integration`.

TalendForge forum

You can find the official Talend forum at `http://www.talendforge.org/`.

The TalendForge forum is a great community tool and will prove invaluable to new and experienced developers alike. Its format is pretty standard, with forum sections for each of Talend's developer tools—*Talend Open Studio for Data Integration, Talend Open Studio for Data Quality,* and so on—and each section has a number of subtopics, so you can choose the area most appropriate to your needs.

The Talend Open Studio for Data Integration is, by far, the most popular section and within this, there are some very active subsections covering installation and usage/operations.

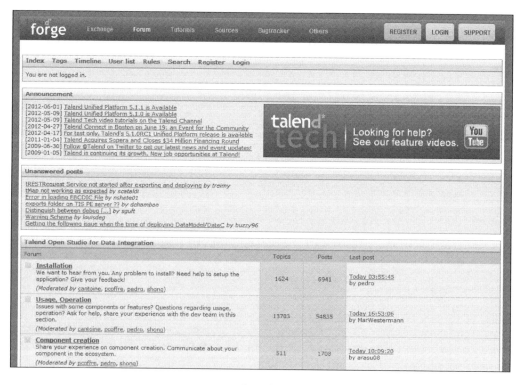

The forum is completely open to browsers and there's a lot of useful information that you can gain by simply reading the queries and answers posted, but in order to get the most out of the forum it is recommended that you register and create a user account. Registered users can post and respond to new topics.

Take a quick look at the **Usage, Operation** subsection. A lot of the topics are of the form "How do I do.....?". You can see that the topics are widely read and often get lots of answers, both from community members and Talend employees, and this is a great place to come when you are stuck on a development task.

Webinars

Talend offers both live and on-demand webinars and these can be accessed at http://www.talend.com/resources/webinars.

The on-demand webinars are recordings of previous live webinars and there's a wide range of topics to view from basic integration techniques to "big data" analytics.

You can create a user account at www.talend.com and sign-up for their regular e-mail communications.

You will be notified by an e-mail when live webinars are due to take place and you simply need a browser and Internet connection to be able to view. The live webinars are often interactive, giving viewers the opportunity to ask questions related to the topic under discussion.

Tutorials

There are a number of worked example tutorials on the TalendForge site and these can be found at http://www.talendforge.org/tutorials/menu.php.

There are three easy tutorials that detail some basic techniques, followed by some more detailed, complex examples. Note that some of the tutorials refer to Talend Enterprise Data Integration, which is an enterprise version of the Studio. Although the functionalities are very similar, the enterprise version offers some features that are not available in Talend Open Studio. As a result, there are some tutorials that you will not be able to complete with Talend Open Studio alone.

Additionally, Talend has a channel on YouTube at http://www.youtube.com/user/TalendChannel.

The instructional videos within the channel are really designed for marketing purposes and are not step-by-step tutorials, but, nonetheless, serve as a good introduction to using Talend in different scenarios.

Talend Exchange

The Studio comes with over 600 built-in connectors and components, but the open nature of the Studio has allowed developers to create their components and made them available to the community. Sometimes, these components get adopted by Talend and make it into the standard Studio product, but others are available for developers to download and use, even though they do not have the "official" stamp of approval.

New components can be downloaded straight into the Studio tool. Follow the given steps to get connected:

1. In the Studio tool, go to **Windows | Preferences**. The **Preferences** dialog box will open.

2. In the search box at the top left, type exchange and press *Enter*. This will reveal the Exchange configuration window.

3. Click on the **Sign In** button to display the TalendForge login window.

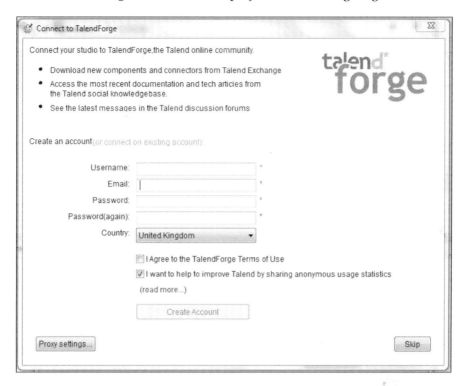

4. On the login window, you can sign in (if you already have an existing TalendForge account) or create a new account.

5. Once you have signed in, you will see your account name in the Exchange Preferences window.

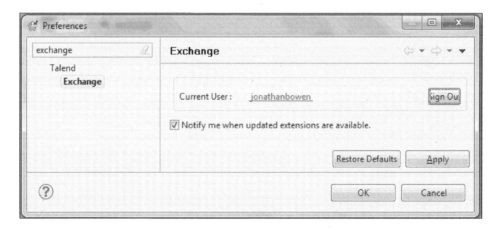

6. Click on **OK** to complete the Exchange setup.

7. Having completed the setup, click on **Exchange** in the menu bar.

8. This will reveal the **Exchange** search window, where you can browse or search for components.

9. Let's install a component for Apache's Solr Search Platform (`http://lucene.apache.org/solr/`). Enter `solr` in the search box and click on the search icon to the right of the textbox.

10. A number of Solr components will be returned. Let's install a `tSolrConnection` component. Click on **View/Download**.

11. You'll see some more details about the component. Click on **Install** to download the component. Once complete you'll get a success notification. You will now be able to search for the component in the Palette and add it to your integration jobs in the normal manner.

Index

Thank you for buying
Getting Started with Talend Open Studio for Data Integration

About Packt Publishing

Packt, pronounced 'packed', published its first book "*Mastering phpMyAdmin for Effective MySQL Management*" in April 2004 and subsequently continued to specialize in publishing highly focused books on specific technologies and solutions.

Our books and publications share the experiences of your fellow IT professionals in adapting and customizing today's systems, applications, and frameworks. Our solution based books give you the knowledge and power to customize the software and technologies you're using to get the job done. Packt books are more specific and less general than the IT books you have seen in the past. Our unique business model allows us to bring you more focused information, giving you more of what you need to know, and less of what you don't.

Packt is a modern, yet unique publishing company, which focuses on producing quality, cutting-edge books for communities of developers, administrators, and newbies alike. For more information, please visit our website: www.packtpub.com.

About Packt Open Source

In 2010, Packt launched two new brands, Packt Open Source and Packt Enterprise, in order to continue its focus on specialization. This book is part of the Packt Open Source brand, home to books published on software built around Open Source licences, and offering information to anybody from advanced developers to budding web designers. The Open Source brand also runs Packt's Open Source Royalty Scheme, by which Packt gives a royalty to each Open Source project about whose software a book is sold.

Writing for Packt

We welcome all inquiries from people who are interested in authoring. Book proposals should be sent to author@packtpub.com. If your book idea is still at an early stage and you would like to discuss it first before writing a formal book proposal, contact us; one of our commissioning editors will get in touch with you.

We're not just looking for published authors; if you have strong technical skills but no writing experience, our experienced editors can help you develop a writing career, or simply get some additional reward for your expertise.

Pentaho Data
Integration 4 Cookbook

Over 70 recipes to solve ETL problems using Pentaho Kettle

Adrián Sergio Pulvirenti
María Carina Roldán

Pentaho Data Integration 4 Cookbook

ISBN: 978-1-84951-524-5   Paperback: 352 pages

Over 70 recipes to solve ETL problems using Pentaho Kettle

1. Manipulate your data by exploring, transforming, validating, integrating, and more

2. Work with all kinds of data sources such as databases, plain files, and XML structures among others

3. Use Kettle in integration with other components of the Pentaho Business Intelligence Suite

Pentaho 3.2 Data Integration

Explore, transform, validate, and integrate your data with ease

Beginner's Guide

María Carina Roldán

Pentaho 3.2 Data Integration: Beginner's Guide

ISBN: 978-1-84719-954-6   Paperback: 492 pages

Explore, transform, validate, and integrate your data with ease

1. Get started with Pentaho Data Integration from scratch.

2. Enrich your data transformation operations by embedding Java and JavaScript code in PDI transformations.

3. Create a simple but complete Datamart Project that will cover all key features of PDI.

Please check **www.PacktPub.com** for information on our titles

Getting Started with Oracle Data Integrator 11g: A Hands-On Tutorial

ISBN: 978-1-84968-068-4   Paperback: 384 pages

Combine high volume data movement, complex transformations and real-time data integration with the robust capabilities of ODI in this practical guide

1. Discover the comprehensive and sophisticated orchestration of data integration tasks made possible with ODI, including monitoring and error-management

2. Get to grips with the product architecture and building data integration processes with technologies including Oracle, Microsoft SQL Server and XML files

3. A comprehensive tutorial packed with tips, images and best practices

Oracle Information Integration, Migration, and Consolidation

ISBN: 978-1-84968-220-6   Paperback: 332 pages

Use Oracle technologies and best practices to manage, maintain, migrate, and mobilize data

1. Learn about integration practices that many IT professionals are not familiar with

2. Evaluate and implement numerous tools like Oracle SOA Suite and Oracle GoldenGate

3. Get to grips with the past, present, and future of Oracle Integration practices

Please check **www.PacktPub.com** for information on our titles